"Teaching our children the 1619 Project, who the oppressor class consists of, and that America and our Judeo-Christian founding is the problem and not the solution makes Randi Weingarten singularly dangerous to our country. Read *The Parent Revolution* to set free our children from her clutches once and for all."

—Mike Pompeo, 70th United States Secretary of State

"Government schools are literal prisons for children, and Corey DeAngelis explains how to set the kids free."

—Michael Malice, author and host of *YOUR WELCOME*

"Corey DeAngelis is considered public enemy number one by Randi Weingarten and the teachers unions for good reason: He thinks parents shouldn't be treated as intruders when they want a voice in their children's education, students shouldn't have their minds colonized by crazy ideologies, and educational monopolies produce the same poor results as do all monopolies. In a world in which victories for freedom lovers are few and far between, the brilliant DeAngelis suggests in this bold manifesto that we can look to the future of education with genuine hope."

—Tom Woods, PhD, *New York Times* bestselling author, and winner, 2019 Hayek Lifetime Achievement Award

"Corey DeAngelis helped us in Arizona become the first state to achieve Milton Friedman's vision of universal school choice. This book lays out the blueprint to bringing education freedom to the rest of America."

—Doug Ducey, 23rd Governor of Arizona

"Today like never before, parents are standing up to teachers unions and progressive activists and reclaiming their right to be the primary decision-makers in their children's education. This is the parent revolution sweeping America, and it's the most important change to our education system in decades. If you're a parent, lawmaker, or citizen who wants to contribute to the fight, read this book."

—Kim Reynolds, 43rd Governor of Iowa

THE PARENT REVOLUTION

THE PARENT REVOLUTION

★ ★ ★

Rescuing Your Kids from the Radicals Ruining Our Schools

Corey A. DeAngelis, PhD

CENTER STREET
New York • Nashville

Cover design by Darren Welch

Center Street
Hachette Book Group
1290 Avenue of the Americas, New York, NY 10104
centerstreet.com
@CenterStreet

First Edition: May 2024

Print book interior designed by Bart Dawson

Library of Congress Cataloging-in-Publication Data
Names: DeAngelis, Corey A., author.
Title: The parent revolution : rescuing your kids from the radicals ruining our schools / Corey A. DeAngelis, PhD.
Description: First edition. | Nashville ; New York : Center Street, [2024] | Includes bibliographical references.
Identifiers: LCCN 2023051341 | ISBN 9781546006862 (hardcover) | ISBN 9781546006886 (ebook)
Subjects: LCSH: School choice—United States. | Education—Parent participation—United States.
Classification: LCC LB1027.9 .D43 2024 | DDC 379.1/110973—dc23/eng/20231128
LC record available at https://lccn.loc.gov/2023051341

ISBN: 9781546006862 (hardcover), 9781546006886 (ebook)

Printed in the United States of America

LSC

Printing 1, 2024

To Randi Weingarten and the teachers unions.
You're doing more to advance freedom in education
than anyone could have ever imagined.
Thank you for overplaying your hand, showing your
true colors, and sparking the Parent Revolution.
America is beyond grateful.

I'd also like to dedicate this book to the sleeping giant awakened
by the power-hungry unions: parents who want more
of a say in their children's education.
For far too long in K–12 education, the only special interests
represented the employees—the adults—in the system.
But now, the kids have a union of their own: their parents.

CONTENTS

INTRODUCTION

THE PARENT REVOLUTION

> An observation: No one in education policy, advocacy, or activism has ever lived rent-free in more heads at once than Corey DeAngelis.
>
> —*Robert Pondiscio, American Enterprise Institute*[1]

It was December 2020. That's when we all realized we had lost our collective mind. Chicago Teachers Union vice president Sarah Chambers was caught vacationing in Puerto Rico while railing against proposals to return to in-person work.[2] Wait. If it was safe enough for Chambers to travel abroad to vacation in real life ("IRL," as the kids say), why wasn't it safe enough for her to go back to work in person? Millions of us asked that very question in our heads. But it was rhetorical. We already knew the two-part answer: First, Chambers didn't really believe COVID was as serious as she made it out to be. Second, it's far more enjoyable to vacation in person than to go to work in person. The perverse incentives baked into the monopolistic government-run school system makes it too easy to be a hypocrite.

That same month, Chicago Teachers Union deleted a tweet—only after immense pushback—claiming that "the push to reopen schools is rooted in sexism, racism and misogyny."[3] Teachers unions were making it abundantly clear that they *really* didn't want to go back to work. That was obvious to just about everyone with more than two brain cells. Teachers-union-enforced "remote learning" (which should instead be called "remote*ly* learning," because kids weren't learning much of anything) provided the unintended benefit of allowing parents to see what was going on in the classroom.

That woke parents up, and, appropriately, they've remained restless and agitated ever since. It was a caffeine injection directly into their hearts. Parents haven't forgotten how powerless they suddenly felt in 2020. Power-hungry teachers unions finally overplayed their hand and sparked a parent revolution. That revolution began toppling in rapid succession the bureaucrats' dominoes, one state after another.

According to polls, a majority of Americans—amid tyrannical COVID mandates and the skyrocketing cost of living—considered the year 2021 "one of the worst of their lives."[4] Nevertheless, when freedom was under siege, the grassroots revolution of parental rights kicked into high gear.

In 2021, heeding the booming call of the parental-rights movement, nineteen states expanded or enacted programs to fund students instead of bureaucrats.[5] Known as "school choice," these programs allow families to take state-funded education dollars to the education providers of their choice, whether a public school, a private school, a charter school, or even a home school. The approach works.

We already fund higher-education students through Pell Grants and the GI Bill, which have proven very successful. The same goes for certain pre-K programs, such as Head Start. The food stamp program is another example of supporting individuals directly. We don't force low-income families to get their food from residentially assigned, government-run grocery stores. Instead, they can shop at Walmart, Trader Joe's, Safeway, or any other store that accepts food stamps. The same approach should apply to primary and secondary education. Nothing short of the future of our nation is at stake.

The Supreme Court actually set the stage for the parental-rights movement the prior year with two seminal cases: *Espinoza v. Montana*

Department of Revenue (5–4) and *Carson v. Makin* (6–3). In the former, the Supreme Court ruled that excluding religious schools from private-school-choice programs was a violation of the Free Exercise Clause of the First Amendment and, therefore, unconstitutional. Similarly, in the latter, it ruled that preventing school-choice families from taking their children's taxpayer-funded education dollars to religious private schools also violated the Free Exercise Clause. As Chief Justice John Roberts put it, a state "need not subsidize private education," but once one decides to do so, "it cannot disqualify some private schools solely because they are religious." Such discrimination is "odious to our Constitution" and "cannot *stand*."[6]

Virginia received significant national attention in 2021, and rightly so. In an increasingly blueish state, former governor Terry McAuliffe was shockingly defeated by Glenn Youngkin, whose campaign, of course, focused on parental rights. Think the various Loudoun County controversies and "I don't think parents should be telling schools what they should teach," which will probably go down in American political history as one of the worse gaffes ever, right alongside George W. Bush's "Mission Accomplished" and Hillary Clinton's "Basket of Deplorables."[7] But the election was just one episode in the remarkable chronicle of the classroom coup, which hasn't yet been told.

West Virginia enjoyed what I believe was the biggest victory of all. At the beginning of 2021, the state had *zero* charter schools and *zero* private-school-choice programs. In March of that year, it enacted legislation allowing all West Virginian families, regardless of income, to choose how to spend their state-funded education dollars. Then in January 2022, a teachers-union-backed legal center filed a lawsuit to halt the program, and it temporarily succeeded when a circuit court judge ruled in its favor, even after three thousand students had been approved to receive state funding. (Lo and behold, that judge had been endorsed and funded by teachers unions.) Thankfully, in October 2022, the state supreme court sided with West Virginian families and reversed the injunction.[8] A month later, they declared the state's Hope Scholarship program to be constitutional.[9]

The year 2021 was just the start; 2022 was the "year of the parent." Officials who supported education freedom won elections in record numbers, which set the stage for 2023 to become the "year of universal school choice." The revolution is underway, and there's nothing the teachers unions can do to stop it.

Why I Wrote This Book: My Terrible Educational Experience Was Your Terrible Experience

I still remember the trails of blood droplets on the stairs and the checkered tiles. Between classes in the cafeteria stairwell, my classmates played "10 Seconds"—a "game" where two kids would fight like banshees bare-knuckle until the timer ran out. They also voluntarily got pummeled in the school restrooms as a form of gang initiation, which was called getting "rolled-in."

I grew up in San Antonio. The government-run middle school I attended was a madhouse. Education was a very distant afterthought. Chaos was the norm. It was actually considered cool to get into fights, to do drugs, and to be in gangs. Some of my closest friends were involved with this stuff. One buddy even tried to help me fit in by coaching me to imitate a limp to walk like a gangsta. Offering to help me with algebra never came up. For whatever reason, a lot of students didn't want to be there. That much was obvious.

Then when I reached high school, I was given the opportunity to attend a magnet school. Communications Arts High School happened to be physically located on the campus of my assigned public school. Every day for four years, I witnessed a night-and-day difference between educational experiences.

In stark contrast, Communications Arts High School, right next door, was ranked the seventeenth best public high school in the entire nation by *Newsweek* the year I graduated. The students actually *wanted* to be there. The culture was one of high expectations and excellence. Apathy and misbehavior were the outlier, shunned and frowned upon. Everyone took AP classes. Older students even paired up with incoming freshmen at the beginning of each school year to help them fit in (and that didn't involve teaching them to walk with a limp).

A map hung in one hallway that proudly displayed where every senior had committed to go to college. I had received a full-ride academic scholarship to play football at Menlo College, a small Division III school southeast of San Francisco. Even though that would mean being around commies for four years, I decided that the offer was too good to turn down. My time on the West Coast lasted for only one semester. But it wasn't radical politics that drove me out. When I went home for winter break, I was confronted with news that shattered my world: My dad had colon cancer. I ended up taking a semester off to be with him. (He miraculously recovered and has been cancer free for over a decade.) To remain close by, I transferred to the University of Texas at San Antonio. I consider my life a testament to the aphorism "Everything happens for a reason."

It was at UTSA that I met John Merrifield, who served as my academic advisor and became a close friend. I consider myself extraordinarily lucky. Few of us on the right have the opportunity to be paired with someone during college who is not just politically aligned, but genuinely interested in mentoring. Most professors hardly bother to even learn the names of their advisees. They simply vacuum up undergraduates to put them to work, undertaking mundane "data collection" tasks of obscure projects that they themselves are too lazy to handle.

John opened my eyes to the problem of monopoly power. He researched school-choice programs and was affiliated with the Friedman Foundation for Educational Choice (now named EdChoice). I came to the conclusion that in America, nowhere was the problem of monopoly power more pronounced—and more harmful to our society—than the nation's government-run school system. I remember thinking, at the most basic level, *What if you similarly had to pick up and move just to visit a different restaurant or grocery store?* One thing was readily apparent. With a captive audience, those restaurants and grocery stores would have little to no incentive to improve or cater to the preferences of their customers. So it goes with our government-run school system.

Dr. Merrifield suggested that I go to the University of Arkansas to pursue a PhD in education policy. Wholly committed to exposing the failures of the government's unchallenged dominance over the minds of young Americans, I took his advice. I studied under school-choice researchers Jay P. Greene (now at Heritage Foundation), Patrick J. Wolf, and Robert Maranto.

I hit the ground running with research on school choice. My first study linked Milwaukee's private-school-choice program to crime reduction later in life. That study and my subsequent research made a splash in the media, thrusting my name into the national spotlight.

I learned very quickly that education academia is a total clown show. For instance, if you're on the "wrong side" of an issue (meaning you're not obviously a person of the left), your "peers" in the "peer-review" process immediately become your enemies. Even worse, they're hidden, disguised behind the double-blind review process. One peer reviewer of my Milwaukee study brazenly pointed out that, while actually admitting my methods were sound, my study had implicitly posed a *problematic* question. In other words, I was at fault because the scientific method produced results that were distasteful to the reviewer's political palate. *Shame on me for offering evidence that the free market in education could help kids stay out of the criminal justice system!*

I weighed becoming a professor, but accepted that higher education in twenty-first-century America had little to do with the pursuit of academic excellence and the improvement of society. It was about ensuring ideological conformity and becoming a good little foot soldier in the left's culture war.

I reached an inflection point when I decided to dedicate myself to social media. It has proven the best career decision I've made. Before that was apparent, many of my close friends in academia told me to get off Twitter. They insisted I was wasting my time—I could instead be doing important work. (By "important work," they meant fifty-page white papers that hardly a soul ever reads.) I'm glad I didn't heed their advice.

Escaping the Ivory Tower allowed me to see how the world really works. The most logical policy solution will not win without the right power dynamics influencing politicians to do the right thing. Getting into state capitols allowed me to figure out the world of political calculations and how to pass policies that empower parents to educate their own children as they see fit. Becoming a regular guest on Fox News and contributor to the *Wall Street Journal* and numerous other publications gave me a platform to advance education freedom and choice for all.

No child should ever be stuck in a school that isn't the right fit for him or her. My terrible educational experience spurred me to fight for policies that would ensure that no child should have to endure a similar situation. Looking back, I'm amazed at how much progress the school-choice movement made in just the past few years. But things had to get much worse before they got better. *The Parent Revolution* would win in the end, but first parents had to wake up to just how bad things had gotten in the public school system. If there was any silver lining to COVID, unleashing freedom in education just might be it...

Chapter 1

HOLDING AMERICA'S KIDS HOSTAGE

Never let a crisis go to waste.

—Rahm Emanuel, chief of staff to President Barack Obama

In 2021, a concerned mom in Brooklyn messaged Randi Weingarten, president of the American Federation of Teachers, simply asking her why she fought to keep schools closed for so long. Weingarten blamed her competitor, the National Education Association. Then, seemingly out of nowhere, she turned on yours truly. "Just look at corey DeAngelis [*sic*] twitter," she told the mother, "every day they attack me."[1]

"Attack" is a strong way to put it. But Weingarten is a high-profile public figure, and her gaslighting campaign is deserving of rebuke. I responded to Weingarten, "You fought to keep schools closed." "This is a lie," she replied, "and you know it." I don't know it. She must have forgotten that the American people have miles of receipts. Parents aren't dumb. They saw with their own eyes what happened over the previous four years, and they aren't going to quickly forget—no matter how much Weingarten wishes they would.

"We spent every day, from February on, trying to get schools open," declared Weingarten before a congressional committee in 2023, defending her organization's role in the COVID-era school shutdowns beginning the spring of 2020.[2]

If life had a narrator, a booming voice would have been heard in the chamber: "No they didn't."

"We knew that remote education was not a substitute for opening schools," Weingarten continued, "but we also knew that people had to be safe."

Only the first half of that statement was true. The second half was a mere pretext, cover for an agenda that put adult interests ahead of children. It was when parents uncovered this terrible truth that they awakened, like a sleeping giant, and became a political force like never before.

The House Select Subcommittee on the Coronavirus Pandemic had convened on April 26, 2023, to determine what had gone wrong. Specifically, the panel was investigating the role Weingarten's organization played in influencing guidance from the Centers for Disease Control and Prevention that helped keep schools closed long past when it made any sense to do so.

"We're investigating the decision-making process behind school closures and the effects it had so that we can do better in the future," said Chairman Brad Wenstrup, a Republican from Ohio, in his opening statement. "Inherently, part of that investigation is evaluating if the Centers for Disease Control and Prevention followed science as they knew it or learned it or merely accepted outside guidance regardless of available data during its guidance drafting and publication process."[3]

The impetus for the investigation was the massive learning loss K–12 students suffered over the previous three years. These losses are often attributed to the pandemic itself, but as I shall show, the reality is that they stem from the way too many schools *handled* the pandemic.

The unions denied the existence of learning loss for as long as they could. "There is no such thing as learning loss," claimed Cecily Myart-Cruz, the head of the United Teachers Los Angeles union—dubbed

"L.A.'s most powerful union" by *Los Angeles Magazine*—during an interview in August 2021.[4] When pressed by the interviewer, she suggested that "learning loss" is (in the interviewer's words) "a fake crisis marketed by shadowy purveyors of clinical and classroom assessments."

Parents knew otherwise, but they needed the data to prove it.

The extent of the learning loss was at least partially revealed by the postpandemic results on the National Assessment of Educational Progress. Often called "the Nation's Report Card," the NAEP is the nation's most respected benchmark for student learning. The assessment is administered regularly by the National Center for Education Statistics, a center within the U.S. Department of Education, to a representative sample of students nationwide.

The results were devastating.

"Two Decades of Progress, Nearly Gone: National Math, Reading Scores Hit Historic Lows," blared the headline at *Education Week* in October 2022, when the first postpandemic NAEP results were announced. Because the NAEP had been suspended due to the pandemic, the first NAEP results since 2019 were for students who took the math and reading tests during the spring of 2022. Those tests showed "the biggest drop in math performance in 4th and 8th grades since the testing program began in 1990."[5] The reading scores were not much better, as students in fourth and eighth grades were shown to be "performing on par with students in the 1990s." As *Education Week* reported, about third of the tested students couldn't "read at even the 'basic' achievement level—the lowest level on the test."[6]

Congress had tried to stem the learning loss with the passage of the Elementary and Secondary School Emergency Relief Fund in 2020, which showered public schools with $190 billion—the equivalent to about a quarter of the federal government's $795 billion annual K–12 budget, or more than $3,650 for each of the nation's 52 million public school students.[7] But funding alone didn't do the job.

The 2023 NAEP results brought even worse news. That year, students took the "long-term trends" version of the NAEP that allows comparisons going back to the 1970s. Not only had students not recovered from the previous results, they appeared to be doing even worse. The performance of thirteen-year-old students on reading fell to levels not seen in thirty years while their math performance dropped lower than any time since the NAEP began in 1971.[8] The abysmal math scores were particularly troubling to Daniel McGrath, the acting associate commissioner for assessments at the National Center for Education Statistics, who warned that "if left unaddressed, [the learning loss] could alter the trajectories and life opportunities of a whole cohort of young people, potentially reducing their abilities to pursue rewarding and productive careers in mathematics, science, and technology."[9]

Learning losses were seen across the board, but they hit some groups worse than others. The black-white achievement gap, which had been narrowing for many years, now burst back open. According to *The 74*, "The gaps in reading and math scores between white and African American students, totaling 23 and 29 points in 2012, grew to 27 and 42 points in 2023."[10] Conventionally, ten points on the NAEP is understood to approximate one year of learning, so the average black student is now about three years behind the average white student in reading and four years behind in math.

The full scale of the negative effects of the school closures are impossible to calculate, but they are almost certainly large and long-lasting. According to research by McKinsey & Company, the learning loss "threatens to depress this generation's prospects and constrict their opportunities far into adulthood."[11] By their estimates, students whose learning was disrupted by the school shutdowns "may earn $49,000 to $61,000 less over their lifetime owing to the impact of the pandemic on their schooling." [12] The learning loss could have broader implications for the U.S. economy as well. McKinsey estimates that the "impact on the US economy could amount to $128 billion to $188 billion every year as this cohort enters the workforce."[13]

Nothing in living memory has come close to the scale of the negative effects on America's K–12 students. In 1983, the U.S. Department of Education issued a report declaring that "the educational foundations of our society are presently being eroded by a rising tide of mediocrity that threatens our very future as a Nation and a People."[14] The report famously concluded: "If an unfriendly foreign power had attempted to impose on America the mediocre educational performance that exists today, we might well have viewed it as an act of war." If so, how should we view policies that caused greater academic harm than any other in the history of American public schooling?

Once the public began to appreciate the scale of the academic catastrophe wrought by the school shutdowns, the teachers unions went into full damage control mode, trying to minimize their role in the shutdowns and arguing that the shutdowns were a necessary evil to ensure the safety of students and school staff. Allies in the media spread Weingarten's version of what had happened. "Rather than championing shutdowns," the *New York Times* columnist Michelle Goldberg claimed in December 2021 that Weingarten had "spent much of her energy, both in public and behind the scenes, trying to get schools open."[15]

In her testimony before Congress, Weingarten claimed that she and her union members knew "how important it was for kids to be in school" so long as they had "the right safety measures," adding that "the safety protocols we advocated for were not an obstacle to reopening schools."[16] Her union even issued talking points, stressing that their goal was "safely reopening, not closing, schools."[17] In their telling, Weingarten and the AFT were working night and day to reopen schools, with ensuring safety as the only obstacle.

That might sound eminently reasonable. It just isn't true.

And parents who lived through it know it.

Pandemic Panic and School Shutdowns

The COVID-era school shutdowns were disastrous. They were also eminently avoidable. To appreciate the duplicity in Weingarten's desperate attempt to rewrite history, it's worth revisiting the early days of the COVID-19 pandemic.

Initially, during the winter break of 2019–20, chatter about the pandemic was just speculative background noise. There had been international outbreaks that had sparked concern in the United States before—

Ebola, SARS, avian flu, Zika virus, and so on—but none that had led to widespread school shutdowns. Schools returned from their winter breaks in January 2020 without incident despite the first recorded COVID-19 infection detected in the United States on January 19.

But by late February 2020, things started to change. On February 25, the Centers for Disease Control and Prevention hosted a press conference in which an official ominously advised parents to "ask your children's schools about their plans for school dismissals or school closures," as well as about their "plans for teleschool."[18] A few days later, the first school in the nation shut down, albeit briefly. Bothell High School in Washington state ceased operations for a few days to disinfect after an employee reported that a relative had gotten COVID. Within a month, the vast majority of school buildings nationwide were shut down. "At their peak, the closures affected at least 55.1 million students in 124,000 U.S. public and private schools," reported *Education Week*.[19] In order to slow the spread of the coronavirus, governors in forty-eight states either ordered or recommended that schools remain closed through the end of the 2019–20 academic year.[20]

It was at this point that we caught the first glimpse that decisions about school closures were driven by considerations other than safety. Certainly the brick-and-mortar school closures were, at this point, driven by genuine concerns about the health of students and staff, but what explained the closure of *virtual* schools?

For example, when Pennsylvania governor Tom Wolf, a Democrat, ordered all public and private schools to close, he also ordered the closure of cyber charter schools serving more than thirty-seven thousand children in the state virtually.[21] This kind of blanket order did nothing to encourage schools to provide educational services to students online during the emergency. Instead, it was clearly intended to protect public schools from competition, even at the cost of kids' learning. Politicians putting the financial (and ideological) interests of adults before the academic interests of children would, sadly, be a running theme throughout the pandemic and beyond.

The shutdowns also began to reveal structural flaws in the nation's public school system. An *Education Next* survey in the late spring of 2020 found that private and charter schools were substantially more likely than traditional public schools to continue providing students with meaningful education services during the lockdown.[22] The survey found that private and charter school teachers were more than twice as likely as teachers at district-run schools to meet with students daily. Private and charter schools were also about 20 percent more likely to introduce new content to their students during the lockdown. In fact, about a quarter of traditional public schools simply provided review material for what students had already learned before the closures. Arlington Public Schools in Virginia, for example, decided in April not to teach students any new material for the rest of the school year.[23]

Another national survey, this one conducted by Common Sense Media, found similar results. Private school students were more than twice as likely to connect with their teachers each day, and about 1.5 times as likely to attend online classes during the closures.[24] Likewise, a report by the Center for Reinventing Public Education in June 2020 found that only one in three school districts examined required teachers to deliver instruction during the lockdown, and less than half of all districts expected teachers to take attendance or check in with students regularly.[25]

Even so, parents were very forgiving at first. The aforementioned *Education Next* survey found that 72 percent of parents were satisfied with how their school was handling the pandemic, even though 71 percent thought that "their kids learned less than they would have had schools remained open."[26] Parents knew that schools were dealing with an unprecedented situation with high levels of uncertainty, danger, and frequently shifting expert guidance, so they were willing to cut schools some slack—even though parents and children were paying a heavy toll.

Parents were willing to do whatever it took to keep their children safe, but keeping their children at home came at a cost. A Morning Consult survey in the late spring of 2020 found that parents' top concern was that their children might be exposed to the coronavirus (70%), but they also worried about their children feeling socially isolated (69%) and falling behind academically (67%).[27] Two out of five parents also expressed concern about missing work while their children were out of school.

But although parents were willing to bear those burdens in the uncertain spring of 2020, they expected that over the summer, schools would figure out how to reopen safely in the fall. In June 2020, a Gallup survey found that 93 percent of K–12 parents wanted their schools to offer in-person instruction, including 56 percent who wanted them open for in-person instruction full time.[28]

Parents had every reason to believe that schools could do it. In June, Randi Weingarten told Fox News that in order to reopen safely, schools would need more resources. "We need the money for PPE [personal protective equipment]," Weingarten said. "We need the money for extra teachers, we need the money for extra cleaning and extra buses."[29] The federal government obliged. The CARES Act included $13.2 billion in emergency funding for schools across the country to use for their core functions as well as for "coordination of preparedness and response to the coronavirus emergency, technology acquisition, mental health services, and activities related to summer learning."[30]

But as back-to-school season arrived, parents were less than impressed. Only 29 percent of parents expressed confidence in their school's reopening plans.[31] Three-fourths of America's one hundred largest school districts, serving more than 9 million students, offered only online instruction.[32]

Students and parents were sick of online learning. A national survey conducted by Common Sense Media in August found that 59 percent of teens reported that they believed online learning is worse than in-person learning, whereas only 19 percent reported the opposite.[33] Some teens disliked remote learning so much that they figured out how to take a screenshot of themselves looking engaged so that they could leave the virtual room without getting in trouble.[34]

Virtual learning also revealed the unhealthy attitudes that some public school officials had about parents as schools tried to exercise control over students and their families at home. For example, a school in Colorado called the police on a twelve-year-old boy because he was playing with a toy Nerf gun during his virtual art class—and the student was suspended for five days.[35] Likewise, police showed up at an eleven-year-old boy's home in Baltimore, Maryland, after his teacher reported him for having a BB gun mounted on the wall behind him during a virtual class.[36]

But it wasn't a two-way street. Although virtual schooling allowed schools to peer into students' homes, school officials didn't appreciate the window it gave parents into the classroom. A school district in Tennessee even demanded that parents sign a form agreeing not to monitor their own children's virtual classes.[37]

Of the public schools that did reopen for in-person instruction, most imposed mask mandates and social-distancing requirements.[38] But even many schools that had reopened were soon closed again, leaving families and students in a lurch.

New York City schools had reopened, but as the *New York Times* explained, Mayor Bill de Blasio "faced enormous headwinds and criticism from the teachers' union, politicians and some parents who said they did not believe schools would be safe and that the city should have started the school year remote-only."[39] By mid-November, de Blasio had closed schools again. But this time, parents were not as sanguine as in the spring. Frustrated parents flooded City Hall to protest the school shutdowns. One parent, Laura Espinoza, explained to the *Times* how the school shutdowns were wreaking havoc on her family. Her then-six-year-old twins both had disabilities, and virtual instruction was no substitute for the care they received in person.

> "They don't adapt to change quickly, all this back and forth has not been good for them," Ms. Espinoza said. She added that remote instruction is also taking a toll on her 15-year-old daughter. "My daughter can't go to class because she's helping me with the twins," she said. "Remote learning is not working."[40]

De Blasio justified his decision as in the interests of safety, but parents were no longer buying it. "The city is not any more safe today than yesterday because schools are closed," said another mother, Daniela Jampel, who lives in Washington Heights with her two children. She joined other parents in pointing the finger at city officials and the special interests who had pushed for school closures over the objections of parents.

> "I am no longer content to let four men—Bill de Blasio, Michael Mulgrew, Richard Carranza and Andrew Cuomo—decide whether my children can go to school and whether I as a working mother can have a job and a career," she added, referring to the president of the teachers' union, the schools chancellor and the governor, along with the mayor.[41]

School districts in several states—including Arizona, Maryland, North Carolina, and Virginia—kept their doors shut for education, but kept them open for day-care services, for which they charged parents, on top of their taxes, hundreds of dollars a week out-of-pocket.[42] You know, COVID was very discerning. If you were learning, it would get you! But if you were just sitting there for day care, it would peacefully pass over you like a wispy cloud on a sunny day.

Nationwide, parents began showing up at school board meetings and school district headquarters to express their displeasure. When the Mequon-Thiensville School District announced that they would offer only remote instruction, more than one hundred parents and students showed up at the district headquarters demanding in-person instruction.

> "Virtual learning is not possible for the majority of parents that work," said Scarlett Johnson, parent.

> "I'm concerned about their social and emotional well being," said Andrea Lorenz, parent.

> "We're out here because this decision should not have been made without the input of the students and [...] parents, not just the teachers," said Rob Wirthlin, parent.[43]

Were the parents' requests unreasonable? Maybe it just wasn't safe to reopen?

But private schools *were* reopening safely. "Public schools plan to open not at all or just a few days a week," reported the *New York Times* in August 2020, "while many neighboring private schools are opening full time."[44] More than eight out of ten private schools associated with the National Association of Independent Schools reopened in the fall of 2020 with full or partial in-person instruction.[45] By mid-October, about 60 percent of independent private schools were fully in-person while just five percent were remote only.[46] Meanwhile, more than nine out of ten Catholic schools reopened for in-person instruction.[47]

Opening wasn't easy, especially in the face of politicians and bureaucrats trying to keep private schools closed.

Kentucky private schools, for example, took the fight to the U.S. Supreme Court for the right to provide in-person services for their customers when Gov. Andy Beshear ordered them to close.[48] Private schools in states such as Michigan, Ohio, and Wisconsin took similar legal actions. A Christian private school in Sacramento even rebranded itself as a day care to get around the government's arbitrary closure rule that applied to schools but not childcare facilities.

If private schools could reopen safely, why couldn't the public schools?

The Force Behind School Closures: Teachers Unions

The long-term closing of schools, and the harm it did to children nationwide, was a decision based not on health but on politics—thanks to teachers unions and the Democratic politicians they fund.

In 2020, Christos Makridis of Stanford University and I conducted the first study to show that public schools in areas with stronger teachers unions were substantially less likely to reopen in person. In our study, we examined the data compiled by *Education Week* on the reopening decisions of 835 public school districts nationwide in the fall of 2020. By that point, it was already common knowledge that children were less at risk for COVID, yet schools were still widely closed—without any relationship to the local COVID infection rates.[49] Not surprisingly, we found that school districts in areas with stronger teachers unions were less likely to reopen in person, even after controlling for differences in local demographics. Indeed, school districts in states that required union membership were 25 percentage points less likely to plan to reopen with full-time in-person instruction available than school districts in right-to-work states. The relationship between unionization and reopening decisions remained substantively and statistically significant even after controlling for school district size, coronavirus deaths, and local infection rates.

In Florida, for example, the largest school districts in the state's biggest cities only offered remote learning at the beginning of the academic year but, statewide, 73 percent of the school districts in the dataset reopened full-time with in-person instruction that fall. By contrast, just 4 percent of districts across California, a state with much stronger teachers unions, offered in-person instruction.[50]

Since the publication of our finding, at least five additional rigorous studies have revealed the same relationship—stronger teachers unions meant more kids locked out of school. For example, a study published by Brown University's Annenberg Institute concluded:

> Contrary to the conventional understanding of school districts as localized and non-partisan actors, we find evidence that politics, far more than science, shaped school district decision-making. Mass partisanship and teacher union strength best explain how school boards approached reopening.[51]

Likewise, a study by researchers at Michigan State University found that when governors left it up to districts whether to have in-person education, the "decisions were more tied to local political partisanship and union strength than to COVID-19 severity."[52] In other words, areas with stronger unions and political control by Democrats were more likely to see their local public schools closed than areas with weaker unions and Republican control.

Americans were told that schools were just "following the science." But to understand why the schools really closed down, we need to follow the political science.

Albert Shanker, the former head of both the American Federation of Teachers and its New York affiliate, supposedly said, "When schoolchildren start paying union dues, that's when I'll start representing the interests of schoolchildren." The quote might be apocryphal, but the sentiment accurately reflects his organization's motivations, incentives, and behavior. Unions represent the interests of their members, not the firms their members work for nor the customers of those firms. In the case of public schools, that means the unions represent the employees, not the students or their families.

It was in the interests of students and their families for schools to reopen, but the unions believed it was in the interests of their members to keep schools closed and to use the *prospect* of reopening as a bargaining chip—under the pretext of "safety"—to extract concessions that were entirely unrelated to COVID safety.

As President Barack Obama's chief of staff Rahm Emanuel said: "Never let a crisis go to waste."

AFT head Randi Weingarten certainly wasn't going to let the COVID crisis go to waste. On July 24, 2020, she declared: "Let's stop the debate about whether safety matters and start rolling up our sleeves so we get the resources to meet the needs of students, whether we are teaching remotely or in person."[53] In other words: "Shut up and show me the money!"

In California, the teachers unions followed Weingarten's lead.

Over the summer of 2020, the two largest school districts in California—Los Angeles Unified and San Diego Unified, which together serve more than six hundred thousand students—announced that they would not reopen for in-person instruction in the fall, claiming that they lacked the necessary "on-demand testing" to safely reopen, and promising that they would reopen "as soon as public health conditions allow."[54] Earlier that year, the teachers union had struck a deal with the Los Angeles school district to require teachers to work only four hours each day in the spring—and that requirement did not include any live video instruction.[55] The unions also shifted the blame for the inability to reopen as other districts and private schools had, declaring that the "federal government must provide schools with the resources we need to reopen in a responsible manner."

But it later became apparent that something else was going on. Unreasonable and politically motivated demands by the teachers unions were making it impossible for schools to reopen.

The unions applauded the school closures, smearing anyone who wanted schools to reopen as "anti-science." "It is time to take a stand against Trump's dangerous, anti-science agenda that puts the lives of our members, our students, and our families at risk," said UTLA President Cecily Myart-Cruz—who, a year later, would be denying the existence of learning loss. "We all want to physically open schools and be back with our students, but lives hang in the balance. Safety has to be the priority. We need to get this right for our communities."[56]

But "safety" was a pretext. The unions had other goals in mind.

That summer, the UTLA published a "study" titled *Same Storm but Different Boats: The Safe and Equitable Conditions for Starting LAUSD in 2020–21*, that purported to look "at the science behind the specific conditions that must be met in the second-largest school district in the nation before staff and students can safely return."[57] The title itself was intended to deflect blame for why the districts it served failed to reopen as others did, but even more egregious was the list of dozens upon dozens of demands the union stated must be met in order for schools to reopen, including:

- **A federal bailout:** "Many experts are calling for at least $500 billion in additional federal assistance this year, and a commitment to continue support over several years."

- **Socialized medicine:** "Coronavirus shows definitively why we need Medicare For All. [. . .] The boundless greed of the for-profit health industry, combined with this country's deeply ingrained racism, has led to race-based health disparities that have resulted in excess deaths especially among Black communities long before the pandemic further widened the health gap."
- **Defunding the police:** "Police violence is a leading cause of death and trauma for Black people, and is a serious public health and moral issue. We must shift the astronomical amount of money devoted to policing, to education and other essential needs such as housing and public health."
- **Tax hikes:** This included hiking California property taxes by about $7.5 to $12 billion as well as raising taxes on high-income earners and creating a new tax on wealth.
- **A moratorium on charter schools:** The union document claims that charter schools "drain resources from district schools."[58]

Who knew that for public schools to reopen safely, we needed to defund the police, tax the rich, remake America's entire health care system, and make it harder for families to enroll their kids elsewhere?

The California unions were far from alone in exploiting the pandemic to make political demands while holding America's students hostage. Unions in Boston, Chicago, Little Rock, Milwaukee, Oakland, Racine, St. Paul, and elsewhere joined with the National Educators United and Democratic Socialists of America in the summer of 2020 to demand that the government "go much further to provide the resources to ensure a safe and equitable school reopening."[59] In addition to demands that there be "no reopening until the scientific data supports it" (i.e., until they *decide* that the scientific data supports it) and that schools provide adequate cleaning, COVID testing, and protective equipment, their list of demands included, in their words:

- **Police-free schools**
- Support for our communities and families, including **canceling rents and mortgages, a moratorium on evictions/ foreclosures**, providing direct cash assistance to those not able to work or who are unemployed, and other critical social needs
- **Moratorium on new charter or voucher programs and standardized testing**
- Massive infusion of federal money to support the reopening funded by **taxing billionaires and Wall Street**[60] [emphases added]

None of these radical left-wing political goals had anything to do with the ability to reopen schools safely.

Parents were furious. They knew that the unions' demands were bogus and self-interested and that the risks were minimal. "More and more research is showing that reopening schools will not overly endanger students and staff," Lance Izumi, senior director of the Center for Education at the Pacific Research Institute told the *Los Angeles Times* in October 2020, adding that "schools are not super-spreaders and school infection rates are low even in places with high community rates."[61] Research by Prof. Emily Oster of Brown University had shown that in early October 2020 "the infection rates were 0.13% for students and 0.22% for staff," indicating a minuscule level of risk.[62]

Meanwhile, distance learning was an absolute disaster for children. Preliminary research was already documenting massive learning loss. In December 2020, a McKinsey report warned of the "high cost of this prolonged period of remote learning, from rising rates of depression and anxiety to the loss of student learning."[63] Their research showed that "the cumulative learning loss could be substantial, especially in mathematics—with students on average likely to lose five to nine months of learning by the end of this school year."[64]

Parents knew it. A poll of California parents showed a massive drop in support for distance learning from 57 percent who thought it was successful in March 2020 to only 35 percent who felt the same in October.[65]

The least satisfied were low-income parents, only 30 percent of whom said distance learning was successful. Moreover, 82 percent of parents told pollsters that they were experiencing higher stress than usual, and 63 percent said their child's stress was higher.

"Parents, we're on edge, some are desperate," said Mary Lee, the mother of a Los Angeles Unified School District graduate with autism, to *The 74*. "Even the ones who don't have to go to a job, they just basically feel like they're failing their kids because they don't know how to do the [distance learning] work."[66]

As parental pressure on public officials mounted, and school districts began preparing to reopen, unions did everything they could to keep schools closed. Despite all the evidence that reopening schools was safe, unions held protests against reopening plans all across the country in which they displayed "mock gravestones, makeshift coffins, and... their own early obituaries."[67] The Florida Education Association sued Gov. Ron DeSantis to block schools from reopening, and members of United Teachers of Dade organized a caravan including a hearse to protest reopening schools. Other unions fearmongered with fake body bags, and protested with ridiculous signs saying things such as, "I can't teach from the grave."[68]

In January 2021, the Chicago Teachers Union (CTU)—the largest union in Illinois—posted a video of its members protesting a return to work through "interpretive dance." No, really, that wasn't a *Babylon Bee* headline. Pradheep Shanker, a radiologist and public-health expert, summed up the country's collective reaction this way: "Dear God." The video was bizarre, creepy, and pathetic. And it spurred nationwide ire. Parents from coast to coast lashed out. While they were trying to make ends meet during lockdowns, the members of the union, dressed in pajamas and socks, were gleefully sliding across the floors of their homes and glitzy apartments. The dance moves were something else. Now we had discovered that Chicago's government-run schools weren't just failing at math and reading. The students wishing to pursue dance were also screwed.

This wasn't the first time the CTU resorted to theatrics to try to score political points. It tweeted that it was "completely in support" of a video of protestors with a guillotine outside of Amazon CEO Jeff Bezos's house. "We are completely frightened by, completely impressed by and completely in support of wherever this is headed," the CTU tweeted.[69] The tweet was later deleted. Maybe because someone finally understood it was sick and demented. Or because someone realized it revealed them to be a bunch of hypocrites. At the time, the Chicago Teachers' Pension Fund owned more than forty-five thousand shares of Amazon stock, worth over $86 million. (The hypocrisy of these union bosses is never-ending. CTU's president, Stacy Davis Gates, decided to send her own son to a private school just a year after she said school choice was for "racists"[70]).

Then in 2022, long after the entire country had returned to normal, the CTU went on strike because its members were still too afraid to go back to work. In Democrat-controlled places like Chicago, "two weeks to slow the spread" turned into two years to flatten a generation.

Nationwide, union shenanigans made it impossible to provide the in-person instruction that parents demanded and students badly needed. School districts in Arizona, Arkansas, New Jersey, New York, Utah, Virginia, Washington, Wisconsin, and elsewhere were forced to delay or abort reopening their schools after the teachers unions staged sickouts or what AFT's Weingarten called "safety strikes."[71]

The unions also worked behind the scenes to influence the federal agencies that school districts relied upon to interpret "the science" surrounding school safety in the age of COVID.

In early 2021, the Centers for Disease Control and Prevention was set to issue new guidance for school closures and reopening. Documents obtained via Freedom of Information Act requests by the watchdog group Americans for Public Trust revealed that the major teachers unions heavily lobbied the CDC to influence the guidance. In fact, emails acquired by the *New York Post* revealed that guidance issued by the CDC regarding school reopenings used the language suggested to them by Randi Weingarten's American Federation of Teachers.[72] In at least two instances, the language adopted by the CDC was almost identical to the AFT's suggestions.

As the *Post* reported, the documents showed that in the days before the CDC released its highly anticipated school-reopening guidelines on February 12, 2021, there was "a flurry of activity between CDC Director Dr. Rochelle Walensky, her top advisors and union officials," while top Biden administration officials were kept informed of their collusion.[73] The emails published by the *Post* demonstrate that the union lobbying paid off:

> "Thank you again for Friday's rich discussion about forthcoming CDC guidance and for your openness to the suggestions made by our president, Randi Weingarten, and the AFT," wrote AFT senior director for health issues Kelly Trautner in a Feb 1 email—which described the union as the CDC's "thought partner."
>
> "We were able to review a copy of the draft guidance document over the weekend and were able to provide some initial feedback to several staff this morning about possible ways to strengthen the document," Trautner continued. "... We believe our experiences on the ground can inform and enrich thinking around what is practicable and prudent in future guidance documents."

On the same day that the CDC released its reopening guidelines, the AFT issued a press release praising the CDC for producing "a rigorous road map, based on science, that our members can use to fight for a safe reopening."[74] The AFT lauded the guidelines for "including compulsory masking, 6 feet of physical distancing, handwashing, cleaning and ventilation, diagnostic testing and contact tracing" as well as "vaccine priority for teachers and school staff." The AFT concluded by applauding the Biden administration for "its $1.9 trillion American Rescue Plan," and for "creating a culture of trust and collaboration" with the union.

The CDC had been preparing to include the phrase "all schools can provide in-person instruction" in their guidance. But in a text message exchange later revealed by a FOIA request by the Fairfax County Parents

Association, AFT's Weingarten raised concerns about this language with CDC Director Walensky.[75] The CDC's final language was significantly watered down, changing the word "can" to "have options to," so that it read: "all schools *have options to* provide in-person instruction" (emphasis added).

The CDC also altered its guidance regarding offering in-person instruction regardless of the local COVID infection rates. After multiple meetings, texts, emails, and phone calls between Walensky and Weingarten's team, the CDC advised that schools could remain closed if they were in "red zones." That sounds benign, but seemingly banal, bureaucratic language can mask radical policy implications. As CNN documented, at the time the CDC released its guidelines, more than 99 percent of America's K–12 students lived in so-called red zones."[76]

When asked by CNN's Jake Tapper whether she could "point to any scientific reason for students in the United States not to return to in person classes" so long as they followed the five CDC-recommended steps for safe reopening, Walensky deflected. "We really don't want to bring community disease into the classroom," she replied. "We also know that mask breaching is among the reasons that we have transmission within schools when it happens. Somewhere around 60 percent of students are reliably masking. That has to be universal. So we have work to do."[77]

Missing from Walensky's answer was any scientific explanation for the CDC's decision regarding red zones, so Tapper pressed her again. "But what's the science?" he asked, noting that she and the director of the National Institute of Allergy and Infectious Diseases, Dr. Anthony Fauci, "have been saying for months that the schools should be open" so long as they followed the CDC's social distancing and other safety guidelines. Walensky again dodged the question, repeating the research about students' masking habits.

Government health officials were even directed by the Biden White House to factor teachers union contract negotiations into their reopening guidance—something that is clearly unrelated to the health of students and school staff, but does affect the unions' coffers. Emails later uncovered by a FOIA request by Americans for Public Trust (APT) showed that White House staffers arranged a meeting between CDC Director Walensky and Becky Pringle, the president of the National Education Association, the nation's largest teachers union.[78] Shortly thereafter, the White House gave "homework assignments" to officials at the U.S. Department of Health and Human Services (HHS), directing them to factor union negotiations into their reopening guidance. Although the emails provided to APT were heavily redacted, Fox News later obtained unredacted versions from a source at the department:

> "Hey team—Just got off a call with the White House and Department of Education regarding the school reopening guidance that is projected to roll out on Friday," Michael Baker, an HHS official, wrote in a Feb. 8 email. "We have some homework assignments."
>
> The assignments Baker listed were redacted in the emails provided to APT. However, an HHS official provided the full email to Fox News. [...] Without the redaction, the email shows that the White House was concerned with issues teachers unions faced that were unrelated to public health experts' determinations on school reopenings.[79]

"These emails show time and time again that the White House inserted itself into the shaping of school guidance with a primary focus of accommodating teachers unions," Caitlin Sutherland, executive director of APT, told Fox News. "However, the only thing the White House should have been focused on was how to get our children safely back into the classroom."[80]

When a reporter asked Washington, DC, mayor Muriel Bowser if trends in the city's COVID-19 cases justified the all-virtual start to the school year, Bowser said the quiet part out loud: "No. I wouldn't say the attention to the health metrics is the only thing that's leading to our decision today," adding that "clearly we want to work with our workforce."[81]

Congress even acceded to the unions' demands for more money, but to no avail. In March, Congress passed yet another COVID-19 relief plan, which included $123 billion for K–12 public schools, supposedly to help them reopen. That's almost the amount the United States dedicated, adjusting for inflation, to the Marshall Plan to rebuild Europe after World War II. And that was on top of the mostly yet-unspent $54 billion federal bailout for public schools a few months earlier and the $13 billion allocation from the spring of 2020.

But money wasn't the issue. In a second analysis with Stanford's Christos Makridis, we examined data from more than twelve thousand school districts nationwide, covering more than 90 percent of school-age children, and found no evidence to suggest that higher revenue or expenditures per student were associated with a higher probability of reopening schools for in-person learning.[82] As before, our study found no relationship between COVID-19 risk in the community and the probability of reopening in person. School reopening was strongly related, however, to county-level voting patterns in the 2016 election.

In fact, an analysis by researchers at Georgetown University found that districts that decided to go remote only generally had financial surpluses. The researchers estimated that Los Angeles Unified School District, which had kept their doors closed under union pressure, had a more than $500 million funding surplus, or about $1,100 a student, for the 2020–21 school year.[83]

The union-induced school closures harmed students academically, mentally, and emotionally, with virtually no reduction in overall coronavirus transmission or child mortality. Parents were understandably furious at the public schools that had broken faith with them during their time of need, and they weren't going to just sit there and take it.

The Parent Revolution had begun.

Chapter 2

THE SLEEPING GIANT AWAKENS

> I fear all we have done is to awaken a sleeping giant and fill him with a terrible resolve.
>
> —*Japanese admiral Isoroku Yamamoto in* Tora! Tora! Tora!

First Shots Fired in the School Board Wars

The teachers unions overplayed their hand. Now it was time for parents to play theirs.

Parents pushed back against the school closures. Across the country, parents organized rallies calling for school districts to reopen. "Parents are outraged," said Danielle Wildstein, a parent who organized a protest rally calling for the Scotch Plains–Fanwood school district in New Jersey to reopen in November 2020. "More and more trust is being lost in the community."[1]

In Davis, California, parents packed school board meetings and demanded that the board reopen the schools. "We're simply asking for the Board of Trustees to listen to, and follow, the science and advice of the experts," said Mike Creedon, a member of the Davis Joint Unified School District Parent Coalition, in February 2021. "Creating arbitrary and excessively strict requirements to keep our children out of classrooms is counterproductive, for both the children and our community."[2] In the end, the board voted 4–1 to adopt a hybrid model, "part in-classroom learning, part distance learning, with small cohorts of students taking turns in a classroom" that had been modified "to increase the amount of airspace between student desks."[3]

In Oak Harbor, Washington, parents stood outside school board meetings in March 2021 with signs reading OPEN SCHOOLS NOW. "I heard another parent say that distance learning is (like) attempting to put Ikea furniture together blindfolded—it's impossible," said Alisha Gollihar. "Open up the schools full time, please, not just for now but for the future of our children."[4] Superintendent Lance Gibbon responded that school officials were working to bring students back to in-person instruction after spring break. Weeks later he announced that he was leaving the district, where he earned nearly $250,000 plus benefits, for a position elsewhere that paid nearly $300,000.[5]

When Des Moines, Iowa's largest school district announced its plans to make schools online-only in the fall of 2020, parents showed up at school board meetings in force. As reported by the *Des Moines Register*, some parents and community leaders implored school board members to at least open schools part time:

> "I believe our families should have a choice between a hybrid model and virtual learning because a 100% virtual does not work for everyone," said Kameron Middlebrooks, president of the NAACP Des Moines chapter.
>
> Virtual classes may work for families that have the resources to send their children to a child care center that can assist with their education, or for families with parents who have the option of working from home, Middlebrooks said.
>
> "But it does not work for the family that has multiple children where both parents are essential workers," he said. "It does not work for the child who has special needs that can only be provided in a classroom setting. It does not work for the child who is falling behind and needs extra attention."

> Nina Richtman said the closure of school buildings has resulted in fewer services for her two special needs children that cannot be made up online. Both of her sons have an individualized education plan and a one-on-one associate when schools [are] in session.[6]

Some community members stepped in to offer support that the district was unwilling or unable to provide. Eugene Kiruhura, a father of Des Moines students and a pastor at Shalom Covenant Church, told the *Des Moines Register* that his congregation began offering educational support services to his mostly refugee community. Fifty students enrolled in the program in the first week, but they could not take on additional students because they lacked enough volunteers.[7]

When school boards didn't listen to parents, parents turned to state elected officials for relief.

For example, frustrated parents in Iowa lobbied Gov. Kim Reynolds, a Republican, for help reopening the schools when school boards wouldn't listen. Reynolds, however, did listen. "Iowa's approach to returning to school must be based on what's in the best interest of students and families," Reynolds said at a press conference announcing her school reopening plan over the summer of 2020. "We've heard from hundreds of Iowa parents who want their children to return to a structured, safe and enriching academic environment."[8] The governor ordered Iowa school districts to conduct at least half of their instruction in-person when classes resumed that fall.

But recalcitrant district officials still didn't listen to parents or the governor. In Des Moines, school officials declared their intent to remain closed for in-person instruction in the fall of 2020, in defiance of the governor's order. The district even sued the governor, seeking to have her reopening order overturned. The district filed a motion in the lawsuit asking the judge to allow their schools to hold classes online only while the litigation was pending. The judge denied the motion, ordering them to reopen schools for in-person instruction per the governor's directive. "The court's decision today recognizes that we are correctly interpreting

Iowa law, and I remain committed to working with Des Moines Public Schools on their return-to-learn plan so that it meets the educational and health needs of Iowa's children," said Reynolds in response to the decision.[9] Another judge denied a similar motion brought in a separate lawsuit by the Iowa City school district and the state's teachers union. Months later, they would drop their lawsuit after losing a hearing and being denied a request to appeal.[10]

Nevertheless, in defiance of both the governor and the judge, the Des Moines school district held classes online only anyway, becoming the only one of Iowa's 327 school districts to flout the law. "Schools that choose not to return to school for at least 50% in-person instruction are not defying me. They are defying the law," Reynolds said. "If schools move to primarily remote learning without approval, according again to the law, those days do not count toward instructional time."[11] Despite the combined pressure of parents, the governor, and the legal system, it was not until October 2020 that any Des Moines students saw the inside of a physical classroom.[12]

In other states, it was the parents who sued to reopen schools. In Utah, eight families filed a lawsuit against Gov. Gary Herbert and the Salt Lake City School Board claiming that their decisions to keep schools closed harmed their children's education to such a degree that it amounted to "an historic deprivation of rights, stripping 21,000 students of basic rights secured by the Utah constitution."[13] The parents lost. A judge ultimately dismissed their lawsuit, ruling that "Utah's children are not entitled under the state constitution to an in-person education."[14]

A lawsuit by California parents met a similar fate. "The State's abdication of responsibility and insufficient response to the challenges of remote learning have denied Plaintiffs the basic educational equality guaranteed to them by the California Constitution," the parents' complaint alleged. "Because the State's pandemic response compels families to use their homes as classrooms, the State's constitutional obligations expand into the home."[15] The California courts rejected their petition.[16]

Parents also sought to replace recalcitrant school board members.

In San Francisco, parents frustrated by the slow pace of reopening efforts organized to recall school board members.

"They seem more focused—in my estimation, anyway—on symbols of equity rather than actual equity, which would mean getting schools open for all the children in San Francisco," said Jennifer Sey, a mother of five who worked on the recall effort.[17] Sey was alluding to the school board's efforts in January 2021 to rename forty-four schools in the district, replacing "controversial" figures like George Washington, Thomas Jefferson, and Abraham Lincoln, the former two for owning slaves and the latter, according to local teacher Jeremiah Jeffries, based on "his treatment of First Nation peoples."[18] Paul Revere was ostensibly removed due to his role in the Penobscot Expedition of 1779, which board members incorrectly believed to be an attempt to colonize Native Americans, rather than an assault on a British fort.[19] Meanwhile, the board appeared to be doing little to nothing about getting kids back in schools.

Parents were outraged. "I don't know anybody personally who doesn't think it's embarrassing," a local parent and pediatrician, Dr. Adam Davis, told the *New York Times*. He called the renaming "a caricature of what people think liberals in San Francisco do."[20]

Facing pressure from woke activists on the one side and angry parents on the other, San Francisco mayor London Breed tried to split the difference, expressing support for the woke renaming effort, but chastising the board for its timing. "What I cannot understand is why the School Board is advancing a plan to have all these schools renamed by April, when there isn't a plan to have our kids back in the classroom by then," Breed said.[21] "Our students are suffering, and we should be talking about getting them in classrooms...Our families are frustrated about a lack of a plan, and they are especially frustrated with the fact that the discussion of these plans weren't even on the agenda for last night's School Board meeting."

Parents had had enough. By wasting time on frivolous virtue signaling instead of doing their jobs and reopening schools, the school board had lost the confidence of parents—so the parents decided to find a new board. "Unfortunately, this board has failed to listen to parents, we made so many good faith efforts to reach out and communicate," said local parent Siva Raj after filing paperwork in January 2021 to initiate a recall of the three board members eligible to be recalled. "Parents are just ready to roll up their sleeves and get involved in every aspect of reopenings."[22]

Parents faced long odds. It was the first recall effort since 1983, when there was a failed attempt to remove then-mayor Dianne Feinstein. (Incidentally, a school named for her was also one of the forty-four slated to be renamed—her supposed sin was replacing a Confederate flag that an activist tore down from a historical display of eighteen American flags outside the San Francisco Civic Center.) But parents were determined and well-organized. A year later, all three challenged board members were successfully recalled.[23]

San Francisco was far from alone. According to Ballotpedia, there were 92 school board recall efforts against 237 board members in 2021, and 52 school board recall efforts against 121 board members in 2022.[24] By contrast, there were only 20 school board recall efforts against 47 board members in 2019.[25] Parents were mad as hell and they weren't going to take it anymore.

But fighting city hall isn't easy. Most of the recall efforts didn't end like San Francisco's. Less than 3 percent of challenged board members in 2021 and 2022 were successfully recalled. Most of the school board members got elected with union support, and the unions were willing to do whatever it took to maintain control over the public schools.

Making Parents the Enemy

How did the unions respond to parental efforts to exert more control of their children's schools? By attacking parents, of course.

No, it wasn't the virus that needed to be defeated. It was you. Mom and Dad.

The unions publicly smeared parents who had the temerity to suggest that schools should do their jobs. In Chicago, home of the nation's third-largest public school system, the local union took to Twitter to demonize those who favored reopening schools: "The push to reopen schools is rooted in sexism, racism and misogyny," tweeted the Chicago Teachers Union (CTU) on December 6, 2020.[26]

A few months later, union member in California named Damian Harmony would say "hold my beer" to the CTU by smearing parents who wanted schools reopened for their supposed "cynical, pearl-clutching, faux-urgency, ableist, structurally white-supremacist hysteria."[27] That same month, the United Teachers of Los Angeles union called California's school reopening plan "a recipe for propagating structural racism," and its president, Cecily "There's No Such Thing As Learning Loss" Myart-Cruz, accused "white, wealthy parents" of "driving the push behind a rushed return."[28]

I'm old enough to remember when the term "white supremacist" referred to those—such as neo-Nazis and members of the Ku Klux Klan—who believed that the white race is superior to other races. Now the unions and their allies were smearing parents as "white supremacists" for the horrible thought crime of wanting their children to go to school.

The smear became a running theme. In Cambridge, Massachusetts, the local union voted to reject the school reopening plan as they endorsed a letter by the Educators of Color Coalition, which claimed that the reopening plan was "rooted in white supremacy norms, values, and culture."[29] Likewise, 140 members of the Pasco Association of Educators in Washington state claimed in January 2021 that the "culture of white supremacy and white privilege can be seen in our very own community in regards to the decision to reopen schools in a hybrid format, despite rising cases and community spread."[30] The *Washington Post* even ran a blog post by a union member in New Haven, Connecticut, lambasting the supposed "racist effects of school reopening" and claiming that "comorbidity is white supremacy."[31]

Not to be outdone, a member of the Chicago Teachers Union, Mike Friedberg, penned an article asking: "Will We Let 'Nice White Parents' Kill Black and Brown Families?"[32] In his telling, it was "white privileged parents" who wanted schools open while "Black and Latine" parents wanted them closed. The reality was that although white parents were, on average, more likely to be ready to return to in-person instruction before minority parents, significant portions of families across the racial and ethnic spectrum wanted in-person instruction. When the Chicago school district conducted a survey of parents in March 2021, more than four in ten wanted to return to in-person instruction.[33] Although the survey did not identify the race or ethnicity of respondents, about three in ten students who returned that month for in-person instruction at campuses were majority black and majority Latino.[34]

Ironically, the Friedberg article spent several paragraphs claiming that "remote learning is not a lost cause" and that the "'learning loss' argument is incredibly flawed."[35] Not only has *massive* learning loss been unquestionably documented, but it's also significantly worse among black students. According to McKinsey, by the end of the 2020–21 academic school year, students "in majority-Black schools ended the school year six months behind in both math and reading, while students in majority-white schools ended up just four months behind in math and three months behind in reading."[36] If any policy had racist results, it was the union-pushed school closures and remote learning—which really should be called *remotely* learning—not parent-backed school reopenings.

The California Teachers Association (CTA) even stooped to spying on parents—conducting what amounts to opposition research, the same as political candidates do on their opponents. A public records request uncovered emails from a union employee asking a public school principal for information about "the ideological leaning of groups that are funding the reopen lawsuits." She noted that she had heard the principal had "lots of information regarding the Parents Association."[37] When another union employee in the email exchange realized that they had accidentally used the principal's work email, they went into damage control mode, asking him to "delete and disregard" the emails.

One union employee was more sanguine, however. "I don't think there will be an issue," she wrote, "unless someone does a record request for his work email." Oops!

The hypocrisy of the unions knows no bounds. In March 2021, while the CTA was still fighting tooth and nail to keep schools closed while spying on parents who wanted them open, the president of the Berkeley

Federation of Teachers, Matt Meyer, was caught on camera taking his own kid to an in-person private preschool.[38] In-person schooling for me, but not for thee!

The unions even did oppo research on parents trying new ways of educating their children during the pandemic. When the unions closed the schools, groups like Prenda helped parents open new "microschools" in their or other parents' homes, church basements, and anywhere they could find space. Rather than embracing the idea, the unions sought to sabotage it.

Prenda was founded in 2018 by Kelly Smith, an MIT grad who was inspired by his kids' experience at an afternoon coding club to create a network of small schools (typically five to ten students each) where learning is self-directed with the assistance of online tools and an in-person "guide." While schools were closed during the pandemic, Prenda received a surge in interest from parents—especially those who wanted the benefits of in-person instruction while limiting their children's potential exposure. Prenda began 2020 with about one thousand students at one hundred microschools and ended the year with four times that.

Where parents saw an opportunity, the unions saw a threat. Prenda's rapid growth sent the unions into a panic. What if the kids who left their public schools liked Prenda better? What if they never came back?

The National Education Association hatched a plan: Scare parents away from trying Prenda in the first place. To do that, they wrote up two "opposition reports" (their words), one on microschools generally and one on Prenda specifically. The first one warned union members and their allies: "The Opposition Report has documented widespread support for micro-schools."[39] *Quelle horreur!*

The report identified more than twenty additional microschool networks and related organizations—including Acton Academy, AltSchool, My Tech High, and Outschool—and recommended that their staff and allies familiarize themselves with a list of anti-microschool talking points the NEA had developed, such as that the microschools "do not guarantee students or educators the same civil rights protections that are required in public schools," their staff are "not required to be credentialed," and their students "are not held accountable to state standards of learning."[40] Of course, none of these issues topped parental concerns about schools being *closed*.

Most amusingly was the union talking point that amounted to an own goal: that microschools would widen the "opportunity gap." As Elliot Kaufman of the *Wall Street Journal* wryly observed: "It's a strange pitch from the teachers union: *Microschools are dangerous—they help their students learn more!*"[41]

The second opposition report focused on Prenda specifically and included personal information about Kelly Smith, including his home address and a picture of his house.[42]

The report also raised concerns about the "safety" of Prenda and other microschool students who might be exposed to guns, drugs, and unfenced swimming pools. Union-backed groups like Save Our Schools Arizona used these talking points to lobby the legislature to regulate Prenda and other microschools.[43] Fortunately, state legislators saw through their absurd and self-serving arguments, and microschools continued to flourish.

It was particularly ironic for the unions to argue that using parents' homes for microschooling was unsafe while the unions were simultaneously arguing that students were not safe at school during the pandemic. Apparently, they weren't safe anywhere!

Friedberg had claimed his support for keeping schools closed was because he did "not want to risk my students' lives, their families' lives, or my own life." He may well have been sincere in his fears, but not all his colleagues were. Some, like CTU executive board and area vice president Sarah Chambers, seemed to have other motivations for working remotely.

"Hearing of an educator revolution happening," tweeted Chambers in late December 2020. "Tons of members are emailing their admin: I'll be asserting my right to continue to work in a safe remote environment on January 4th, 2021. I have signed the pledge, along with over 8,000+ union educators to continue to work remotely[.]"

How remotely? Thousands of miles, apparently, as Chambers was tweeting from poolside at a resort in Puerto Rico. "Spending the last day of 2020 poolside," Chambers wrote from her @sarah4justice Instagram account alongside a selfie of herself lounging by the pool, adding: "We have the whole pool to ourselves."[44]

In the wake of unnecessarily long school closures and attacks on parents, many frustrated parents were ready to let the unions have the public schools to themselves, too.

The Public School Exodus Begins

Parents noticed that private schools were open while public schools were closed. If school boards wouldn't listen to their voice, some parents decided to exercise their choice.

For example, Joe and Jennifer Clayton had never considered private school for their six-year-old son, Robbie. The Claytons were a family of limited means living in Lake Hopatcong, a small town in New Jersey. When their public school closed for in-person instruction during the spring of 2020, Jennifer had to take a leave of absence from her job at a local restaurant to take care of their son. She was planning to return to work in the fall, but "at the very last minute, the township went all virtual," Jennifer told CNBC, adding that upon hearing the news, she "had a slight nervous breakdown."[45] As CNBC reported:

> That day, "I called every single Catholic school in the area," Clayton said. "I wasn't working and I needed to get back," she added. "Something had to give."[46]

She managed to find a Catholic school that was offering fully in-person instruction, for which she and her husband paid close to $1,000 a month over the course of the school year. "I am working to pay for [Robbie] to go to school," Jennifer told CNBC. "But I just think it's all working out for the best for our family. The money that I'm paying is one million percent worth it."[47]

It certainly was. While the Nation's Report Card in 2023 showed that public school kids were falling behind, Catholic school students continued to make progress. Indeed, as Kathleen Porter-Magee observed, "If all

U.S. Catholic schools were a state, their 1.6 million students would rank first in the nation across the NAEP reading and math tests for fourth and eighth graders."[48] On average, Catholic school students in fourth and eighth grades performed seventeen to twenty points higher than the national public school average—the equivalent of about one and a half to two grade levels higher.

The Claytons weren't alone in fleeing the closed public schools. The situation had gotten so bad that families were fleeing traditional public schools in droves for the first time in modern U.S. history. Several school districts across the country reported substantial reductions in enrollment during the fall of 2020. These enrollment drops ranged from around 3 percent in Clark County, Nevada, to around 9 percent in Orange County, Florida.[49] Homeschool filings were also through the roof just about everywhere, including Texas, where they jumped nearly 400 percent from the same time the previous year.[50]

By December 2020, an analysis by Chalkbeat and The Associated Press of data from 33 states showed that, during the fall of 2020, public K-12 enrollment "dropped across those states by more than 500,000 students, or 2%, since the same time last year."[51]

The public school exodus had begun.

By the fall of 2021, public school enrollment nationwide was down by more than 1.5 million students.[52] In New York City alone, district school enrollment dropped by about 64,000 students, or about 4.7 percent, from pre-pandemic levels to the end of 2021, while charter school enrollment increased 3.2 percent.[53] It would only get worse for traditional public schools in the coming years.

The push to close public schools backfired for power-hungry unions by enticing families to vote with their feet. In a study I conducted with Christos Makridis of Stanford University and Clara Piano of Samford University, we found that—independent of COVID risk and several other factors—school closures significantly shifted families toward homeschooling and private education.[54] These effects had nothing to do with differences across states in demographic factors or rates of infection or death, among many other variables. By the spring of 2021, the proportion of households who homeschooled their children was more than triple the prepandemic rate—even after many schools returned to in-person learning.[55]

Another study found some evidence to suggest that public school remote instruction was associated with private school enrollment boosts.[56] As noted above, private schools were much more likely than public schools to provide in-person services, and staying open for business probably attracted new customers. A study published in the *Journal of School Choice* similarly found that private schools in areas with closed public school districts were more likely to experience enrollment increases in the fall of 2020.[57]

Now it was public school officials' turn to notice.

The public school exodus spurred some districts to start listening to parents. In Wausau, Wisconsin, schools were open only for remote instruction in the fall of 2020. That prompted more than 430 students—just over 5 percent of the students in the district—to unenroll and go elsewhere, whether another district or private school. As the *New York Times* reported, that got the attention of local school officials:

> In Wisconsin, where funding is tied to enrollment, the exodus raised alarms over the future of the district. At the same time, parents pointed out that the spread of the virus in Wausau was comparable to that of nearby communities where students were attending in person. [...]
>
> After months of debate, the board voted to open the schools for hybrid learning in early November, giving families the option for students to be taught in the classroom on certain days or virtually.[58]

When schools are paid based on enrollment, school officials must pay attention when parents start leaving. In fact, a study published by Brown University's Annenberg Institute found that public schools with more Catholic school competition nearby were less likely to shut down and more likely to reopen in person in 2020.[59]

Facing competition from private schools that were open for business, you might think that all public schools would respond by quickly getting their act together and giving parents what they wanted.

If so, you would be wrong.

When You Can't Beat 'Em, Shut 'Em Down

Teachers unions all across America shut down public schools using COVID-19 as a pretext. When parents tried bringing their children to private schools instead, the unions and their political allies tried to shut them down, too.

For example, in July 2020, New Mexico governor Michelle Lujan Grisham, a Democrat, told private schools that they could operate only at 25 percent capacity.[60] That was in line with a public health order for businesses in the state, but public schools were allowed to operate at 50 percent capacity, despite generally having more students per classroom.[61] If that was safe for public school students, why wasn't it safe for private school students?

The question answers itself. "Safety" wasn't the motivation. Protecting public schools from competition was.

If New Mexico's public schools were operating at half capacity—which often meant going to school for half a day or every other day—some parents might decide to enroll their children somewhere else, like a private school that managed to reopen safely at full capacity. One way to prevent that is to ensure that private schools are operating at well below their full capacity so parents have nowhere else to go.

Even better—at least for the unions—would be shutting down the private schools entirely.

Take the case of Montgomery County, Maryland. The county is the most populous in Maryland with more than one million residents. As elsewhere, public schools remained closed in the fall of 2020 while private schools were reopening. That was when Montgomery County's health officer, Dr. Travis Gayles, issued an order in early August to keep all private schools closed through October 1. But as the attorney representing parents who sued to overturn the order noted, private and parochial schools "had been closely following the state's guidelines for safely reopening schools, and had invested millions of dollars in retrofitting buildings."[62] Despite the fact private schools didn't get anything close to their fair share of federal emergency COVID funds, they still managed to install the requisite air-filtration systems and hand-sanitizing stations while public schools sitting on piles of federal largesse dithered.

In his order, Gayles provided no metrics justifying the closures, nor any road map for reopening. Worse, the order was issued on a Friday evening, making it all but impossible for parents and school leaders to reach any government officials to object before the schools were set to resume on Monday morning. Nevertheless, furious parents appealed directly to Gov. Larry Hogan, who quickly issued an executive order blocking county officials from closing private schools.[63] "As long as schools develop safe and detailed plans that follow CDC and state guidelines, they should be empowered to do what's best for their community," the governor said.[64]

That should have been the end of it, but it wasn't. A few days later, Gayles again ordered private schools closed, in defiance of the governor.[65] Gayles cited rising COVID infection rates, but simultaneously permitted massage and tattoo parlors to reopen, thereby telegraphing that the school closures were about something other than mere "safety."[66] Angry parents again mobilized, and eventually the order was rescinded.

"This had nothing to do with public health, and everything to do with their own notions of fairness and equity," said Timothy Maloney, the attorney for parents suing Gayles and his office over the school closure order.[67]

Indeed, the *New York Times* coverage of the controversy barely focused on the issue of safety at all. Instead, the *Times* journo-activists fretted about the "inequality in American society," stemming from private schools that "find ways to move ahead with reopening plans that are outside the grasp of public school systems."[68] To ensure readers drew the proper conclusion, the *Times* cited Christopher Lubienski, a professor of education policy at Indiana University, who claimed that allowing private schools to open while public schools were closed proved that private schools are "engines of inequality."

In other words, if the public schools are unable or unwilling to reopen, then "equality" demands that private schools remain closed, too. This perverse understanding of equality is like trying to solve the problem of homelessness by kicking everyone out on the street. No one would be better off, and the vast majority of people would be far worse off—but the *Times* would surely applaud that everyone was equal!

Instead of focusing on the root causes of the public school closures, their media allies lamented the so-called privilege of students at schools that actually did their job. The closest the *Times* article got to addressing the real issue at hand was a passing reference to how public schools "must also negotiate with teachers' unions, many of which have pushed for their schools to remain online or adopt more stringent health measures."[69] Do tell!

The "engines of inequality" narrative is also absurd in another way: many private schools—especially parochial schools—serve as engines of *opportunity*. For example, Catholic schools disproportionately serve disadvantaged students and produce much better results than the public schools while spending significantly less per pupil. As Ashley McGuire of the Catholic Association observed, far from being "engines of inequality," Catholic schools are "accessible pathways out of poverty for some of America's most disadvantaged students."[70]

There may also have been another, viler motive behind the attempts to shut down the private schools. Why did the Montgomery County health officer choose the seemingly arbitrary reopening date of October 1, which was nearly two months later, rather than basing his decision on COVID infection rates or some other metric? The Cato Institute's Walter Olson, a resident of Maryland, had a theory: "September 30 is the cutoff date in Maryland to count official public school enrollment," he observed. "Many real-world consequences, including but not limited to the magnitude of state and federal grants, depend on the count as of that date."[71] By preventing parents from enrolling their children in private schools until after September 30, county officials kept state and federal funds flowing to the closed-down public schools.

In other words, government officials might have put adults' financial interests before students' welfare during their time of need. If anything, the real engines of inequality are the government-run schools.

Chapter 3

PUBLIC SCHOOLS ARE GOVERNMENT SCHOOLS

> Government schooling is the most radical adventure in history. It kills the family by monopolizing the best times of childhood and by teaching disrespect for home and parents.
>
> —*John Taylor Gatto, former New York State Teacher of the Year*[1]

In his final State of the Union Address in February 2020, President Donald Trump declared that "no parent should be forced to send their child to a failing government school."[2] Although journo-activists in the corporate media lost their collective minds over this statement,[3] Trump was absolutely right to call them "government schools" instead of "public schools." Indeed, if the pandemic made one thing clear to parents, it was that what they had thought of as their local, neighborhood public school was just as bureaucratic as the DMV and as political as Congress, because so-called public schools are really government schools.

Defenders of government schools bristle at this term, but it is the most accurate term to describe schools that are run by the government. Although the federal government does not directly operate individual schools, they are controlled by school districts, which are local government entities. These schools are also funded by a mix of federal, state, and local tax dollars that come with large amounts of regulations from various government agencies.

It is important to call things what they are, especially in conversations about public policy. It's clear how schools operated by the government are government schools, but in what sense are they "public schools," as their defenders would have us call them? Are the schools in question truly open to all members of the public? Are they public goods? Do they best serve the public interest? Are they accountable to the public? If even one of these questions were plausibly answered in the affirmative, then calling them public schools might be warranted. But as we'll see, all these claims fall flat.

Government Schools Are Not Truly Open to the Public

Perhaps the most common claim about government schools is that they are open to all members of the public.[4] That might be true in theory, but as Yogi Berra reportedly said, "In theory there is no difference between theory and practice, but in practice there is."

Imagine that a group of people believed it was vital that all people have access to open spaces where people could enjoy fresh air and get in touch with nature. After years of grassroots activism, they succeeded in persuading a majority of the citizens in their state to amend the state constitution to create a system of "free public parks" to which every single citizen was guaranteed access. The government then divided the entire state into separate districts, and told each citizen which park they could use based on the location of their home. But there were striking differences between parks—citizens in wealthier areas had access to the nicest parks, with lots of shady trees, water features, and well-designed playgrounds. Meanwhile, lower-income citizens were assigned to smaller parks with few trees and old, rusted equipment. When low-income families tried to access the better parks, they were refused. When some snuck in anyway, they were arrested. When some citizens sued, claiming their rights to a free public park were being denied, the courts rejected their arguments, noting that the state constitution made no guarantees about quality. Would you say that these parks are truly "public" parks?

This is essentially our system of "public" schools. Children are generally assigned to schools in the United States based on the location of their parents' home, and government-run schools regularly exclude students who live outside of the district. Wealthier families can afford to live in districts that have better government schools than those available to lower-income families. In many cases, parents who have resorted to lying about their residences to get their children into better "public" schools have been fined and even sent to jail.[5] For example, Kelley Williams-Bolar was sent to jail for using her father's address to enroll her daughters in the well-regarded Copley-Fairlawn School District in Ohio, rather than the failing Akron district to which they would have been assigned.[6] In twenty-four states, parents face criminal prosecution—including steep fines and jail time—if they use a fake address to enroll their children in "public" school.[7] Privately owned shopping malls are more open to the public than so-called public schools.

Moreover, although most states have compulsory education laws and constitutional provisions requiring a system of free schools open to the public, there is no guarantee of quality.[8] The government also compels us to attend schools and pay for their services regardless of how satisfied we are with the product. Fifty years ago, in *San Antonio Independent School District v. Rodriguez*, the U.S. Supreme Court ruled that there is no "fundamental right" to an education, nor are all schools within a government's school system required to be equal.[9]

In theory, every American child has access to a public school. In practice, there is no school that is truly open to all children, and the schools that children can access vary wildly in terms of quality. There's no such thing as a public school.

Government Schools Are Not Public Goods

Some claim that government schools are "public" in that they are "public goods." Colloquially, people often mean this in the sense that they are open to the public (which, as we've seen, they are not) or that they serve the public interest. But when economists and political scientists use the term "public good," they are referring to a good that is both "nonrivalrous," meaning that one person's enjoyment of a good does not detract from another person's enjoyment, and "nonexcludable," meaning that it is impossible or impractical to prevent nonpayers from benefiting from the good.[10] National defense is a classic example of a public good. It is nonrivalrous because one individual's benefit from the military's defense of a given area does not detract from anyone else's benefit. Likewise, it is nonexcludable because when the government or another entity defends a given geographic area, it is impractical to exclude specific individuals within that area from the blanket of protection. By contrast, schools fail both conditions. There are only a limited number of seats in each classroom, and schools can (and do) exclude people.

Why does it matter? Public goods might go unproduced unless the government provides the service and forced everyone to pay for it. Since public goods are nonexcludable, there is a real risk of "free riders" benefiting without paying. And the more that payers see that free riders are benefiting without paying, the greater the risk that they will stop paying as well. If an insufficient number of people are willing to pay for a service, then the service might go unprovided. If the public good in question is something like fireworks, then the stakes are relatively low. But if the public good is something vital like national defense, then there is—in theory—a more compelling societal interest in funding it via taxes.

Education is a vital service, especially in a democracy. Self-government depends on having a populace that is sufficiently educated to make wise decisions about public policy. If schooling were truly a public good, then there might be a compelling government interest in providing education directly. But schooling is not a public good.

If one student is in a seat in a classroom, they take up another child's ability to sit in the same seat. As a result, schooling fails the first part of the definition. Second, and perhaps most important, it is not difficult to exclude a person from a school, or any other type of institution. If someone does not pay you to educate them, you can simply deny him or her the benefits of your service. This already occurs with private schools and tutoring services. Hence, there is no free rider problem in education.

Government Schools Do Not Best Serve the Public Interest

Schools are not public goods, but is there still a case for government provision of education? Sure, there may not be a free rider problem, so education will not go unprovided entirely, but it might still go *under*provided if some people are unable to afford a quality education for their children. If so, it might still be in the public interest for the government to provide schooling.

Education has positive externalities. When something has an externality, it means that third parties either benefit or are harmed. Sometimes, there is an economic case to subsidize cases of positive externalities which might otherwise be underproduced, or to tax or regulate negative externalities, which might be overproduced. When a factory pollutes a river, third parties who have nothing to do with buying the factory's products or selling raw materials to the factory are harmed by the negative externality of the pollution that the factory produces. Depending on the level of harm caused by the pollution, there could be a compelling interest in regulating the factory. However, not every externality warrants government intervention. Although pedestrians passing by a bakery can benefit from the positive externality of the aromas they produce, there is no need for the government to subsidize the bakery's production.

Education theoretically produces positive externalities beyond the benefits accrued by the educator and their students. For example, higher levels of education can result in higher overall economic productivity, higher tax revenues, and lower rates of crime. Moreover, as noted above, democratic societies depend on at least a minimal level of education for self-government. As a result, the government may have a compelling interest in funding schooling to ensure that all its citizens have access to at least some minimal level of education.

However, as the Nobel laureate economist Milton Friedman observed, it does not follow that the government must operate schools as well. In his landmark 1955 essay, "The Role of Government in Education," Friedman argued that "the administration of schools is neither required by the financing of education, nor justifiable in its own right in a predominantly free enterprise society," by which Friedman meant a society that "takes freedom of the individual, or more realistically the family, as its ultimate objective."[11] Given both the inefficiencies of government provision generally, and the potential threats to liberty posed by the government's provision of education in particular, Friedman argued that a free society is best served by having the government *fund* education but not *operate* schools. Instead, he proposed that the government "give each child, through his parents, a specified sum to be used solely in paying for his general education," and then "the parents would be free to spend this sum at a school of their own choice."[12] Friedman predicted that such an arrangement—now called school choice—would lead to wider educational opportunities, healthy competition among education providers, and overall improvement in education.

For about forty years after Friedman published his essay, little progress was made in enacting school-choice policies. Yet in the past twenty years, more than thirty states plus Washington, DC, have enacted some form of private school choice program. Initially, these mostly took the form of Friedman's voucher proposal, in which families can use a portion of the state funding associated with their child to pay for private school tuition. Even more popular has been the tax-credit scholarship policy, which provides tax credits (often dollar-for-dollar) to individual and corporate taxpayers who contribute to nonprofit scholarship organizations. More recently, states have followed Friedman's later suggestion of creating "partial vouchers" in the form of K–12 education savings accounts (ESAs). Families can use ESAs to pay for a wide variety of education expenses, including private school tuition, tutoring, textbooks, online courses, special-needs therapy, and more, and can roll over unused funds from year to year.

By all accounts, the research literature on school choice has proven Friedman correct.[13] School choice provides access to greater educational opportunity. Out of seventeen random-assignment studies on the effects of school-choice policies on the academic performance of participating students, eleven find statistically significant positive effects while only three found any negative effects. Two of the negative findings were from Louisiana, which implemented a highly regulated voucher program that was very far from Friedman's free market ideal.[14] As Dr. Lindsey Burke and I demonstrated in a study published in 2021, Louisiana-style regulations such as open admissions mandates and requiring the state test have the unintended consequence of reducing the number and quality of private schools willing to participate in a school-choice program.[15] Additionally, five out of seven studies found statistically significant positive effects on participating students' attainment—that is, increased rates of high school graduation and college matriculation—while two studies found no visible effects and none found any negative effects.

Friedman was also right that school choice fosters healthy competition. Out of twenty-nine studies of the effects of school choice on the academic performance of government school students, twenty-six found statistically significant positive effects, one found no visible effect, and only two found negative effects. One of the supposedly negative findings was of a voucher program in Florida that never actually went into effect due to a lawsuit, while several studies of the school-choice policies actually operating in Florida found positive effects. The overwhelming conclusion of the research literature is that competition produces better results for everyone, whether they receive a voucher or attend their assigned government school.

But perhaps government schools better serve the public interest in other ways. Private schools might do a better job teaching skills, like reading and math, which will benefit individual students in the marketplace, but perhaps government schools are still necessary. Government schools may theoretically ensure a certain level of civic knowledge and instill civic values, such as political tolerance, patriotism, and voluntarism. As government school advocates Carol Burris and Diane Ravitch put it, "Public governance of our schools matters for the health of our democracy" because government schools are "designed to serve and promote the common good."[16]

Yet here too, school-choice policies have proven to do a better job promoting the common good than government schools. Out of ninety-three findings in studies of the effects of private school choice or private schooling on various civic outcomes, fifty-six showed a private advantage and thirty-four found no visible difference, while only three found a government school advantage.[17] A free society is best served by an education system rooted in freedom, not compulsion.

Contrary to Chicken Littles like Prof. David Berliner of Arizona State University, who once predicted that "voucher programs could end up resembling the ethnic cleansing now occurring in Kosovo,"[18] thirteen measures found that private schools did a better job at instilling political tolerance, while only a single measure found a government school advantage and ten found no difference. When it comes to political participation and civic knowledge and skills, there were eighteen findings of a private advantage and twelve found no difference. Not a single study found a government school advantage.

Among studies of the effects of education systems of voluntarism and social capital, nineteen findings showed a private advantage and eleven showed no difference, while only two showed a government school advantage. One of my own studies with Dr. Patrick Wolf found that participants in Milwaukee's school-choice program were 86 percent less likely than nonparticipants to be convicted of property crimes, 53 percent less likely to be convicted of drug crimes, and 38 percent less likely to be the subject of paternity suits.[19]

Not only are government-run schools not justified on the grounds of being public goods, but they are also not justified on the grounds of best furthering the public interest. To a great extent, that is because government schools have been captured by special interests, like the teachers unions. Although most people assume that government schools are accountable to the public, in reality they are accountable to those special interests.

Government Schools Are Not Accountable to the Public

People like to think of government schools as neighborhood schools that are isolated from political agendas and accountable to parents and local communities via nonpartisan school board races, parent-teacher conferences, and groups like the Parent Teacher Association.

This is the fairy-tale model of democratic accountability. It's a myth.

In reality, as parents learned the hard way during the COVID shutdowns, government schools aren't accountable to parents or to the public at all. They're not designed to be. Instead, they're designed to place the interests of the adults in the system first—before the interests of the children they're supposed to serve or their parents.

Under the status quo, if families are dissatisfied with their child's public school, they only have a few options, all of which are either costly or ineffective: (1) pay out-of-pocket for private school tuition and fees while still paying for the assigned government-run school through taxes, (2) move to a residence assigned to a better public school, (3) complain to the school board (which might pretend to care or, worse, label you a domestic terrorist), or (4) vote for school board members who say they will advocate for certain policies, which could take several years to implement, if they're ever implemented at all. The unions negotiate with elected officials and administrations they hand-picked. Their lobbying doesn't involve bargaining as much as it does rubber-stamping.

The unions get the policies they want without any consideration for the taxpayers and the actual beneficiaries of their services. This is the inner workings of special interest politics. As economist Mancur Olson Jr. has described, where benefits are concentrated to a particular group and costs are diffuse or dispersed among the general public, the smaller group will typically get its way politically because it has a very strong interest in achieving its aims, while each member of the public has a much smaller interest in stopping them.[20] For example, if the city budget will require raising taxes by $10 per citizen and will result in a $1,000 pay raise per city employee, the city employee union will have a very strong incentive to push for the budget while each taxpayer has a very minimal interest in opposing it.

Many policies that hurt society get implemented because the costs (e.g., bad education) are dispersed while the benefits (e.g., job security for teachers) are concentrated. Public school teachers are strongly incentivized to push for policies and politicians that benefit, first and foremost, themselves.

Unions are formed to serve the interests of their members, particularly through collective bargaining. When unions don't get their way, they engage in various forms of collective action, like strikes or work stoppages, to strengthen their position. In the private sector, unions are constrained by the profitability and sustainability of their firm—ask for too much and the firm could lose its competitive edge and fold. But the government faces no competition, so it is not nearly so constrained. Moreover, the public sector unions have a tool at their disposal that private sector unions do not: the ability to choose with whom they negotiate.

Elected school boards are supposed to hold government schools accountable, but school board elections are designed to favor entrenched interests by keeping turnout down and voters in the dark. About three out of four school board elections are held "off-cycle," meaning on a date other than statewide and federal elections in November. As Michael Hartney of Boston College observed in a report for the Brookings Institution, research shows that off-cycle elections drive down turnout, which means that organized interests like teachers unions have a big advantage.[21] Likewise, around 90 percent of school board elections in the nation's nearly 13,200 K–12 school districts are nonpartisan, meaning that no party affiliation is listed on the ballot.[22] Of course, that doesn't mean the candidates don't have political ideologies or party loyalties—it just means that the average voter is kept in the dark about what those ideologies and loyalties are.

Because the unions have a stronger interest in the general public in knowing when the elections are and which candidates will favor their interests than the general voter, they have a decided advantage in the elections. As Stanford University political scientist Terry Moe described in his book *Special Interest*:

> The Michigan Education Association, for example, distributes a forty-page instructional (and hortatory) document to its local leaders, filled with operational details about how to evaluate and screen school board candidates, recruit friendly ones, run entire campaigns, set up phone banks, engage in door-to-door canvassing, get out the vote, and more. Its title: "Electing Your Own Employer, It's as Easy as 1, 2, 3."[23]

Not surprisingly, the union-backed candidates usually win. According to Hartney's analysis of more than five thousand union endorsements in school board elections in three of the four largest states over twenty-five years, the union-backed candidates won the vast majority of competitive elections—64 percent in Florida, 71 percent in California, and 80 percent in New York.[24] If you include races where the unions scared off would-be challengers, the union's win rate is as high as 90 percent. As Hartney notes, "Union-favored candidates tend to win in both strong (CA, NY) and weak (FL) union states and in conservative and liberal school districts."[25] This means that in both red and blue states, and both red and blue areas within states, the unions typically choose the school board members who are tasked with holding them accountable. Whose interests are those board members more likely to represent, the parents' or the union's?

Although most of the races are officially nonpartisan, one political party is the primary beneficiary of the teachers unions' largesse: the Democrats.

It's a symbiotic relationship: The Democrats use their political positions to favor the unions, and the unions use their resources to elect more Democrats. Over 99 percent of campaign contributions from the American Federation of Teachers went to Democrats in the 2022 election cycle.[26] According to OpenSecrets, a nonprofit research group that tracks money in U.S. politics, this is not a new trend. An average 96 percent of the teacher unions' contributions have gone to Democrats every election cycle over the past *three decades*.[27] Teachers unions exert tremendous political influence over Democrats, who turn around and vote for additional funding for government-run schools that are staffed by unions. That money then makes its way back to the elected officials through political contributions from the unions—and the cycle continues. It's a form of money laundering. It should be illegal.

The laundered money doesn't even go to teachers in the form of better salaries. Indeed, more union dues are spent on *political activity* rather than member representation. A recent analysis by Americans for Fair Treatment found that the National Education Association (which is the largest public-sector union in the country) spent twice as much on politics than member needs in 2021.[28] Also consider that inflation-adjusted government-school spending per student increased by 155 percent between 1970 and 2020.[29] Inflation-adjusted teacher salaries have increased by a meager 9 percent over the same period.[30]

Why do teachers unions push for more staffing rather than better salaries? Because more staffing means more dues-paying members, which means more revenue for political activities. Teachers unions also opt to advocate for additional hidden benefits like pensions. That allows them to continue to propagate the narrative that America's teachers are "undervalued."

Ultimately, our kids suffer the most from the unchecked greed of the teachers unions. The unions pushed to close schools (and keep them shuttered), pay the best employees the same as the worst, make it impossible to fire the worst employees, lower standards, and essentially brand zip codes onto the skins of our children to prevent them from moving. In fact, the nation's largest teachers union, the National Education Association, defeated a business item at its 2019 annual meeting to "rededicate itself to the pursuit of increased student learning in every public school in America."[31] To that point, I uncovered a whistleblower email from a public school employee in Colorado showing just that. A teachers union leader in Durango had urged staff to "please think about signing up to speak" about "whether we need another charter school in our small town," after claims that "less students = less $$."[32] To the unions, our children are nothing more than dollar signs.

In December 2022, I went on *Dr. Phil* to talk about the myriad and deep harms of school closures. It was meant to be a debate against the teachers unions...only every single teachers union representative declined to participate. Weingarten's team had even quietly reached out to *Dr. Phil*'s producers to ask whether I would be participating. Apparently my presence was the deciding factor, because Weingarten was a no-show. The unions can't defend their positions because they're indefensible. They exist to meet the needs of their dues-paying constituents. To heck with them kids.

The government school system is neither accountable to the public nor to parents. If we want to hold schools accountable, we'll have to change how they're funded.

Fund Students, Not Systems

Government schools are not public schools. They are not truly open to all members of the public; they are not public goods; they are far from the best means of serving the public interest; and they are not accountable to the public. Again: there's no such thing as a public school.

If we want schools that better serve the public interest and are accountable to parents, we should heed Milton Friedman's advice: Give the money to the parents and let them choose the schools that work best for their children. In short, fund students, not systems.

Imagine if you still had to pay Walmart the same amount of money each week regardless of whether it reopened for in-person shopping and provided you with adequate and fresh groceries for your family. The grocery store would have a very different set of incentives than it does today. Because fresh groceries are more costly to provide and buildings are expensive to maintain, the store would profit from remaining closed—and giving you subpar produce when it opened.

But that's not what happened. Walmart and other private stores know you can take your money elsewhere. Schools need to know that you can do the same.

School choice does just that. Choice policies create a feedback mechanism that provides accountability from the bottom up. Allowing families to vote with their feet gives schools a financial incentive to cater to the needs and goals of children. No longer are parents captive audiences. When schools and school boards know that dissatisfied parents can easily take their money and leave, they suddenly allocate resources differently, putting money into the classroom as opposed to administrative bloat. School districts also feel some pressure whenever bad policies come to light. Competition fundamentally changes the power balance, ejecting teachers unions and putting parents in the cockpit.

We saw this dynamic at work during the pandemic: Choice and competition empowered parents, while the lack of choice and competition empowered entrenched interests. Private schools had a powerful bottom-up incentive to cater to the needs of families. Teachers unions had a perverse top-down incentive to bolster their monopolistic institutions by holding children's education hostage. This divide highlights a major fault line in America: the vast gulf between the incentives guiding public schools versus those guiding private establishments. After all, the major difference between these services is that one of them receives your money through property taxes regardless of how well their decisions meet the needs of families.

The unions know that education choice policies pose a mortal threat to their stranglehold over education. Their entire business model depends on parents being a captive audience. Education choice sets them free. That's why, when the NEA released its "2020 Policy Playbook for Congress and the Biden-Harris Administration," one of its top priorities was persuading policymakers nationwide to "oppose the enactment of any new voucher program, including education savings accounts and tuition tax credit schemes, or the expansion of existing [education choice] programs."[33] As Inez Stepman of the Independent Women's Forum put it, the NEA was essentially telling parents: "We will close the schools and keep your money, how dare you try to find alternatives for your children!"[34]

The pandemic exposed the main problem with our country's K–12 education system: a massive power imbalance between the government school monopoly and individual families. And the only way that we're ever going to fix the messed-up set of incentives that's baked into the government school system is to fund students directly and empower families with options.

We already fund students directly when it comes to Pell Grants for higher education. The funding follows the student to the public or private, religious or nonreligious, higher education provider of their choosing. The same goes for taxpayer-funded pre-K programs such as Head Start. We already fund individuals directly when it comes to other taxpayer-funded initiatives such as food stamps and Medicaid.

We don't force low-income families to spend their food stamp dollars at residentially assigned government-run grocery stores. Instead, families are allowed to choose to take the funding to Walmart, Trader Joe's, Safeway, or just about any other provider of groceries. We should apply the same logic to K–12 education and fund students, not systems.

The implications of whether to fund students or systems extend to far more than just reopening decisions. Whether schools are accountable to parents or special interests determines what is taught in the classroom, what policies schools adopt, and the extent to which schools consult with parents about their curricular and policy decisions—or if they even bother to inform them at all.

Chapter 4

THE SCHOOL WARS: OUR CHILDREN, OUR CHOICE

There's no such thing as someone else's child. Our nation's children are all our children.

—President Joe Biden[1]

We cannot continue to send our children to Caesar for their education and be surprised when they come home as Romans.

—Voddie Baucham Jr.

When parents organized to reopen their kids' schools, they initially thought that was the end goal. They didn't realize that reopening schools was just the beginning of *the Parent Revolution*.

The fight over school closures opened parents' eyes to the fact that government schools were not really accountable to them. When the schools broke trust with parents, the parents didn't just forgive and forget once the schools were reopened—especially since "Zoom school" gave parents a window into the classroom. Many didn't like what they saw. Rainbow flags, activities involving Gender Unicorns, lessons in "white privilege" in math class—what was going on?! That was when parents realized that the real fight was over which values should be taught in government schools and who should decide—parents or so-called experts?

"The purpose of public education in public schools is not to teach kids only what parents want them to be taught," declared the Michigan Democratic Party on its Facebook page in January 2022. "It is to teach them what society needs them to know. The client of the public school is not the parent, but the entire community, the public."[2] It's great when your opponents say the quiet part out loud—it takes the imperfect art of guesswork out of determining their intentions. Only after enormous blowback did the Democrats delete the post and issue some semblance of an apology, claiming that "the post does not reflect the views of Michigan Democrats and should not be misinterpreted as a statement of support from our elected officials or candidates." In other words: "Please don't hold us accountable for saying what we really believe."

But parents intended to do exactly that.

The Mask Slips: CRT and Gender Ideology in the Classroom

"My daughter will never go back to public school," said Michelle Walker of McMinnville, Oregon, in the spring of 2021.[3] Walker was serious; she even took out a loan to enroll her daughter, MacKenzie, in a private school. After fighting to reopen schools through her group Open Schools USA—a network with more than 180,000 participants—she felt that the government schools were too far gone to save. Although she was a Democrat, she believed the left-wing ideology being pushed in the government schools was too much.

"Parents want children to learn about racism. We don't want it taught necessarily in the way that it is," said Walker. "If you're going to tell the bad and the ugly, you need to tell the good and the beautiful."[4] Yet government schools seemed far more interested in the bad and ugly. Why? Three little letters: CRT.

Most parents first learned about "critical race theory," or CRT, in late 2020 and early 2021. In the wake of the death of George Floyd at the hands of a Minneapolis police officer in May 2020, the issue of race in America understandably took center stage. But soon, parents started noticing that many schools were exploiting the tragedy to sneak a radical ideology into the classroom.

As Heritage Foundation scholars Jonathan Butcher and Mike Gonzalez explain, CRT is an offshoot of critical theory, a Marxist academic theory that holds that America's legal system and society writ large are irredeemably "structurally racist," and therefore must be dismantled, not merely reformed.[5] Like other strains of critical theory, CRT sees society as "made up of categories of oppressors and oppressed" and seeks to "dismantle all societal norms through relentless criticism."

The societal norms that CRT seeks to dismantle are regularly labeled "whiteness" or "white supremacy." This isn't the KKK's white supremacy, the noxious notion that people with white skin are somehow superior to those with a darker complexion. So what is it? Well, here's a list of things that the Smithsonian National Museum of African American History and Culture declare to be "aspects and assumptions of whiteness" (i.e., Bad Things):

- "Rugged Individualism," including "self-reliance, independence, and autonomy,"
- "Family Structure," including "the nuclear family," and "children should have own rooms, be independent,"
- "Emphasis on Scientific Method," including "objective, rational linear thinking," and "cause and effect relationships," and
- "Protestant Work Ethic," including the notion that "hard work is the key to success" and that we should "work hard before play."[6]

The list goes on. Other things that fall under the awful category of "whiteness" include the Judeo-Christian tradition, delayed gratification, and being polite.[7] Seriously, I wish I were making this up, but I'm not.

Indeed, CRT seeks to undo the entire American project. But again, don't take my word for it. Listen to the proponents of CRT. Harvard Law professor Derrick Bell, widely seen as the "godfather of CRT," wrote in *Who's Afraid of Critical Race Theory?* that CRT's proponents are "highly suspicious of the liberal agenda, distrust its method, and want to retain what they see as a valuable strain of egalitarianism which may exist despite, and not because of, liberalism."[8] In *Critical Race Theory: An Introduction*, CRT proponents Richard Delgado and Jean Stefanic write that "critical race theory questions the very foundations of the liberal order, including equality theory, legal reasoning, Enlightenment rationalism, and neutral principles of constitutional law."[9]

What does all that jargon mean in practical terms? For one thing, it means opposition to the right of freedom of speech enshrined in the First Amendment. "Being committed to 'free speech' may seem like a neutral principle, but it is not," wrote Bell. "Thus, proclaiming that 'I am committed equally to allowing free speech for the KKK and 2LiveCrew' is a nonneutral value judgment, one that asserts that the freedom to say hateful things is more important than the freedom to be free from the victimization, stigma, and humiliation that free speech entails."[10] As Butcher and Gonzalez wryly observe: "Thus we arrive at today's cancel culture."[11]

It's not just First Amendment rights that CRT proponents oppose. It's all of them. Proponents of CRT are hostile to the concept of political rights itself. Delgado and Stefanic explain how "CRT scholars with roots in racial realism and an economic view of history believe that moral and legal rights are apt to do the right holder much less good than we like to think."[12] Why? Because rights are "alienating." Rights supposedly "separate people from each other—'stay away, I've got my rights'—rather than encouraging to form close, respectful communities."

CRT is radically opposed to the very foundations of America, including the Constitution and the Bill of Rights. CRT is fundamentally un-American. So what is it doing in our schools?

At first the legacy media narrative was that CRT wasn't really in K–12 schools. "Teaching Critical Race Theory Isn't Happening in Classrooms, Teachers Say in Survey," reported NBC in June 2021.[13] "Schools

Not Teaching Race Theory, Some Want to Ban It Anyway," read an Associated Press headline a month later.[14] But before long, the evidence that lessons crafted through the prism of CRT were pervasive in government school classrooms became undeniable.[15] That's when the media narrative quickly shifted from "it isn't happening" to "it's good that it is." Shortly before the Associated Press claimed CRT wasn't in the classroom, the National Education Association adopted New Business Item 39 at its national convention, calling on the NEA to defend the teaching of CRT from attempts to ban it: "It is reasonable and appropriate for curriculum to be informed by academic frameworks for understanding and interpreting the impact of the past on current society, including critical race theory."[16] It even adopted a measure to spend $127,000 promoting CRT.

Ironically, while the NEA supports CRT, it doesn't support making student learning a priority. Two years earlier, the NEA voted down a New Business Item to "make student learning the priority of the Association."[17]

The NEA also pledged in 2021 to spend $56,500 on conducting opposition research on groups opposed to CRT.[18] It also pledged to provide a study "that critiques empire, white supremacy, anti-Blackness, anti-Indigeneity, racism, patriarchy, cisheteropatriarchy, capitalism, ableism, anthropocentrism, and other forms of power and oppression at the intersections of our society."[19]

The unions' radical CRT agenda was not confined to left-wing strongholds like San Francisco and Portland. Even in deep red states, parents were shocked by the racialist agenda that government schools were pushing on their children. For example, Utah Parents United collected hundreds of pages of testimonials from parents statewide documenting CRT in the classroom.[20] In the Canyons school district, an A.P. American History class's first assignments were almost entirely drawn from the discredited "1619 Project," which pushed an error-riddled narrative that the American colonists "declared their independence from Britain was because they wanted to protect the institution of slavery in the colonies."[21] According to a parent in the Davis school district, a teacher told a student that "all the white children attending the school needed to acknowledge their own racism" because "whites are inherently racist" due to their "white privilege."[22] Freshmen honors English students in the Alpine school district were asked to write an essay on reparations, but were only given articles in favor of the controversial proposal. The parent of a student in the Jordan school district described how students were forced to do a "Privilege Walk":

> The teacher had all the kids standing in a row and then asked them questions and if they could answer yes to the question then they took one step forward. Now obviously the point of this was to have all the white kids in the front at the end and then have the "black and brown" kids in the back to show how their life is so hard and white kids have it so easy. The questions asked were things like, "Take one step forward if you can drive your car without being pulled over because of your race" or "Take one step forward if you live with both of your parents." Some of the questions were a bit more personal and shocking. One question was "Take one step forward if you have never been sexually assaulted." My daughter, who is black, came home very upset that day. She said she knew exactly what the teacher was after and it was just all around uncomfortable for everyone in the class room. [...] As black Americans and with a long history of our family and ancestors fighting for civil rights, this was just very insulting and offensive.[23]

Nationwide, it became an all-too-common practice for teachers to fly Black Lives Matters flags in their classrooms, even though BLM is an explicitly political movement with a radical political agenda.[24] It's one thing to express support for diversity and students who have suffered discrimination. It's another thing entirely to hang up the symbols of a political organization whose list of demands includes "disrupt[ing] the Western-prescribed nuclear-family-structure requirement," abolishing all police and prisons, legalizing drugs and prostitution, massive wealth redistribution, and more.[25]

The BLM flags weren't the only political flags flying in classrooms alongside—or instead of—Old Glory. Rainbow flags—often with a blue, pink, and white triangle symbolizing transgenderism—announced the presence of radical gender ideology.

What is gender ideology? Heritage Foundation scholar Jay Richards has defined gender ideology as "the theory that the sex binary doesn't capture the complexity of the human species, and that human individuals are properly described in terms of an 'internal sense of gender' called 'gender identity' that may be incongruent with their 'sex assigned at birth.'"[26]

In other words, schools are teaching children that their gender has nothing to do with their biological sex, that boys can become girls and girls can become boys, and that there are an infinite number of genders beyond "male" and female." So-called nonbinary people might use "they/them" pronouns, or "ze/zer," or "ay/em," or . . . well, you get the point. PronounsList.com contains literally hundreds of pronouns.[27] If ze don't believe me, ze should check it out for zirself.

Indoctrinating children in gender ideology starts as young as possible. The "Gender Unicorn" and "Genderbread Person" are used to teach children as young as kindergarten that gender is a spectrum and is not tied to biology. "For transgender people, their sex assigned at birth and their own internal sense of gender identity are not the same," reads a Gender Unicorn worksheet. "Female, woman, and girl and male, man, and boy are also NOT necessarily linked to each other but are just six common gender identities."[28] These lessons aren't confined to the fringe. Indeed, they've even been made available to teachers by the Pennsylvania Department of Education.[29]

Many of the most popular books pushing gender ideology veer into pornographic territory. For example, *Gender Queer* is a graphic novel (in both senses of the word "graphic") that depicts a gender-confused teen wearing a strap-on dildo that another teen fellates.[30] Other pages contain images of the narrator masturbating—including while driving—and having homosexual sex. In several school board meetings, outraged parents have read shockingly explicit excerpts from *Me and Earl and the Dying Girl.* [31] For example, one character in the book describes to a child—at great length and in the vulgarest of terms—how to perform oral sex on women. Yet although some districts eventually removed the book for violating rules around explicit content, some school districts voted to keep the book anyway.[32]

Some books being pushed in schools are even instruction manuals that groom kids for sex. For example, *This Book Is Gay* teaches kids how to have anal sex, use butt plugs and other sex toys, and even how to meet people for sexual encounters on sex apps.[33] It's so shocking as to be literally unbelievable. Even when confronted with the piles of evidence, people instinctively recoil from the reality of what's happening in our schools. It's just too radical, too perverted, too surreal. Can this really be happening?

It is. And parents are mad as hell and they're not going to take it anymore.

Parents Fight Back

All across the country, parents poured back into their school board meetings. Before, they were upset that schools were closed. Now some were wondering whether they were worth opening at all. "Once considered tame, even boring," reported ProPublica, the school board meetings had "become polarized battlegrounds over COVID-19 safety measures, LGBTQ+ student rights, 'obscene' library books and attempts to teach children about systemic racism in America."[34]

But school boards by and large weren't interested in hearing parents' concerns. Parents who tried to read from the books in their children's school were censored for being obscene. (If the books were too obscene for a public meeting, what were they doing in schools?) School boards sharply limited the time allotted for parents to speak and cut off parents whose critiques were deemed out of bounds, such as criticizing school board members by name.[35] Other times, public comment periods were closed early. Parents left the meetings even more frustrated than when they'd arrived.

But they didn't despair. They organized. "There is nothing more frustrating than seeing your children denied the education they deserve and feeling powerless to change it," wrote Tiffany Justice and Tina Descovich in the *Washington Post*.[36] Together, they founded Moms for Liberty in January 2021 to give parents a voice and work to take back America's schools. They organized parents, informed the public about what was going on in government schools, trained their members on how to be effective at school board meetings or run for school board, and even sued school boards that employed illegal tactics to stifle dissent.[37] By November, they had grown to more than 150 chapters in 33 states, with more than 60,000 members.

Seeing the massive parental support for reeling in radical ideology and getting back to focusing on basics, the unions readily complied with the parents' wishes.

Just kidding.

The unions instantly recognized the organized parents as a threat and set about shooting the messenger. In their minds, the problem isn't what they're doing to our kids—the problem is that parents are noticing. "Who Is Behind the Attacks on Educators and Public Schools?" asked an NEA report, which blamed the supposedly "manufactured outrage" on "dark money networks."[38] In the NEA's telling, "radical groups" were "using social media to spread disinformation and stoke fear about race in the classroom, pushing for laws to ban books about Ruby Bridges, Martin Luther King, Jr. and other civil rights figures, and seeking to censor teachers and deny students the right to a truthful and honest education." Months after the NEA adopted resolutions supporting CRT in the classroom, the NEA report decried "the false notion that children are being taught 'critical race theory.'"

The only disinformation was coming from the NEA. But they were just getting started.

The unions and their allies weaponized "safety," claiming that the angry parents posed a threat and therefore the authorities needed to crack down on them. "This peddling of misinformation and fear has led to a sharp increase in threats aimed at educators and school board officials," claimed the NEA, "many of whom have been intimidated and threatened in alarming numbers across the country—outside school grounds, across social media, and, most notoriously, at local school board meetings."[39] The NEA even sent a letter to social media executives asking them to censor accounts that raised awareness about the radical agenda being pushed in government schools, claiming their "safety" was at stake if Facebook and Twitter didn't censor their critics.[40]

Even more egregious was the effort to get the federal government to crack down on parents. In September 2021, the National School Boards Association sent a letter to President Joe Biden requesting federal assistance to protect school boards and school employees who were supposedly "under an immediate threat" because of "propaganda purporting the false inclusion of critical race theory within classroom instruction . . . despite the fact that [CRT] is not taught in public schools."[41]

The NSBA letter requested that the president direct the FBI, the U.S. Department of Homeland Security, and the U.S. Secret Service's National Threat Assessment Center to help school boards investigate and monitor critical parents, whom the NSBA libeled as "extremist hate groups" and even argued that the federal government should deem their actions "a form of domestic terrorism and hate crimes." It was later revealed that an earlier, even more unhinged draft of the letter requested that the president deploy Army National Guard and military police to guard school board meetings.[42]

Days later, U.S. Attorney General Merrick Garland issued a memo ordering the FBI to investigate the supposed surge in "harassment, intimidation, and threats of violence" and promised to "launch a series of additional efforts in the coming days designed to address the rise in criminal conduct directed toward school personnel."[43] (Astoundingly, two years later, after Hamas terrorists slaughtered more than 1,400 Israelis, the White House issued a statement declaring that people making violent antisemitic threats were *not* being classified as "domestic terrorists."[44])

The pushback was swift and fierce. Outraged parents began appearing at school board meetings with T-shirts saying PARENTS ARE NOT DOMESTIC TERRORISTS.[45] The Republicans on the U.S. House Judiciary

Committee condemned Garland and the DOJ for engaging in "intimidation" of concerned parents and for "chilling free speech."[46] Likewise, the Republican attorneys general of seventeen states denounced the DOJ for, in their words, attempting to "chill lawful dissent by parents voiced during local school board meetings."[47] The attorneys general noted that "anyone who attacks or threatens violence against school administrators, board members, teachers, or staff should be prosecuted," but that "in its letter demanding action, the NSBA fails to document a single legitimate instance of violence," let alone anything approaching "the burning, looting, police assaults, vandalism and other criminal activity that occurred in the summer of 2020," which the feds had done nothing to address.

It later came out that the Biden administration had colluded with the NSBA *before* they sent the infamous "domestic terrorist" letter—just as the administration had colluded with the unions over COVID guidance. As the *Washington Free Beacon* reported, emails obtained by Parents Defending Education via public records requests revealed that top NSBA officials had "collaborated with the Biden White House before sending a controversial letter calling on the FBI to investigate parents as potential domestic terrorists." The emails also uncovered that the NSBA's president and CEO "sent the letter to Biden on Sept. 29 without approval from the organization's board."[48]

After an investigation, the House Judiciary Committee later issued a report concluding that there was "no legitimate basis" for using Justice Department resources to investigate concerned parents or supposed "threats" to school boards, and that "it is apparent that the Biden administration misused federal law-enforcement and counterterrorism resources for political purposes."[49]

The NSBA eventually apologized for their letter, conceding that "there was no justification for some of the language included in the letter."[50] But it was too little, too late. The damage had been done. Parents were justly outraged, and state affiliates of the NSBA began jumping ship. According to the *Washington Examiner*, by the end of 2021, seventeen states had left the NSBA, which was "looking at a shortfall of at least $1.1 million."[51] Within just a year, *twenty-six states* left the NSBA.

Parents were not to be trifled with.

The NSBA's collapse sent a strong message, but it wasn't enough. There's still a lot of work left to do to reclaim our schools for our children.

Reclaiming Our Schools

Why are the government schools doing this? Government schools have been captured by the political left, which has been implementing its "long march through the institutions" for decades.[52] And at its core, the left is socialist.

"Socialists regard your property as their property, but even more nefariously regard your children as their property," observed Ukrainian-American author Michael Malice. Lo and behold, America's government-run education system refuses to accept that government schools are not the right fit for every child, for doing so would present a direct challenge to its existence. The system, guarded and perpetuated by the teachers unions, is tantamount to a dictatorship. This is not an exaggeration. That's because it is stridently opposed to allowing citizens—citizens who are, after all, endowed with rights—the very freedom to *choose*.

This is not an attack on government-run schools in and of themselves. Many families and kids throughout America are happy with them. The clarion call of *The Parent Revolution* is *choice*; if you like your public school, you can keep your public school. Allowing low-income parents on food stamps to choose their grocery store isn't an attack on Walmart or Trader Joe's. Similarly, allowing families the opportunity to choose where their kids are educated isn't an attack on government-run schools.

Higher-education students can take their Pell Grant or GI Bill funding to a community college or public university, but they can also take it to a religious or nonreligious private university. We should apply the same logic to K–12 education and fund students, not radical activists and bureaucrats. Education funding is supposed to be meant for educating children, not for lining the pockets of bureaucrats and spreading propaganda.

The past several years have demonstrated that the more effective argument for school choice is focused on values rather than performance.

Are the values taught at your child's school the same as yours? American pastor and educator Voddie Baucham Jr. said it best: "We cannot continue to send our children to Caesar for their education and be surprised when they come home as Romans." Thirteen years of government indoctrination immensely harms society. Conservatives—and anyone else concerned with preserving a civilization rooted in reason and critical thinking—must strike back.

Millions of families still have no option for getting out of government-run schools. Our nation is diverse, so families inevitably differ over how they want their children to be raised and to be educated. That's totally fine. But their aspirations are hopelessly betrayed by the government's one-size-fits-all approach. The only way forward is more freedom—to fund students *directly* and empower families to choose the education providers that best meet their needs and align with their values.

We must fight to retake control of local school boards. The left has spent decades infiltrating and co-opting these critical institutions that are right in our own backyards. Their activists have long used our government-run school system to indoctrinate children into socialism. This is a war to save our country. We've already lost countless souls and minds. This is the moment we say, "That's it!" We can't surrender another generation of our children to the left.

Yet taking over school boards is just one part of the fix. Moms and dads must also show up at the ballot box to support candidates who respect parental rights, and, further, organize and demonstrate to let lawmakers know they must pass bills allowing greater freedom and choice in education. Politicians respond to power. Parents have power in numbers.

Parents also have power when they have options. Counterintuitively, making it easier for parents to leave can give them the leverage they need to reform government schools so their children can stay.

Some critics of woke schools have also been suspicious of education choice policies. One of their concerns is that with a school-choice policy, all the parents upset about the ideology infecting the government schools would leave, thereby making it harder to reform the government schools. Instead, like Spanish conquistadors, they want to burn the proverbial boats so that parents have no option but to fight. This argument is understandable, but as a tactic it asks too much of families. We're talking about children, not soldiers. Some government schools are just too far gone, and the only hope parents have for their children is to escape. It's too much to expect those parents to sacrifice their children at the altar of wokeness just to improve the odds of taking back another school.

Moreover, the "burn the boats" strategy is self-defeating. Parents will have a better chance of taking back government schools when those schools aren't their only option. Economist Albert O. Hirschman described more than half a century ago that there are two ways that members of organizations in decline—such as government schools—can reverse the decline: exit or voice.[53] A regular customer of a restaurant that declines in quality can either speak to the manager or another employee (voice) or start eating elsewhere (exit). But what if there were no other restaurants? Monopolists can ignore the concerns raised by their customers because those customers have nowhere else to go.

A major reason that school boards were so dismissive of parents is because they knew they had a captive audience. Sure, some parents could afford to enroll their children in a private school, but doing so came at a big cost—too big for many families. With school choice, parents who wanted to send their child somewhere else could take the public funds associated with their child with them. That makes switching schools much easier for parents—and thereby gives them much greater leverage with school boards. But that doesn't mean parents will flee at the drop of a hat. Parents don't switch schools lightly—it's expensive, time-consuming, and entails separating their child from a school where, for all its faults, they might have made lots of friends. They prefer to exercise voice first. Exit is always Plan B at best.

Hirschman himself was initially skeptical of Milton Friedman's school voucher proposal because he believed schools were more responsive to voice than exit, and that—similar to some choice skeptics today—an exit option would reduce the likelihood that they would first exercise voice.[54] But Hirschman later reversed himself, observing that "the opening up of previously unavailable opportunities of choice or exit may generate feelings of empowerment in parents, who as a result are more ready than before to participate in school affairs and to speak out."[55] In other words, choice enhances voice. The ability to exit makes parents more likely to speak up because they know that school boards are more likely to listen.

Taking back control of school boards and pushing for school choice are strategies that go hand in hand. Parents concerned about the state of K–12 education and the future of our nation need to do both. To achieve those goals, we must first understand what we're up against.

Union Strategy in Red, Purple, and Blue States

When I first got involved in the school-choice movement, something puzzled me. The Republican Party tended to be much more supportive of school choice than the Democrats, so one would expect that the redder the state, the more school choice it would have, but that wasn't the case. Deep red states like Alabama, Mississippi, Texas, Utah, and West Virginia had little to no school choice to speak of. Most of the states with school-choice policies tended to be purple states that had gotten redder over time, like Arizona, Florida, Ohio, and Wisconsin. Why?

I asked my friend Jason Bedrick, a former state legislator who is currently a research fellow at the Heritage Foundation, who explained as follows:[56] In purple states, where political control shifts back and forth between the two parties, the teachers unions and government school establishment tend to side with the Democrats because they are the party of government. The Democrats are more likely to favor increased school spending and a host of policies and regulations that favor the unions, so it's no shock that the unions reward them with their political support. There's an even stronger incentive for unions to get into bed with the Democrats in blue states, where their control of the government is rarely challenged. This means that the unions are nearly always able to block school-choice legislation in blue states, but every now and then the Republicans gain a sufficient control in purple states to pass a school-choice policy.

But what about red states? The unions aren't stupid. They're not going to put all their eggs in the Democratic basket when they know that the basket will almost certainly get run over by an eighteen-wheeler. In red states, therefore, the unions play in the Republican primaries—especially in rural areas—supporting candidates who are down-the-line conservatives on issues like abortion, guns, and taxes, but who support the union's K–12 education agenda, including their opposition to school choice.

And it's not just the unions. Superintendents in rural areas, where government schools are often the single largest employer, often wield outsized influence with state legislators. The unions might be the face of the opposition to school choice, but superintendents work quietly behind the scenes. When a school-choice bill comes up for a vote, the superintendents will meet with the state legislators representing their districts and warn of the supposedly dire consequences of passing school choice. Why, if parents could leave and take their money with them, there will be a mass exodus! We'll be forced to fire teachers and cut the football team! The whole school could collapse! And do you know whom the voters will blame in November? You! Unless lots of voters are in the legislator's other ear explaining the need for school choice, the superintendents' whisper campaign is usually sufficient to persuade rural legislators to vote no.

But what if the unions in a deep red state broke faith with the Republicans? What if instead of playing in Republican primaries, they thought they could replace the Republicans with Democrats who are more ideologically aligned with them on a host of issues beyond opposition to school choice? And what if the government schools broke faith with parents—such as by closing down or teaching things that ran counter to families' values—spurring them to ask their local legislators for greater education choice? Such a scenario might just produce the perfect opportunity to usher in a wave of education reforms in red states that had thus far been impervious to them. But taking advantage of that opportunity would require school-choice advocates to adopt a new strategy designed to mobilize frustrated parents and the GOP's base.

The Red State Strategy

For decades, school-choice supporters had tried to make the bipartisan case for choice. They pointed out, correctly, that the policy is an equalizer.

Rich people already have school choice because they can already afford to pay out-of-pocket for private school tuition and fees or to live in neighborhoods with the best public schools. Funding students directly allows more families to access educational options. The policy should not be a partisan issue—and it isn't if you ask voters directly. But the average voter doesn't wield nearly as much political influence as do special interests like the teachers unions. Almost all campaign contributions from teachers unions go to Democrats. The same goes for their formidable grassroots organizing. That means the unions form a core constituency that the Democratic Party dares not cross—even if a majority of registered Democrats disagree with them. The Democrats in office respond to power as opposed to logic. That doesn't mean they're bad people, they are just rational actors responding to political incentives.

Decades of appealing to Democrats using liberal arguments for school choice—for example, that it expands educational opportunity for the most disadvantaged—had failed to result in more than token support from a small number of elected Democrats. The bipartisan approach had a certain appeal to it, but it was not enough to form a winning coalition. Meanwhile, the school-choice movement writ large was avoiding the very arguments that might appeal to conservative, rural Republicans out of a concern that those arguments would turn off Democrats. But if the Democrats weren't on board anyway, what did we have to lose?

Moreover, it wasn't clear that the education reform coalition was really as bipartisan as it claimed to be anymore.[57] Over time, the education reform movement had begun to drift to the political left—and spurn the political right. In 2019, my PhD mentor Jay P. Greene and Rick Hess of the American Enterprise Institute analyzed the political giving among staff at major education reform organizations. Twenty years earlier, political-campaign contributions by education reform advocates was nearly "evenly split between Democratic and Republican candidates."[58] But by 2019, more than 90 percent of the contributions were going to Democrats, even though Republican legislators were much more likely to support education reforms like school choice. As Greene and Hess observed, education reform organizations that had bent over backward to avoid alienating liberals suddenly had no compunction about alienating conservatives or even the median voter:

> In seeking to win the intramural fight on the left, both union and reform Democrats have taken to one-upping each other by staking out positions farther and farther left on hot-button cultural issues. As they've done so, reformers have seemingly gone out of their way to alienate Republicans. Indeed, today's reformers have been engaged in noteworthy efforts to soften school discipline, conscript schools into progressive battles over sexual orientation and gender identity, and enlist schools as outspoken advocates for DACA and critics of ICE.[59]

Some left-wing education reform advocates had even organized efforts to excommunicate prominent conservatives, like Robert Pondiscio (then of the Fordham Institute, and later the American Enterprise Institute) for the sin of daring to question the left-wing racialist orthodoxy.[60] Greene and Hess warned that "winning coalitions aren't formed by belittling potential partners" but that the ed reform movement's "politically correct monoculture" was making it hard for conservatives to stay in the coalition "when their potential partners are busy demonizing their views and values."[61] I couldn't agree more.

Instead of playing the same old advocacy game, I went rogue. In 2020, I began coordinating regularly with a small group of like-minded education choice advocates to discuss the future of our movement. We all recognized that the union response to COVID had provided a unique window of opportunity—parents were more aware than ever before of the problems with government schooling and they wanted solutions. Taking over school boards was not enough. They needed education choice, too. That required forming a winning political coalition.

America has two major political parties. To get anything done politically, you need at least one party on board. Most Republicans already were on board for school choice as it aligns with their general support for families, freedom, and market competition. But there were enough GOP holdouts in deep red states' legislatures to block reform. Forming a winning coalition would require either persuading a sizable number of Democrats to buck one of their most powerful constituencies, or persuading a similar number of Republicans to side *with* their base, key coalitional allies, and a majority of parents. Which seems like the easier lift?

We decided that the **first step** to winning on school choice was to show frustrated families that school choice was a solution to their problems. Parents who had been upset about a host of issues—mask mandates, CRT, and gender ideology in the classroom; secret transgender policies; males in the girls' locker rooms, and so on—tended first to try to get schools or school boards to reverse the policies, then to go to the legislature to force their hands. We needed to show them how school-choice policies provided them with additional leverage with school officials and school boards, and an immediate escape hatch when they still wouldn't listen.

The **second step** was to help parents turn up the heat on state legislators, especially Republicans. If we amplified the voices of frustrated parents and the GOP's conservative base, then Republican politicians would feel pressure to vote for school choice. Until now, many GOP legislators had only been hearing from union lobbyists and their local superintendents. Now they needed to hear from a host of their actual constituents.

The **third step** to winning on school choice is to make the policy a litmus test for Republicans. Despite the pressure, some GOP legislators would probably continue to vote against it. We needed to let their constituents know who they were so the voters could replace those Republicans who adhered to the party platform on school choice. We needed to transform the Grand Old Party into the Parents' Party.

If we were right that school choice was popular among the general population, then the voters would reward the Republican Party in the general elections. The **fourth step** would be capitalizing on those electoral victories. Success begets success. When legislators saw that school choice was a winning issue among voters, some of the holdouts would flip their views on the issue or risk being thrown out of office.

We presented our strategy to many of the legacy education reform groups but did not find a receptive audience. Even if it worked in a few deep red states, they argued, this hyperpartisan strategy was going to backfire in the long run. Tying school choice too closely to one party would make it impossible for anyone associated with the other party to embrace it. Red states might eventually come on board, but blue states would be lost forever.

We disagreed. First, the blue states were already nowhere near making any progress on school choice and were highly unlikely to do so in even the distant future. If all we managed to do was pick up a few red states, that was already better than the stagnant status quo. And second, our strategy was only hyperpartisan in the short term. In the long term, our strategy was bipartisan, too, just in a more realistic fashion. How so? Those who championed bipartisanship appealed to the left's ideals. That's nice, but insufficient. We were appealing to interests. With a few notable and admirable exceptions, Democratic politicians were not going to embrace choice because we persuaded them that it was the morally right thing to do. They were going to come on board because the voters forced them to.

If we passed school-choice laws in enough red states, then we would normalize them. As citizens of those states became accustomed to more education freedom, voters in other states would start demanding school choice, too. And if the issue of school choice gave the Republicans a significant enough advantage in elections, then Democrats would eventually get tired of losing and tell the unions they weren't going to die on that hill anymore. But we would never get to that point unless the school-choice movement—or at least some elements of it—was willing to make school choice a culture war issue.

The Red State Strategy was not only the most effective way to expand education choice, it was also the right thing to do. As Jay P. Greene and Jason Bedrick of the Heritage Foundation explained:

> Emphasizing that parents need to be empowered with options to ensure that their children's education aligns with their own

> values [is] the right thing for strengthening families. Allowing different families to select among educational options that serve different values is also essential for promoting diversity and harmony in our pluralistic society.
>
> Parental choice has always been at the heart of the school-choice movement. Parents care about much more than optimizing test scores; they often care even more about the values with which their children are educated. Making this connection between education and family values the focus of the choice movement's political strategy [entails] placing the moral imperative of parental choice at the center of our efforts.[62]

Whether the legacy ed reformers liked it or not, we were about to test the Red State Strategy in 2021 and beyond…

Chapter 5

A NEW HOPE FOR PARENTS IN WEST VIRGINIA

> If it is our intention as a state to fund education . . . then of course it should go where the child gets the best education possible.
>
> —*West Virginia state Senator Patricia Rucker*[1]

In 2021, *the Parent Revolution* swept the nation.

Throughout 2020 and 2021, my friends and I put the Red State Strategy into effect. We wrote op-eds in the *Wall Street Journal* and dozens of other outlets showing parents how school choice was the solution to their problems.[2] We called out Randi Weingarten and hypocritical anti-school-choice politicians on social media. Those Twitter tussles attracted a great deal of attention, and soon I was leading an online army. Media outlets noticed, and before long I was a regular guest on several shows on Fox News and Fox Business, where I raised awareness about the gap between parents' values and what the government schools were pushing, and how school choice offered a solution. I flew all over the country, speaking about school choice at scores of state capitols, rallies, and events.

Whenever I spoke about *the Parent Revolution*, the excitement in the air was palpable.

But again, don't take my word for it. A couple years later, the liberal media finally figured out what I was doing. As Vox reported in late 2023: "Corey DeAngelis, a senior fellow at AFC, became the public face of the effort, traveling from state to state, holding rallies, making media appearances, and tweeting constantly."[3]

The results exceeded even my wildest expectations. Nationwide, state lawmakers passed more education choice policies than ever before. Tired of being ignored by government school officials and school boards, exasperated parents turned to state lawmakers for relief. Inundated by a wave of calls and emails from angry constituents, the legislators complied. In Kentucky, a bill to create a new education choice policy passed by a vote of 48–47 with the crucial support of a lone Democrat, Rep. Al Gentry. "I personally don't like this bill," Gentry said on the House floor, explaining his vote. "I do not support many things in this bill. However, the majority of those who sent me here do support this bill. So I voted yes for them."[4]

Kentucky governor Andy Beshear vetoed the bill, stating, "I am a proud product of public education. A proud graduate of Kentucky's public schools."[5] What he conveniently left out was that he also attended private school in Kentucky: Capital Day School. I found the yearbook photos. They were from 1987. I posted them on social media in 2021.[6] Fortunately, his hypocrisy did not stand. The Kentucky legislature overturned his veto shortly thereafter.

By the end of the 2021 legislative session, nineteen states enacted thirty-two new or expanded education choice policies, including new ESAs in Indiana, Kentucky, Missouri, New Hampshire, and West Virginia, and new tax-credit scholarship policies in Arkansas and Ohio.[7] It was the most progress the school-choice movement had ever made in a single year—and almost all the progress was in red states, where elected Republicans were responding to the demands of frustrated parents. The Red State Strategy was working.

We could prove it, too. In a report for the American Enterprise Institute, Jay P. Greene and James D. Paul analyzed whether school-choice policies required bipartisan support among elected officials to pass. Of seventy votes considered, including those from the 2021 legislative session, they found that Republicans did not need support from any Democrats more than 95 percent of the time.[8] Their takeaway was that school-choice advocates should devote far more resources toward getting Republican lawmakers in line than converting Democrats to the cause. This might sound obvious, but it was nothing short of revelatory to have it in writing and backed by data. We already knew Democrats weren't going to come out against their union backers. Now we could show that we didn't need them. Republicans, on the other hand, could win because school choice was deeply rooted in the values of their party and the philosophy of liberty. It was just a matter of letting the GOP base know when a legislator with an "R" next to his or her name went off the reservation.

Among all the states to empower families with more education choice in 2021, one stood out: West Virginia.

Mountain State policymakers threw off the yoke of union control and empowered families with greater control over their children's education via the Hope Scholarships, the nation's first publicly funded education choice policy for *all* students. It was a stunning victory. Just two years earlier, the teachers unions had thwarted a far less ambitious proposal. What happened in between is the perfect case study of how policymakers should respond to union hubris and overreach.

Red for Ed's Pyrrhic Victory

In early 2018, the teachers unions in West Virginia threatened to strike if they didn't receive significant pay increases. In most states, teacher compensation is set locally, but in West Virginia, the pay scale is centralized. State lawmakers offered to raise salaries by 2 percent that year with 1 percent increases in the following two years. But the unions rejected the proposal, saying that it wasn't enough.[9] On February 22, 2018, more than 22,000 West Virginia teachers went on strike in all 55 counties, leaving about 270,000 students and their families in a lurch. Thousands of crimson-clad union members holding "Red4Ed" signs took to the streets around the state capitol, telling state lawmakers that they wouldn't return until their demands were met.

According to the National Education Association, the nation's largest teachers union, the average teacher salary in West Virginia in 2018 was $44,700.[10] That might sound low, but school is open only about 180 days a year and, according to the U.S. Census Bureau, the median household income in West Virginia that year was $44,097.[11] In other words, without even factoring in government benefits, the average *individual* teacher in West Virginia working *thirty-six weeks per year* was making slightly more than the average *household* working *all year*. And that was using the NEA's own figures. The Bureau of Labor Statistics reports that the average teacher salaries for West Virginia teachers was somewhat higher in 2018—about $45,250 for high school teachers and about $47,350 for elementary school teachers.[12]

Moreover, teacher salaries are more a function of resource allocation than total resources. Over the past three decades, K–12 government school enrollment in West Virginia has fallen by about 20 percent, yet school staff has *grown* by 7.5 percent.[13] Had Mountain State government schools simply not created new positions as the student population declined, then they would have been able to give significant raises to current staff. But they chose instead to hire new staff. It's worth remembering that unions get more money when they sign up new dues-paying members, not when current members get pay increases.

After more than a week of striking, the unions reached a deal with Gov. Jim Justice and the state legislature to boost teacher pay by 5 percent. On March 7, teachers returned to the classroom. But victory only whetted the unions' appetite. Not only did they face no repercussions for engaging in a strike that the state attorney general had declared to be unlawful, but the unions also saw that they could force state lawmakers to give them what they wanted if they just applied enough pressure.

Teachers unions in other states and their allies in the press had been watching closely. In the wake of the deal, the *New York Times* editorial board crowed: "West Virginia Teachers Give a Lesson in Union Power."[14]

Soon, similar union-backed "Red for Ed" movements were threatening strikes in Arizona, Kentucky, and Oklahoma. Meanwhile, the West Virginia unions were plotting their next move. The AFT's Randi Weingarten even called the deal "a starting point."[15]

The unions' goals were as much about changing the political makeup of the state legislature as they were about extracting financial concessions. Indeed, the political goals might even have been a higher priority. "I don't think this is a strike or a work stoppage. I think this is a movement for a better future for West Virginia," union member Steve Buford told the *Intercept* during the strike.[16] He went on to predict a "'landslide' win for local pro-labor Democrats." As the *Intercept* observed, the unions and their political allies had "overwhelmingly blamed Republican Gov. Jim Justice and the GOP-held state legislature for meager teacher pay and shrinking benefits," while striking protesters frequently held signs reading "We will remember in November!"

During the 2018 midterm election, the NEA and AFT, along with their local affiliates, poured money into political action committees, like Mountain State Values and ReSet West Virginia, that backed Democrats in state legislative races.[17] The political winds nationwide seemed to be pointing toward a blue wave, and the unions thought this just might be their chance to turn West Virginia blue, too. In the end, the Democrats picked up two seats in the state senate and six in the House of Delegates, but the GOP kept its majorities in both chambers.[18]

As with their strike, the unions didn't get everything they wanted, but they felt they were moving in the right direction. Now they were on the lookout for another excuse to flex their political muscle, extracting more legislative concessions and building popular support to help the Democrats take over the statehouse and the governor's mansion. Not long into the 2019 legislative session, they thought they had found the perfect target: an education choice bill filed by a freshman legislator.

They had no idea how badly their plan was going to backfire. They had picked a fight and won a battle. They were about to pick another fight and lose the war.

The Unions Meet Their Match

The bill's sponsor was state senator Patricia Puertas Rucker, a former social studies teacher who homeschooled her five children. Born in Caracas, Venezuela, Rucker and her family moved to the United States when she was six years old due to her father's job as a journalist, but they never returned because of how communism had wrecked the country. "I mention it as a cautionary tale," Rucker told the *Daily Signal*, "because so many Americans believe that we could never go down the road of Venezuela or other countries and I can tell you, I never would've thought that would've happened to Venezuela either."[19] Now Rucker was on a mission to ensure that the country she loved did not go down the same, dark path to socialist misery as the nation her family had left behind.

Concerned that then-senator Barack Obama's rhetoric during the 2008 presidential campaign was reminiscent of Venezuela's Hugo Chavez, Rucker decided to get involved politically. That year, she founded We the People of Jefferson County, a local Tea Party group dedicated to defending the freedoms enshrined in the U.S. Constitution. A few years later, she ran for the West Virginia House of Delegates, losing by just over one hundred votes. In 2016, she won election to the West Virginia Senate by more than 2,300 votes.

At the heart of her agenda was education. She had attended government schools that she believed did a great job, and she initially enrolled her eldest daughter in one. But when her daughter was diagnosed with autism and placed in special education classes, Rucker realized that her daughter's assigned government school "really did not have a handle on how to handle autism."[20] After her daughter came home from school with bite marks and bruises, she approached school officials with her concerns but was told that "the only way to keep her safe" was to "lock her up in a high chair so that she is separated from the other kids."[21] Rucker was shocked. "So your answer to keep her safe is to punish her?" she asked the school officials incredulously. "That's not an acceptable answer." In order to ensure her daughter was safe and got the education she deserved, Rucker decided to homeschool her. It was that experience that made her realize that a one-size-fits-all system doesn't actually fit all. "If [a] child is somehow not getting the education they need in the traditional public school, our priority as a state and as a people is to make certain that child gets what they need," said Rucker. "That should be what is most important."[22]

Rucker quickly earned the respect of her state senate colleagues. In 2019, she was appointed chair of the West Virginia Senate Education Committee, which put her in a strong position to reform the state's education system and expand educational opportunities for Mountain State children. West Virginia was one of the few states without any school-choice policy, not even a charter school law that would allow private entities to manage public schools as in more than forty other states. Rucker set out to change that.

Rucker's comprehensive reform bill would have shifted some decision-making from the state to local school districts, modified the state's funding formula, legalized the creation of charter schools, allowed families to enroll their children in out-of-district government schools with open seats, and given teachers another 5 percent pay raise and sick day bonuses along with tax credits for purchasing classroom supplies. It also would have created a modest education savings account (ESA) policy—something the unions opposed vociferously. "The bad really outweighs the good," said Joy Jenkins, staff representative for the West Virginia American Federation of Teachers. "The money follows the students, and we're already facing massive cuts statewide due to declining enrollment."[23] In other words, the unions were afraid that, given the choice between a government school and something else, parents would choose something else.

Like school vouchers, ESAs let families tap into the funds that the state would have spent on their child to pay for a private education. But whereas traditional vouchers are like tickets that can only be redeemed at a private school, ESAs empower families to truly customize their child's education. Families can use ESAs for private school tuition, tutoring, textbooks, homeschool curriculum, online courses, special-needs therapy, and more. Arizona had pioneered the ESA concept in 2011, and by

2019 there were also ESA policies in force in Florida, Mississippi, North Carolina, and Tennessee.[24] All the ESA policies except for Arizona's were limited to students with special needs. In Arizona, several categories were eligible, including students with special needs, students assigned to low-performing government schools, children living on Native American reservations, foster children, and the children of active-duty military personnel or those killed in the line of duty. Rucker's bill would have made about one thousand ESAs available to students with special needs or victims of bullying or abuse.

Despite the vocal opposition of the unions, the bill easily cleared Rucker's committee and then the entire state senate. It was the first time a school-choice bill had ever cleared a legislative chamber in West Virginia.[25] But the unions did not appreciate the historic achievement. "That seems like retaliation for last year," AFT's Jenkins said in response to the bill's passage. "They are basically holding your pay raise hostage in this bill."

In retaliation, the unions decided to hold West Virginia's children hostage. If the unions didn't get exactly what they wanted from the legislature, they weren't going to educate children. "We are left with no other choice," declared Fred Albert, president of the American Federation of Teachers' West Virginia chapter, announcing alongside Randi Weingarten and the state's two other teachers unions that they would be going on strike to protest the legislation.[26]

After just two days of the unions striking, Republican legislators in the House of Delegates buckled under the union pressure. The lower house indefinitely tabled the state senate's education reform bill and instead passed legislation to raise teacher pay 5 percent without any other reforms.[27] Even though school choice was a Republican platform issue and the GOP had supermajorities in both legislative chambers, the prospects for expanding educational opportunities seemed slim.

But Rucker and her senate colleagues did not give up. Unlike their House colleagues, as Rucker later explained, the senators were ready to play hardball: "In the Senate we were very clear when we said, 'Well, we want education reform. If we're not going to get education reform, we're not going to pass that teacher pay raise.'"[28] The senate rejected the house bill, and the legislative session ended without any teacher pay raises or education reforms—but not before the governor called for a special session on education. The senate, for its part, set aside the money for the pay raises in anticipation of the special session.

The senate's hardline approach had put the governor in a quandary. Governor Justice had promised the teachers another pay raise, but when he asked senate leadership before the legislative session began what it would take to pass the pay raises, they responded that they wanted comprehensive education reform. That threw a monkey wrench into his plans, as his union allies hated the proposed reforms. The governor had even threatened to veto Rucker's reform bill, calling it "a dog's mess for the sake of creating a dog's mess to hit back," implicitly echoing the union's baseless charge that seeking to expand educational opportunities for children was merely "retaliation."[29]

But now it was clear that Senator Rucker and her colleagues meant business. If the unions wanted pay raises, they would have to accept some reforms. A few months later, after a great deal of wrangling, the legislature finally agreed on the Student Success Act, which included a pay raise and several of the reforms Rucker had initially proposed, including more local control and a modest charter school law that allowed up to ten brick-and-mortar charter schools and two virtual charter schools.[30] By the 2023–24 school year, only seven charter schools had been approved statewide.[31] Notably absent from the education reform bill was any ESA component. Although the state senate separately passed an ESA policy as a standalone bill, it did not receive support from the lower chamber—or even the vote that House leadership had promised.

Knowing that there was insufficient appetite in the House of Delegates for a robust education choice bill, Rucker bided her time and focused on other issues during the 2020 legislative session, which wrapped up in early March before COVID shut down state legislatures nationwide. Desperate families would, unfortunately, have to wait. Rucker decided to make education choice a campaign issue. A day after the House tabled her ESA bill, she went on a statewide radio program and promised her constituents that if reelected, she would work to pass a much more ambitious ESA policy. But achieving that goal would require a new legislature.

A new legislature was exactly what the unions had in mind as well, although their ideal legislative makeup differed markedly from Rucker's. Once again, the unions poured hundreds of thousands of dollars into the Mountain State Values PAC, which spent nearly $4 million on state election contests in 2020.[32] Rucker was a prime target, with the PAC spending nearly a quarter-million dollars trying to knock her out.

They failed.

Not only did Rucker win reelection, but the GOP expanded its majority in both legislative chambers to a wider margin than they'd had after the 2016 elections, gaining three seats in the state senate and a whopping seventeen seats in the House of Delegates, producing 23–11 and 76–24 supermajorities, respectively. Ralph Waldo Emerson famously said, "When you strike at a king, you must kill him." The unions struck and missed. Now they would reap the consequences.

West Virginia Goes from 0 to 100

By going all in for the Democrats even after raising their pay two years straight, the unions lost any remaining goodwill they'd had with the Republicans. And worse, by putting their all into defeating the Republicans and coming up short, they revealed themselves to be paper tigers. In 2019, a two-day strike struck enough fear in the hearts of the GOP-controlled House of Delegates that they killed the education reform bill. Now, no one feared them.

One of the legislature's first acts was to pass a bill, sponsored by Senator Rucker, clarifying what the attorney general had explained two years ago: Work stoppages and strikes by government employees are illegal.[33] Now the prohibition would be explicit in statute in addition to common law. Only one Republican state senator voted against the measure. An amended version later passed the House of Delegates on a 55–44 vote, with about twenty Republicans voting with the Democrats in opposition. In the end, the bill became law without Governor Justice's signature.

Much more important, Rucker took another shot at passing an education choice bill. This time, she filed the Hope Scholarship Act to create an ESA worth about $4,600 per year for every child in the state who was switching out of a public school or entering kindergarten—what would be the most expansive education choice policy in the nation. At the time, only five other states—Arizona, Florida, Mississippi, Tennessee, and North Carolina—had ESA policies, and all but Arizona's were limited to students with special needs. "I really am excited about the Hope Scholarship, which is going to be our legislation this year to provide an opportunity of choice for every family [in] West Virginia that shows that we care about every student," Rucker said. "It doesn't matter where they are. It doesn't matter where they live. It doesn't matter what their income is. It doesn't matter what their background is. We want to make certain every child has an opportunity for a good education."[34] About 93 percent of K–12 students in the state would be eligible for a Hope Scholarship in the first year of its implementation, and the bill would automatically expand eligibility to all students after a few years.

This time, Rucker had the support of a coalition of local and national groups behind her, including the American Federation for Children, Americans for Prosperity of West Virginia, the Association of Christian Schools International, the Cardinal Institute for West Virginia Policy, Catholic Education Partners, ExcelinEd in Action, EdChoice, Education Choice West Virginia, and the West Virginia Christian Education Association.[35] "This coalition . . . firmly believes that ESAs offer West Virginia the best opportunity for families to tailor an education that best fits the learning needs and styles of their children," said Garrett Ballengee, executive director of the Cardinal Institute. "Empowered with ESAs, thousands of families in West Virginia could—for the first time in West Virginia's history—have the ability to create an education that will help each child realize his or her potential, regardless of the family's income or ZIP code."[36]

Parents also rose to support the Hope Scholarships. Rucker had heard from countless parents who supported education choice during her first term in office, and now she let them know there was a bill that would give them greater education freedom. "During the strikes, I saved a folder of all the people who wrote to me in support of the education reform. I kept all of their emails," Rucker told Jayme Metzgar of the *Federalist* in an interview. "The vast majority of them said something like, 'Please don't use my name. Don't tell anyone I wrote to you.' They were so scared and intimidated by the teachers' unions."[37]

The school-choice coalition also helped to organize parents. The Cardinal Institute and the Institute for Justice partnered to create Education Choice West Virginia, a group of dozens of parents and educators who collaborated to spread awareness about the concept of school choice and the Hope Scholarships.[38] The more the parents reached out to their legislators, the more it seemed the Hope Scholarships were likely to pass.

The unions and their political and media allies freaked out. The president of the AFT's state affiliate warned of a "slow death spiral" for government schools, while the West Virginia Education Association branded Rucker's bill as "an attempt to destroy public education."[39] State lawmakers echoed the unions' apocalyptic language. Democratic Delegate Ed Evans predicted the Hope Scholarships would "seriously cripple" government schools, while Sen. Michael Romano lamented that the scholarships would "suck money out of the public-school education till it falls flat on its face."[40] Media outlets did their best to turn union talking points into the official narrative. Locally, Susan Johnson of the *West Virginia Gazette* warned readers about the supposed "weakening of public schools" and predicted "cuts in teacher positions, salaries, and benefits."[41] Meanwhile, national education blogger Diane Ravitch shrieked that West Virginia was "hurtling backward into the nineteenth century," whatever that means.

Perhaps most amusing was the concern trolling from politicians who pretended to oppose the Hope Scholarships because they weren't targeted to students in need, but who had voted against the prior ESA bill, which had been targeted. "This particular bill is not a targeted bill," whined Democratic Senate Minority Leader Stephen Baldwin. "It's wide open. So it doesn't target the aid towards the students who need it the most."[42]

But the wailing and gnashing of teeth was all for naught. In March, the Hope Scholarship bill cleared the state senate along party lines with only two Republican defections, Senators Bill Hamilton and Eric Nelson.[43] Later that month, it passed the House of Delegates with a comfortable margin of 57–42, including about twenty Republican defections. This time, Gov. Justice signed the bill into law.

"I'm very proud of the legislation we passed," said Rucker in a message to her constituents on social media. "The Hope Scholarship provides an opportunity for students in our state to get the education that they need, no matter whether it comes through the public school, private school, individualized home education, or any other option that fits their unique needs."[44] Rucker concluded by thanking all of the parents who had written and called their legislators in support of the Hope Scholarships: "We couldn't have done it without your support."

It was the dawn of a new era for education in West Virginia. And just as the Red for Ed movement had inspired protests and strikes in other states, the passage of the Hope Scholarships showed parents and policymakers nationwide that passing a universal education choice policy was within the realm of possibility. Once considered a political fantasy, West Virginia made universal education choice a political reality.

The Mountain State had busted a hole in the dam. Soon, the floodgates would break wide open.

Chapter 6

RISE OF THE PARENTS' PARTY

> I don't think parents should be telling schools what they should teach.
>
> —*Terry McAuliffe, former governor of Virginia*

Terry McAuliffe seemed to be on the glidepath to victory. By late September 2021, the Democratic former governor of Virginia was already measuring drapes for his old office. After all, he was well ahead of Glenn Youngkin in all the polls, and Virginia had gone from red to purple in recent years. The Old Dominion had even favored Biden over Trump by ten points in the 2020 presidential election.

Then, during the final debate, McAuliffe's momentum came to a screeching halt.

"I don't think parents should be telling schools what they should teach," McAuliffe haughtily declared during an exchange about education.[1] His opponent, Glenn Youngkin, pounded him and turned the sound bite into a campaign ad that turned the tide. And luckily for Youngkin, McAuliffe quadrupled down on his anti-parent rhetoric until Election Day. Inexplicable? No. The teachers unions were behind him all the way. He even had teachers union president Randi Weingarten stumping for him the night before the election. Youngkin ended up winning in what has been considered one of the biggest upsets in recent history.

Shortly after the votes had been tallied, a Virginia mother went on CNN and said that Weingarten stumping for McAuliffe was the "nail in the coffin" for her. *Washington Post* exit polling attested that education was the number two issue of importance to voters—second only to jobs and the economy. Youngkin won by two points overall, and by six points with voters who ranked education as their most important issue.

McAuliffe made a serious mistake by digging in even deeper against parents during the campaign. But it was more complicated than that. McAuliffe was in a bind. Switching on the issue, right before the election, might have been even worse for him if the general public hadn't believed in the authenticity of the switch. He might well have ended up with two powerful groups upset with him (parents and the unions) as opposed to just parents. In this way, McAuliffe's refusal to admit he was wrong to oppose parents during the final gubernatorial debate was likely the result of cold hard political calculation. Maybe he should have had a better math teacher.

But to understand why McAuliffe's gaffe was particularly salient, we have to understand what happened in a government school in Loudoun County.

The Reckoning in Loudoun County

On June 22, 2021, *the Parent Revolution* came to the Loudoun County School Board.

For months, parents had been raising concerns about CRT in the classroom and other signs of an ideological agenda that took precedence over learning. "Critical race theory is racist. It is abusive. It discriminates against one's color," said Loudoun County mom Shawntel Cooper, who is black, at a school board meeting a month earlier.[2] The district had also recently been sued by five local parents over their twenty-two-page "equity plan" that called for "implicit bias training," a Soviet-style "bias reporting system" that encouraged students to report other students for any statements or behavior they deemed "racist."[3] Now the board was considering a contentious new transgender policy that would allow biological males into the girls' bathrooms and locker rooms and require staff to call students by whatever pronouns they chose. One teacher who had criticized the proposed policy was put on administrative leave until reinstated by a judge a month later.[4]

Parents weren't going to just sit there and take it anymore.

Loudoun parents packed the school board meeting, holding signs saying, WE THE PARENTS STAND UP, EDUCATION NOT INDOCTRINATION, and THERE ARE TWO GENDERS: MALE AND FEMALE. TRUST (TEACH) THE SCIENCE.[5] More than 250 parents had signed up to speak, but after only an hour the board voted unanimously to cut off public comments prematurely.

"The meeting has degenerated," claimed a school district spokesperson as the board ordered people to leave.[6] Parents chanted "Shame on you," and some gave the board the bird.

Barely a fifth of the parents who had registered to speak were given the opportunity to do so. "I'm a mom of 11," said local mom Beverly McCauley, "I took a lot of time to write my speech. I put a lot of heart into it. And then I'm not allowed to speak?"[7]

After the meeting, school board chair Brenda Sheridan blasted the parents. "Tonight, the Loudoun County School Board meeting was interrupted by those who wish to use the public comment period to disrupt our work and disrespect each other," she said. "Dog-whistle politics will not delay our work. We will not back down from fighting for the rights of our students and continuing our focus on equity. We will continue to work toward making Virginia, specifically Loudoun, the best place to raise a family."[8] She also blamed "opponents of the school board" for "pushing false stories about 'critical race theory'" and lamented the supposed "rise in hateful messages and violent threats aimed at progressive members of the school board."[9]

In other words, instead of listening to the concerns of parents who disagreed with the board's policy, the school board president dismissed their concerns and smeared parents as violent, hateful racists.

Much of the media attention focused on the arrest of Scott T. Smith, a forty-eight-year-old father from Leesburg, who was charged with disorderly conduct and obstruction of justice. Two years later, Governor Youngkin would pardon him.[10] News outlets circulated a picture of the bald-headed Smith being held by police with his shirt pulled up and lip busted up. As Luke Rosiak of the Daily Wire observed, in the coming days "Smith became the poster child for what the National School Boards Association has since suggested could be a form of 'domestic terrorism': a white blue-collar male who showed up to harangue obscure public servants on his local school board." Indeed, the NSBA even cited Smith's arrest in its infamous "domestic terrorism" letter three months later.[11]

But Rosiak did something that no one in the mainstream media had bothered to do: ask Smith why he was so upset that evening in June. Smith's answer upended both the media narrative and the Virginia gubernatorial campaign.

Just a few weeks before the school board meeting, Smith's daughter was sexually assaulted in a bathroom at Stone Bridge High School (SBHS) by a "gender fluid" boy wearing a skirt. Although the transgender bathroom policy was not yet officially in effect, it was widely expected to be adopted and schools were already behaving accordingly. Smith was concerned that the policy was putting girls in danger. "My wife and I are gay- and lesbian-friendly," Smith told Rosiak. "We're not into this children transgender stuff. The person that attacked our daughter is apparently bisexual and occasionally wears dresses because he likes them. So this kid is technically not what the school board was fighting about. The point is kids are using it as an advantage to get into the bathrooms."[12]

In the immediate aftermath of the assault, school officials recognized that it *was* related to the transgender bathroom policy. Indeed, a grand jury report would later observe that shortly after being informed of the assault, the district's chief operating officer emailed several district officials, including the superintendent, saying that "the incident at SBHS is related to policy 8040 [the transgender bathroom policy]."[13] The administrator then scheduled a meeting for the district's top brass to discuss the incident. Months later, the grand jury report would excoriate the administrators, calling this meeting "the beginning of the complete lack of transparency by [Loudoun County Public Schools] surrounding this situation."[14]

The boy who assaulted Smith's daughter was arrested and charged with one count of anal sodomy and one count of forcible fellatio, but—as the grand jury report later concluded—the school board covered it up and lied to the public about it. That was what had set off Smith at the school board meeting.

Shortly before Smith's arrest, school board member Beth Barts had dismissed parents' concerns about the dangers of letting boys into girls' bathrooms and locker rooms. "Our students do not need to be protected, and they are not in danger," she said. "Do we have assaults in our bathrooms or locker rooms regularly?"[15] Ziegler replied: "To my knowledge, we don't have any record of assaults occurring in our restrooms." The grand jury later concluded that this statement was "a bald-faced lie."[16] At that point, board chair Brenda Sheridan turned to Loudoun County Public Schools Superintendent Scott Ziegler and asked, "Have we had any issues involving transgender students in our bathrooms or locker rooms?" Ziegler then proceeded to lecture the assembled parents:

> *Time* Magazine in 2016 called that a red herring, that the data was simply not playing out that transgender students were more likely to assault cisgender students in restrooms than were other students. In fact, regardless of the gender identity of the student, if a crime or violation of the rules were committed, that would be investigated and dealt with to the full extent of the rules or the law . . . I think it's important to keep our perspective on this, we've heard it several times tonight from our public speakers but the predator transgender student or person simply does not exist.[17]

Smith could barely contain himself. The superintendent *knew* that his daughter had been assaulted by a boy wearing a skirt in the girls' bathroom. In fact, when he was first called into school and informed about his daughter's "altercation," school administrators told Smith that they would deal with the matter "in-house," meaning that they were not planning to go to the police. He was furious. When he began shouting at the principal and calling him names, school staff called the police. Later, they issued a public statement that, without naming him (or mentioning the sexual assault against his daughter), painted him as the villain. Later that evening, a hospital administered a rape kit on his daughter. The results would later help the prosecution's case against her assailant—he was ultimately convicted, sent to a residential treatment facility, and forced to register as a sex offender for the rest of his life.[18] But now government school officials were pretending it never happened while the parents of the rape victim were sitting in the very same room.

It was at that moment that Jackie Schworm, a far-left community activist wearing a rainbow heart shirt, approached Smith and his wife, Jess, who had mentored Schworm's daughter in the Girl Scouts. Schworm demanded to know which side they were on. The Daily Wire's Rosiak recounted what happened next:

> Smith tried to tell her what happened to his daughter, he said. "And she looks me dead in the eyes and says 'that's not what happened.'"
>
> Schworm noticed that Smith was wearing a shirt with the name of his plumbing business on it, "And she goes 'Oh... I'm going to ruin your business on social media,'" he said.
>
> "You're a bitch," Smith told her, video shows. A police officer monitoring the tension-filled exchange pulled on Smith's arm, he yanked it away, and soon, Smith and the officer were wrestling. Other officers pinned Smith to the ground, bloodying his lip in the process, as Smith uttered, "I can't breathe."
>
> Jess cried out, in words lost in the chaos: "My child was raped at school, and this is what happens!"[19]

Smith was arrested and charged with disorderly conduct and resisting arrest. Months went by without anyone bothering to ask the Smiths to tell their side of the story. It looked like the school board was going to get away with endangering children and lying to the public—until Luke Rosiak published the Smiths' story in the Daily Wire in mid-October, right in the midst of Virginia's gubernatorial contest.

The story was explosive. The truth reignited parents' anger and gave it added force. Adding fuel to the fire was the revelation that the same boy had transferred to another school and committed *another* sexual assault.[20] Apparently, despite credible accusations of sexual assault and a series of disturbing behaviors that other students had reported to school officials, the perpetrator was given only a verbal warning by school administrators and otherwise allowed to roam freely. As *the Parent Revolution* ignited nationwide, Virginia's Loudoun County quickly became the flashpoint.

A group called Citizens of the Leesburg District filed a petition to remove school board member Beth Barts—the one who had haughtily dismissed parents' concerns at the June meeting—arguing that her "neglect of duty, misuse of office, and incompetence in the performance of her duties" made her unfit for office.[21] The petition also claimed Barts "crossed the line when she urged members of a private Facebook group to compile a list and expose information about people against critical race theory."[22] Barts conceded that the member of the Facebook group who called for hacking the anti-CRT parents "unfortunately took it a step too far," but claims that she did not ever personally "advocate for anything illegal or aggressive."[23] In a sign of things to come, a member of that Facebook group—"The Anti-Racist Parents of Loudoun County," or what became known to local critics as "Chardonnay Antifa"—urged fellow members to persuade the Southern Poverty Law Center to list disfavored conservative groups as "hate groups," then weaponize that designation to convince the school board to "have them banned from speaking publicly at meetings."[24] The petition to remove Barts received more than 1,850 signatures. Seeing the writing on the wall, Barts resigned shortly thereafter.

It was a great start, but there was far more work to do for *the Parent Revolution*. As Ian Prior, executive director of the group Fight for Schools, noted, "The problems at Loudoun County Public Schools and on the school board go well beyond one school board member."[25] Prior's group had worked tirelessly to oust Barts, and he promised that his group would "continue to shine a light on Loudoun County Public Schools and will keep fighting until we have a school board of common sense, nonpartisan members and a superintendent who is accountable to parents and tells the truth."[26]

Months later, the grand jury report would condemn the Loudoun school district administration for widespread institutional failures, including "a remarkable lack of curiosity and adherence to operating in silos."[27] The report also slammed top administrators "looking out for their own interests instead of the best interests" of the district or the students they served, which "led to a stunning lack of openness, transparency, and accountability both to the public and the special grand jury."[28] The report specifically reprimanded Loudoun superintendent Scott Ziegler, whom the grand jury accused of lying to the public about having no knowledge of sexual assaults in girls' bathrooms related to the district's transgender policy.[29] The day after the grand jury report was published, the school board unanimously fired Ziegler.

The Youngkin-McAuliffe Election: Parents vs. Unions

The repercussions of L'Affaire Loudoun were felt at the state level, too. The concerns that had mobilized families to show up at school board meetings also brought them out to the ballot box.

A Monmouth University poll released on October 20—shortly after the Daily Wire published Rosiak's story about the Loudoun scandal—found a shift among registered voters from a five-point McAuliffe lead to a tie. "Youngkin's improved position," according to Monmouth, "comes from a widening partisan gap in voter engagement and a shift in voters' issue priorities, particularly around schools and the pandemic."[30] In September, 14 percent of registered voters ranked education and schools as their top issue. In the October poll, that number jumped to 21 percent.

For months, Youngkin had positioned himself as the champion of parents. His campaign website even had an entire section titled "Parents

Matter." Standing in front of a Loudoun County Public Schools headquarters, Youngkin promised that if elected, "on day one, I will issue an order banning the teaching of critical race theory in our schools."[31] Meanwhile McAuliffe championed the teachers unions. The unions were much more organized and well-funded than ordinary parents, but many more voters were parents. As the education issue rose in prominence, so did Youngkin's fortunes. "This is no longer a campaign," Youngkin declared at a campaign rally in Winchester, Virginia. "This is a movement. It's a movement led by parents."[32]

A CBS News poll from early October found that 62 percent of likely Virginia voters reported that "school curriculums on race and history" were a "major factor" in their vote for governor—higher than those who said their most salient issue was abortion (58%), masking (54%), and even taxes (60%).[33] The same survey found that these curriculum concerns were substantially more likely to mobilize conservatives than liberals, with 77 percent of conservatives and 51 percent of liberals indicating curriculum was a major factor.

Then came McAuliffe's biggest blunder. During the final gubernatorial debate, Youngkin brought up the fact that families had been voicing opposition to sexually explicit books in school libraries:

> What we've seen over the course of this last 20 months is our school systems refusing to engage with parents. In fact, in Fairfax County this past week, we watched parents so upset because there was such sexually explicit material in the library they had never seen, it was shocking. And in fact, you vetoed the bill that would have informed parents that they were there. You believe school systems should tell children what to do. I believe parents should be in charge of their kids' education.[34]

McAuliffe responded: "I'm not going to let parents come into schools and actually take books out and make their own decision . . . I don't think parents should be telling schools what they should teach."[35]

That kind of rhetoric might go over well in the faculty lounge, but it was ballot box poison—and the Youngkin team knew it. The team immediately seized on McAuliffe's verbal self-own, turning his comment into a campaign ad which asked voters: "Are you a parent who wants to have a say in your child's education? Too bad. Terry McAuliffe says you have to sit down and shut up."

Youngkin also took to Twitter to sharpen the contrast between him and his opponent, highlighting his comments during the debate when he sided with families: "I believe parents should be in charge of their kids' education."[36]

Youngkin's gambit worked. A poll conducted by the Trafalgar Group a week after the debate found that 54 percent of likely voters disagreed with McAuliffe's statement, while only 37 percent agreed.[37] The same survey found that respondents were more than twice as likely to "strongly disagree" (45%) than they were to "strongly agree" (20%) with McAuliffe's statement. Shortly thereafter, polls showed that Youngkin had taken the lead, as voters' trust regarding handling schools and education shifted from his opponent to him. [38]

A mid-October Fox News poll indicated that likely voters were more likely to agree than to disagree with the idea that parents should "be telling schools what to teach."[39] Again, Youngkin supporters were substantially more mobilized around this topic than McAuliffe supporters, with 79 percent of Youngkin supporters agreeing and 61 percent of McAuliffe supporters disagreeing. At the same time, Youngkin supporters were more than five times as likely to agree than to disagree with parents telling schools what to teach, while McAuliffe supporters were less than 2.5 times as likely to disagree than to agree with the same concept.

As Fox News correspondent Dagen McDowell noted, his tone-deaf debate comment "might be the 'basket of deplorables' moment for Terry McAuliffe."[40]

McAuliffe went into damage-control mode. Three weeks after the debate blunder, and just two weeks before Election Day, McAuliffe's team responded with an ad desperately claiming that Youngkin took

McAuliffe's words "out of context"—a classic example of political gaslighting.[41] As CNN reporter Chris Cillizza commented, "This strategic decision suggests the Youngkin ads on education are hurting [McAuliffe]."[42] Indeed they were.

The Youngkin team probably couldn't believe their good fortune. The more McAuliffe talked about the issue, the more the voters didn't like what they heard. On the same day that McAuliffe released his ad claiming he didn't say what he had said, Team Youngkin responded with an ad showing that McAuliffe did, in fact, say it—he even *reiterated* his anti-parent remarks in multiple interviews *after* the debate.[43]

Voters were especially annoyed by the hypocrisy. McAuliffe had exclusively attended private schools and sent his children to private schools.[44] He had obviously had a say in his children's education. But as Virginia's former governor, he vetoed nine school-choice bills that made their way to his desk, three in 2016 and six in 2017, blocking access to educational options for less advantaged families.[45] Now he was saying that parents shouldn't even have a say in the government schools.

His stance against educational choice hadn't changed, either. On CNN in mid-October, when mentioning Youngkin's support of private-school-choice programs, McAuliffe said, "I will never allow that as governor."[46]

Of course, there is nothing wrong with the McAuliffes seeking out the best educational opportunities for their children. But why does he fight against school choice for others?

The answer is politics. The teachers unions were among McAuliffe's biggest donors, and they fight tooth and nail against allowing families to take their children's education dollars to nonunion private and charter school competition.[47] According to the Virginia Public Access Project, the nation's two largest teachers unions contributed nearly a million dollars to McAuliffe and nothing to Youngkin.[48] The American Federation of Teachers even launched an ad in support of McAuliffe after he embraced them in the debate, and its president, Randi Weingarten, stumped for the former governor the night before Election Day.[49]

The unions might have liked McAuliffe's "school choice for me, but not for thee" position, but the voters didn't. In fact, a nationwide poll conducted by RealClear Opinion Research found that 62 percent of registered voters would be less likely to vote for candidates who send their own children to private school while opposing school choice for other families.[50] This rejection of school-choice hypocrisy is held across party lines as well, with 66 percent of Republicans, 65 percent of independents, and 56 percent of Democrats saying they would be less likely to vote for such a candidate.

It appears McAuliffe knew the hypocrisy of his opposition to school choice could hurt him. In an interview on NBC's *Meet the Press*, he implied that he sent his children to public schools in Virginia.[51] "Chuck," McAuliffe said to the anchor, "we have a great school system in Virginia. Dorothy and I have raised our five children. Of course parents are involved in it."[52] But voters saw through his charade.

In the end, after months of trailing in the polls, Youngkin beat McAuliffe by two points. Exit polling by the *Washington Post* found that 24 percent of voters said education was their top issue, making it the second most important issue in the race, behind the economy and jobs.[53] Among those who said education was their top issue, Youngkin led McAuliffe by 6 points. The final polling by Echelon Insights and Cygnal similarly found Youngkin won among parents by a whopping 15 and 17 percentage points, respectively.[54]

Youngkin had made the GOP the Parents' Party.

After election night, much of the legacy media, and many Democrats, were in denial about the significance of their defeat. Instead of looking inward to figure out why voters changed their minds, many chose instead to fall back on their favorite tactics: gaslighting parents upset about their children's education and smearing them as "white supremacists."[55]

Although the media generally conceded that the election had *something* to do with parents upset about their children's educational experiences, news anchors consistently repeated McAuliffe's lie that critical race theory "is not being taught in Virginia public schools."[56] Whether they were intentionally lying or just useful idiots was not always clear.

Either way, mainstream media figures seemed impervious to the fact. All that mattered was the union-approved narrative. For example, in an exchange between CNN's Brianna Keilar and Sen. Rick Scott, the Florida Republican pointed out that one of the major factors contributing to McAuliffe's loss was his insistence—despite a mountain of evidence to the contrary—that critical race theory wasn't in Virginia schools.[57] To prove that CRT was in Virginia government schools, Scott shared a 2015 training document from the Virginia Department of Education website instructing staff to "embrace critical race theory" and to "re-engineer attitudes and belief systems."[58] In the face of such clear evidence, what did Keilar do? Exactly what she was programmed to do: quickly change the subject, but not before repeating, just one last time, the union-approved message that critical race theory "is not in the curriculum." No wonder trust in media is at an all-time low.[59]

Fortunately, parents are seeing through the media narrative, so this kind of gaslighting isn't going to work anymore. As Scott pointed out in the interview, "[CRT] is happening. And I hope Democrats continue to say it's not happening because parents aren't dumb. They can see it...I hope Democrats keep doing that all across the country."

The media no longer have the power to control the narrative in the face of *the Parent Revolution*. Parents aren't going to forget how powerless they felt over their children's education during the COVID-era union school shutdowns. Parents aren't going to forget how power-hungry unions pushed to keep schools closed, holding their kids hostage in order to secure billions of dollars in ransom payments from the federal government. Parents aren't going to forget what they saw when they had the opportunity to peer into the classrooms during remote instruction. Democrats and their allies can play definitional games and call the curriculum whatever they want, but at the end of the day, parents know what they saw and they didn't like it.

Siding with the unions has been politically profitable for Democrats for decades, but overreliance on teachers unions puts them in a sticky situation today. Parents have emerged as a new special interest group, and Republicans are now in position to make education a winning issue.

Democrats who have long opposed educational freedom find themselves in a Catch-22: If they come out in favor of parental rights, they will get pushback from the teachers unions; if they come out against parental rights, as McAuliffe did, they will get pushback from parents and suffer for it at the voting booth.

Youngkin Proves the DeSantis Playbook Works

Virginia's gubernatorial election wasn't the first example of educational freedom helping a Republican win a gubernatorial race. There is similarly compelling evidence that Florida governor Ron DeSantis owes his 2018 victory to unexpected support from "school choice moms."

As Bill Mattox of the James Madison Institute explained in the *Wall Street Journal*, DeSantis owed his gubernatorial victory "to about 100,000 African American women who unexpectedly chose him over the black Democratic candidate, Andrew Gillum." In a race with a margin of fewer than forty thousand votes, that proved decisive. Exit polls showed that DeSantis had received more than double the support among black women (18%) as black men (8%). Likewise, Republican U.S. Senate candidate Rick Scott won the support of only 9% of black women.

What accounted for DeSantis's surprising overperformance among this demographic? As Mattox noted, more than one hundred thousand students from low-income families, most of whom were black or brown, participated in the state's school-choice program. Gillum had threatened to eliminate the school-choice program, while DeSantis had promised to expand it. Parents who might otherwise have been inclined to support Gillum decided to vote for their children instead, and that meant voting for DeSantis.

The DeSantis win showed Republican politicians that the school-choice issue could help the GOP electorally, especially among nontraditional constituencies. The Youngkin victory provided further proof that parents were becoming a potent political force, and that transforming the Grand Old Party into the Parents' Party was a path to electoral success. Now it was time to take this strategy nationwide. *The Parent Revolution* was well underway.

Taking the DeSantis-Youngkin Playbook Nationwide

DeSantis and Youngkin created a playbook for political success for Republicans. Youngkin put his opponent in a bind: McAuliffe would catch flak from teachers unions for reversing course by coming out in favor of parental rights in education, and, conversely, he would catch flak from families by coming out against parents having more of a say in their kids' education. Because Democratic politicians—who have been overly reliant on backing from teachers unions—lose ground either way, it's in the best interest of Republicans to make parental rights in education a centerpiece of future campaigns.

Republicans nationwide got the message. In the months after Virginia's election, more than two hundred lawmakers from over twenty-five states signed an Education Freedom Pledge to support policies promoting parental rights in education, such as "the right of parents to voice their opinions at school board meetings and to take their children's taxpayer-funded education dollars to the education providers of their choosing—whether it be a public, private, charter, or home school."[60]

There will be no more hiding. Politicians are going to have to take a stance on parental rights from here on out. Parents are the new education special interest in town, and they aren't going away anytime soon. Politicians from all parties would be wise to take their side. After all, parents are going to fight for the right to educate their children as they see fit harder than anyone else will fight to take that right away from them.

DeSantis and Youngkin proved that transforming the Republican Party into the Parents' Party was a winning strategy. In the years that followed, the GOP would take the DeSantis-Youngkin playbook and run with it.

Chapter 7

THE KIDS GET THEIR OWN UNION

The Most Powerful Moms in America Are the New Face of the Republican Party.

—Mother Jones *magazine headline, August 2022*[1]

The way you solve things is by making it politically profitable for the wrong people to do the right things.

—Milton Friedman, Nobel Prize laureate in economics

The Parent Revolution was underway. In 2021, state lawmakers nationwide recognized that they needed to give parents more options for educating their children. The result was the Year of Education Choice, in which nineteen states passed new or expanded education choice policies—the crown jewel being West Virginia's Hope Scholarship for all K–12 students. In November, Virginia's gubernatorial election proved that siding with parents was a winning strategy, and the GOP sought to claim the mantle of the Parents' Party. In the following year, those trends would accelerate as Arizona enacted the nation's second universal education savings account and Republican primary voters added school choice to their list of litmus test issues.

Arizona: Education Freedom Pioneer

For decades, Arizona had blazed the school-choice trail that other states had followed. In 1997, it became the first state to adopt a tax-credit scholarship policy. In 2011, it became the first to enact an education savings account policy. But now, West Virginia had gone from the back of the pack to take the lead in empowering families to choose the learning environments that work best for their children. Arizona policymakers weren't going to let that stand.

A few years earlier, Arizona had nearly been the first to implement a universal ESA policy. When Arizona's ESA was first enacted in 2011, it was available only to students with special needs. The program proved popular—parents liked the freedom and flexibility the ESAs offered. The first survey of ESA families found that nine out of ten respondents reported being satisfied (19%) or very satisfied (71%) with the ESA program, while fewer than three in ten said the same of their child's prior government school.[2] Before long, the legislature expanded eligibility for the ESAs to several additional categories of students, including those assigned to government schools that received a D or F rating on the state accountability system, foster children, children on Native American reservations, the children of active-duty military personnel or those killed in the line of duty, and more.

In 2017, the Arizona legislature passed a bill to expand ESA eligibility to all the state's 1.1 million K–12 students, albeit with a cap limiting the total number of students who could participate to about 5,500. "When parents have more choices, kids win," Arizona Governor Doug Ducey, a Republican, tweeted hours before signing the bill.[3] Meanwhile, opponents like far-left *Arizona Republic* columnist E. J. Montini shrieked that the ESA expansion would "destroy Arizona's public schools" and "ruin . . . kids' chances for a decent education."[4]

But the unions and their allies weren't going down without a fight. Opponents of school choice quickly formed a group called Save Our Schools Arizona (SOS) and launched a campaign to refer the ESA expansion to the ballot. In Arizona, citizens can refer any recently enacted law to the ballot for voter approval if they gather the signatures of more than

5 percent of the number of votes cast in the prior gubernatorial election. In 2017, they needed about seventy-five thousand valid signatures to successfully refer a new law for voter approval. In August 2017, SOS theatrically used a yellow school bus and a little red wagon to deliver seventy-six bankers boxes full of petition sheets containing about 111,000 signatures.[5] That was enough to put implementation of the ESA expansion on hold pending the results of the ballot question, Proposition 305, in the 2018 general election.

This put the school-choice movement in a severe quandary. Due to another Arizona law called the Voter Protection Act, any law passed by the voters is essentially set in stone, requiring a three-fourths supermajority of the legislature to make any changes. That's practically impossible even in states where a single party has a supermajority in both chambers of the legislature, let alone a purplish state like Arizona. This was particularly concerning to school-choice advocates for two reasons. First, the ESA expansion bill extended the cap on ESA participation that was otherwise set to expire. The coalition had hoped to raise the cap within a few years, but if the law were enacted via the ballot, that would be nearly impossible. This predicament was particularly concerning to parents of students with special needs because if the cap on enrollment did not increase, future applicants with special needs might be unable to get access to an ESA. That possibility would reduce support for Prop 305 among parents of students with special needs, who had been one of the core constituencies of the ESA until that point.

Second, ESA policies are fairly new, so policymakers are learning what works and what doesn't as parents share their feedback about how they're utilizing the scholarships for their children. Already in the first six years, there had been several bills making technical changes to how the ESA policy worked. Although program expansions had been controversial, the technical fix bills had not. Passing Prop 305 would mean that even such technical fixes would be a major uphill fight. Compounding the matter, the Voter Protection Act said that any legislative changes to a law approved by the voters had to "further the purpose" of the law. What would that mean for technical fixes? The courts would have to decide. In other words, even minor changes would require an incredible expenditure of political capital, after which would likely come an expensive court battle.

Some school-choice supporters decided that, despite all the obstacles, it was still worth fighting to pass Prop 305 to expand the ESA. But others—including my employer, the American Federation for Children—calculated that even a ballot win would be a pyrrhic victory. Better to lose at the ballot this time, they reasoned, and then come back in the coming years and pass a truly universal ESA without any enrollment caps. If school choice was going to go to the ballot, let it be a policy that would benefit everyone from the outset instead of one that would divide the school-choice coalition.

Predictably, Prop 305 failed by a margin of 65 to 35 percent.[6] "This result sends a message to the state and the nation that Arizona supports public education, not privatization schemes that hurt our children and our communities," crowed Beth Lewis, cofounder of SOS. "Thousands of volunteers have poured blood, sweat, and tears into this effort for nearly two years in order to protect public education from continued attacks."[7]

The ballot fight was a wake-up call to parents. Soon after, Arizona saw the launch of new parent-led nonprofit advocacy groups, like Love Your School, founded by ESA parent and mom of five, Jenny Clark, who had been the spokesperson for the 2018 Yes Prop 305 campaign known as Yes for Ed. "I started Love Your School immediately after the loss of Prop 305 in January of 2019," said Clark.[8] "I knew how amazing options like ESAs were for our family, and that so many parents wanted access to an ESA but didn't qualify. I wasn't willing to give up the vision that Governor Ducey and many of us parents had to see every single Arizona family have access to the program."

Love Your School began statewide support of parents navigating school options, and later played a critical role in 2020 in mobilizing parents to stop the first initiative against the ESA program. Their foundation of grassroots parent support became even more important in 2022 when a universal ESA would come back around.

In 2019, Arizona legislators passed a very minor technical fix bill to address an issue that had arisen on a Native American reservation. Under newly installed Superintendent of Public Instruction Kathy Hoffman, a Democrat, the Arizona Department of Education (ADE) was cracking down on a few low-income Navajo families, demanding that they repay thousands of dollars to the state over supposedly misused ESA funds. What was their crime? Paying for their children's education at a Christian school on the Navajo reservation—just a quarter mile beyond the Arizona–New Mexico border. (As I revealed on Twitter in January 2020, school-choice opponent Kathy Hoffman graduated from a private school, St. Mary's Academy.)

The ESA statute permitted paying for brick-and-mortar schooling only within the boundaries of Arizona, though online learning providers could be based anywhere in the world. The previous ADE administration had permitted the Navajo families to enroll their children at the Navajo-run Christian school, but Hoffman was a close ally of SOS, which was demanding strict compliance. (In another episode of bureaucratic chicanery, ADE denied the application of the adopted son of a member of the military because department officials mistakenly thought that only biological children were eligible even though the ESA statute clearly includes all legal guardians.[9]) After a public outcry, state legislators passed a bill holding the families harmless for one academic year, through July 2020.[10] After that, they would have to find new schools or pay out-of-pocket. All the local government schools in their district received grades of D or F on the state rating system with only 10 to 20 percent of students passing the state math and English tests, despite the schools' spending 60 percent more per pupil than the state average.[11]

Gov. Ducey was not satisfied. If the purpose of the ESA was to empower families to choose the learning environments that worked best for their children, why should it matter where the school was located? To bring attention to the Navajo families' fight and spur the legislature to act, Ducey invited one of the affected parents and her daughter to attend his 2020 State of the State Address. Noting that their chosen school had served their daughter well, Ducey asked the assembled lawmakers to imagine "their surprise when they received a letter from the heavy hand of government declaring the school was out of bounds, and demanding repayment of funds from their education savings account."[12] According to Ducey, this was "an example of government losing sight of the people it's supposed to serve."

The legislature agreed. Shortly thereafter, the legislative committees held hearings on a narrowly tailored bill that would allow students on Native American reservations to attend schools that were within two miles of the Arizona border so long as the school was also on the reservation. It would have been better to eliminate any restrictions on the location of private schools, but the margins in the legislature were thin, and some squishy legislators bought the SOS talking point that the 2018 referendum proved that the "will of the voters" was against any expansion of the ESA. This compromise served as a permanent solution for the affected families without expanding it.

But it was still too much for SOS. "We now have this year's first ESA voucher expansion," their newsletter breathlessly announced. "Senate Bill 1224 aims to expand ESA vouchers across state lines, which would make Arizona the first state in the nation to allow tax dollars to pay for private, religious schools in other states."[13]

It's amazing how many falsehoods they managed to cram into just two sentences. As Jason Bedrick (then of EdChoice) and the Goldwater Institute's Matt Beienburg explained, not one single additional student would have become eligible from the legislation. Moreover, ESA funds were *already* used to purchase lots of educational products and services across state lines, and school-choice programs in other states already permitted even paying tuition at brick-and-mortar schools in other states.[14] But SOS hated the prospect of families choosing their children's school so much that they were either willing to lie or couldn't be bothered to look up very basic, verifiable facts.

The legislature passed the law in February 2020, and SOS—feigning outrage as they grasped at any opportunity to flex their political muscle—filed paperwork for a ballot initiative asking voters to place restrictions on the ESA policy, including limiting enrollment to 1 percent of students statewide and banning the use of ESAs at out-of-state schools. Last time they were seeking to prevent a million kids from getting access to ESAs, which they claimed would destroy the government school system. This time, they wanted voters to kick eight kids from low-income Navajo families out of the school that was serving them so well back to failing government schools.

One of SOS's chief media cheerleaders, Laurie Roberts of the *Arizona Republic*, predicted in February 2020 that gathering the necessary signatures would "be no sweat."[15] She was dead wrong. In May, SOS suspended their campaign as it became clear they wouldn't be able to gather enough signatures.[16] SOS blamed their failure on COVID and a nearly unanimous state supreme court decision not to rewrite state election laws to permit online signature gathering—but nearly all the other major ballot initiatives that year succeeded in gathering enough *actual* signatures to get on the ballot. The voters just weren't interested in what SOS was selling.

Arizona Loses the School-Choice Crown

Legislators took notice. Cracks began to appear in SOS's narrative that the 2018 ballot measure proved the voters didn't want more school choice. A survey by Morning Consult in January 2021 found that two-thirds of Arizona citizens supported the state's ESA policy.[17] If the COVID school shutdowns had made anything clear to parents and policymakers, it was the importance of having lots of educational options. Moreover, contrary to the doom-and-gloom predictions of SOS and other school-choice critics, education in Arizona was *significantly improving*. Over the previous decade, Arizona was first in the nation for academic growth on the National Assessment of Educational Progress.[18] Republicans decided it was time to go big or go home.

In February 2021, the Arizona state senate passed a bill expanding the Empowerment Scholarship Account policy to students assigned to "Title I schools" which serve a high proportion of low-income students. About two-thirds of Arizona's government schools qualified as Title I schools.[19] The vote was along party lines, 16–14.

Opponents of school choice freaked out. State Sen. Rebecca Rios, the leader of the Arizona Senate Democrats, called the bill a "calculated movement to resegregate schools" done under the "guise of helping poor children and people of color."[20] Ironically—and hypocritically—Rios sent her own child to a private school.[21] Was she trying to segregate her own child? Dawn Penich-Thacker, spokesperson for SOS, vowed her organization would "take all steps necessary to stop this attack on our public schools, whether by citizen's initiative, referral to the 2022 ballot, or litigation."[22]

Unfortunately, the House Republicans were not as supportive of school choice as the Senate Republicans. With a narrow 31–29 majority, the GOP needed every party member to vote together for school choice, but three representatives—Michelle Udall, Joanne Osborne, and Joel John—all defected. The ESA expansion bill was dead on arrival in the lower house. Although the state senate responded by including an ESA expansion in their version of the state budget, House lawmakers stripped it out. After tense and drawn-out deliberations, the two chambers compromised on a small but important change to ESA eligibility, exempting low-income families from the requirement that they first enroll their child in a government or charter school for forty-five days before becoming eligible for an ESA.[23]

But even that was still too much for Democrats like Sen. Jamescita Peshlakai, who predictably and ridiculously bemoaned that the tiny change was "defunding public education." Like Rios, Peshlakai sent her own child to private school—a decision that has the exact same fiscal effect on local government schools whether the child receives an ESA or not.[24] Was Peshlakai trying to defund government schools with her own family's schooling decisions? More likely she was just another school-choice hypocrite—choice for me, not for thee.

Governor Ducey wasn't satisfied with the small-ball compromise, especially as West Virginia had now taken away Arizona's school-choice crown with its universal Hope Scholarships. The governor had promised voters he would deliver on education choice, and he only had one year left as governor to do it. In January 2022, Ducey used his State of the State

Address to make clear to the state legislature and the citizens of Arizona that expanding education choice was his top priority: "This session, let's expand school choice any way we can... Send me the bills, and I'll sign them."

Yet again, the entire Republican caucus in both chambers of the legislature supported a bill to expand ESAs to all students, except for the Three Union Stooges: Representatives Udall, Osborne, and John. The stooges even filed legislation that would add unnecessary regulations on Arizona's existing education choice policies.[25] They knew it wasn't going anywhere. They were laying down a marker. Hope of taking back the school-choice crown appeared to be slipping away.

A New Challenger Appears: Governor Reynolds Lays Down the Gauntlet in Iowa

Arizona wasn't the only state looking to follow West Virginia's lead in 2021. In Iowa, Gov. Kim Reynolds, a Republican, championed an education-savings account bill as one of her top legislative priorities. "If education truly is the great equalizer," Reynolds declared, "we should create opportunities for more families to provide their children with the education choice that's best for them. That's exactly what this legislation does."[26]

Reynolds's bill would have created state-funded ESAs similar to Arizona's that Iowa families could use to customize their child's education. Under Reynolds's proposal, up to ten thousand ESAs worth about $5,000 annually would have been available to students with special needs or those from households earning up to four times the federal poverty line (about $110,000 for a family of four).

The bill handily passed the GOP-controlled Senate in a vote of 31 to 18, with only one Republican joining the Democrats in opposition. However, the bill soon encountered fierce opposition in the House. Although Republicans held a supermajority of sixty out of one hundred seats in the Iowa House of Representatives—and despite the fact that the Iowa GOP and national Republican party platforms endorsed school choice—they failed to pass the bill.

But Reynolds didn't give up. To pressure Republican holdouts, Reynolds held up the budget, even waiting until after the 110th day of the legislative session, beyond which legislators were no longer paid their per diem for meals and housing. Nevertheless, legislators in the House held firm against it, citing concerns about the effects of school choice on traditional public schools.

Both sides believed voters were with them. A *Des Moines Register* poll found that 52 percent of Iowans opposed the governor's plan, while a Morning Consult poll showed that 66 percent supported ESAs.[27] But even the first poll found that 57 percent of Iowa Republicans favored the proposal, up 8 points since the prior year. The stalemate broke when Reynolds agreed to sign the budget without the legislature passing her ESA proposal.

Reynolds might have lost the battle, but she was determined to win the war. If the legislature wouldn't support her agenda, she'd assemble a new one that would. In a rare and daring move, the governor backed nine pro-school-choice candidates in the Iowa GOP primary elections that June, including several challengers to incumbent legislators in her own party who had blocked her proposal. She took her case on the road, appealing directly to voters—especially parents who had been expressing frustration with the woke ideology being pushed in the government schools even in deep red rural areas. For example, Reynolds visited the rural community of Marion, where the Linn-Mar Community School District had recently adopted a controversial transgender policy. "I want to hear from parents," Reynolds said when asked about the meeting. "It's the right thing to do. We want to make sure parents understand what's involved in the bill I'm putting forward. It was an opportunity to hear from parents to hear how important it is for them to make the decision on what is the best environment for their child."[28]

The governor explained to the voters how her education choice proposal would solve the issues they'd been facing in government schools, from X-rated books to biological males in the girls' locker rooms to critical race theory in the classroom. A school-choice policy would provide an immediate escape hatch for kids who would otherwise be stuck in those government schools—and it gave parents greater leverage when negotiating with school boards who had ignored them. According to Samantha Fett, the Warren County chapter chair for Moms for Liberty, her organization first became active in an effort to pull sexually explicit books from elementary school libraries. "The public school administrators and school boards would just ignore us and hope we'd go away," she explained.[29] After raising multiple concerns with school boards and getting nowhere, she realized she needed other options. "The frustration we had [with] the local level not making any progress, not getting any answers, and being pushed away, drove us to look for solutions outside the district system."[30] Reynolds's message made perfect sense to Fett and the other frustrated parents in her group.

Her message resonated with GOP primary voters, too. Of the nine primary challengers Reynolds endorsed, eight won.

The most prominent scalp belonged to Iowa House Representative Dustin Hite, chair of the education committee, who was funded by the teachers union and had been instrumental in blocking Governor Reynolds's school-choice proposal in 2022. He lost his primary to Reynolds-backed school-choice champion Helena Hayes by a whopping fourteen points.[31]

Legislators got the message. "I might as well come out and say it," admitted Rep. Dennis Bush, who had opposed Reynolds's proposal. "The governor is trying to use this election as a referendum for her voucher bill."[32] He was right, but he didn't realize that the voters were with Reynolds until it was too late. In a three-way primary race, Bush secured less than a quarter of the vote, while the Reynolds-backed candidate, Zachary Dieken, won handily with over 55 percent of the vote.[33]

School choice emerged as a litmus-test issue for GOP voters in Iowa and nationwide, stoking red states to compete against each other to earn the crown of the nation's undisputed champion of parental rights and education choice. But Iowa would still have to wait until the next legislative session in 2023 to take another shot at passing a school-choice bill. Meanwhile, Arizona's legislature was still in session.

Arizona Takes Back the Crown

Arizona was down but not out. Speaker of the House Ben Toma, the sponsor of the universal ESA expansion, still had a card to play—a card very similar to the one played by West Virginia's Senator Rucker when she brokered a compromise to enact the Hope Scholarships. The state of Arizona was flush with cash, and the government schools were clamoring for more money. The Three Union Stooges wanted desperately to give it to them. Legislative leadership proposed a win-win compromise: $1 billion in new funding for the state's school finance formula in return for expanding the ESAs to all students.[34]

The GOP holdouts agreed. On June 24, 2022, the Arizona legislature passed a bill to truly fund students, not just systems. All families, regardless of income or background, were finally able to take their children's state-funded education dollars to the education providers of their choosing. "This is a monumental moment for all of Arizona's students," declared Governor Ducey, as he excitedly signed the ESA expansion. "With this legislation, Arizona cements itself as the top state for school choice and as the first state in the nation to offer all families the option to choose the school setting that works best for them."[35] Arizona's accomplishment even exceeded West Virginia's, as Arizona also eliminated the requirement that students enroll at a government school before becoming eligible for an ESA.

Arizona families were ecstatic. In fact, so many families applied for an ESA in the first week after the expansion took effect that the Arizona Department of Education website crashed.[36] Families submitted more than twenty-five thousand applications within the first two months of program expansion, representing about a tripling of the number of students already using the program.

But one obstacle remained: SOS moved quickly to file paperwork to refer the ESA expansion to the ballot. Local pundits who bought the SOS narrative expected a repeat of 2018: SOS would easily gather signatures and soundly defeat the unpopular "school voucher" measure at the ballot. Instead, it was a repeat of 2020—all thanks to *the Parent Revolution*.

Arizona parents quickly organized to thwart SOS's attempt to block the ESA expansion, urging voters to "Decline to Sign" the SOS petitions. They used social media to coordinate their efforts. If someone saw SOS signature gatherers at a public library or outside a supermarket, they would inform the group, and soon parent activists would be there, too. "If SOS showed up to gather signatures, there was a Decline to Sign parent volunteer also there," said Grant Botma, a father of three from Gilbert, Arizona. "The energy and effort that these pro-ESA parents put forth helped properly educate our community to limit SOS petition signatures."[37]

Fully informed voters were much less likely to sign the SOS petition. In fact, many of them wanted to learn more about ESAs. Christine Emmanuel, a mother of four ESA students, said the voters she spoke with frequently wanted to learn more "about what the ESA can do for their children." When she was done speaking with them, she said, "The only signing they wanted to do was to sign up for an Empowerment Scholarship Account."[38]

SOS was totally unprepared for *the Parent Revolution*. Beth Lewis, executive director of Save Our Schools Arizona, expressed her aggravation with the "Decline to Sign" activists in an interview with *Salon*:

> In the meantime, the final weeks of petition gathering have turned hostile, as groups backed by the Goldwater Institute and AFC have launched a massive "Decline to Sign" campaign, holding protests at petition gathering spots, urging supporters to call businesses near petition sites to complain that "this is hurting our children's education" and videotaping both petition circulators and voters who sign, posting clips of those interactions online. In this atmosphere, petition volunteers say they've been surrounded, harassed and followed for blocks on end, while pro-ESA protesters say they've been insulted or sworn at by referendum supporters.
>
> While Lewis said there wasn't "any organized opposition" to the [2018] petition process . . . this year, "It's like a war zone at some of these events."[39]

The parent activists saw things differently. Local ESA mom Taylor Hoffman described how "hundreds of volunteer parents from all different backgrounds have come together to peacefully hold signs and talk to voters about the ESA program."[40] SOS even lied about its goals, claiming in 2022 that it supported the ESA as it was supposedly "originally intended to serve students with special needs," and merely opposed the expansion.[41] But even back in 2018, when the ESA primarily served students with special needs, SOS complained that ESA policies "siphon funds away from" government schools—they didn't say, "Oh, except for vouchers for kids with special needs."[42] I mean, remember when they went to war over a handful of low-income Navajo kids assigned to failing government schools using ESA funds?

SOS even tweeted in February 2023 that they had "always supported ESA vouchers for students with special needs."[43] Yeah, and Oceania had always been at war with Eastasia.

But Lewis got one thing right: When comparing the 2018 and 2022 ballot initiatives, it was parents who made the difference.

On the day of the deadline, SOS claimed they had turned in 141,714 signatures—more than the 118,823 signatures needed to refer the ESA expansion to the ballot. At a celebratory press conference in front of the state capitol, a seemingly jubilant Beth Lewis declared victory, speaking as though the referendum had already been won: "These voters have repudiated the schemes of Governor Ducey and the Republican-led legislature that continually work to defund our public schools in service to special interests," she squealed.[44] Shortly thereafter, then Secretary of State Katie Hobbs—an avowed opponent of school choice and the Democratic nominee for governor—ordered the processing of ESA applications to halt as her office began reviewing and verifying the petitions.

It looked like a significant setback for school choice—that is, at least, until school-choice supporters acquired all the petition sheets from the secretary of state's office via public-records requests. Although SOS had claimed to have submitted 10,200 sheets of signatures, the secretary of state's office revealed that only 8,175 sheets were turned in. By counting the number of signatures on a random sample of one hundred of those sheets, I estimated the total number at 92,623. The Goldwater Institute hand-counted all signatures and found only 88,866.[45]

Just days after declaring victory, SOS admitted defeat. Its executive director, Beth Lewis, conceded to reporters that the attempt to block the ESA expansion would "end up short." Hilariously, SOS then released a statement explaining that the initial counts they had trumpeted "were necessarily estimates." Apparently, no one at Save Our Schools Arizona could do basic math.

With the last obstacle out of the way, parents flocked to the ESA program. In the first two weeks since the ESA expansion went into effect, the families of more than 6,000 students applied.[46] At the time, there were about 12,000 students already in the ESA program. That fall, more than 32,000 students signed up for an ESA.[47] By the summer of 2023, there were more than 65,000 ESA students. As more and more parents sought alternative learning environments for their children, the number of options they could choose from expanded. In the wake of the ESA expansion, all sorts of new schools opened and expanded, including classical education schools, microschools run by the Black Mothers Forum, schools that leverage virtual reality to teach ancient history and science, and more. [48]

It's plain as day: Families want education choice. This kind of government school exodus is why the unions and their allies, like SOS, are absolutely terrified of providing families a wide variety of options. They know that given the opportunity, moms and dads will pull their kids from government-run schools that fail to meet their kids' needs in a heartbeat.

They'll also vote against lawmakers who vote against their interests. Although the Three Union Stooges ultimately voted for the ESA expansion, GOP primary voters held them accountable for being obstacles to school choice in the first place. Earlier that year, the Republican Party in Maricopa County—the largest county in the state—rebuked them in a resolution condemning "Republicans who campaign as conservatives while voting against school choice and against the best interests of students and parents—specifically Representatives Joanne Osborne,

Michelle Udall, and Joel John."[49] All three lost their primaries—Udall for superintendent of public instruction, Osborne for state senate, and John for reelection to the statehouse—by double digits.[50] Now every single Republican elected to the Arizona legislature was a supporter of education freedom and choice.

Republican Voters Makes School Choice a Litmus Test Issue

Arizona and Iowa were far from alone. Across the country, Republican primary voters were remaking the Grand Old Party into the Parents' Party, as school choice became a litmus test issue on par with being pro-life. Indeed, GOP primary voters in Texas displayed higher support for a pro-school-choice ballot proposition (88%) than a pro-life one (83%).[51] Likewise, a poll of Republicans in Oklahoma found even higher levels of support for school choice (78%) than for pro-life policies (68%).[52]

Republican legislators who had locked arms with the Democrats and the unions to block school-choice bills in recent years were hoping against all hope that the polls were wrong. Unfortunately for them, the polls were right. In the 2022 primaries, GOP voters consistently threw their support to candidates who supported choice, even if it meant tossing out otherwise conservative incumbents.

School choice was the clear dividing line for many primary runoff races in Texas. Rep. Phil Stephenson, an incumbent backed by the teachers union, lost to school-choice supporter Stan Kitzman, who secured 58 percent of the vote despite spending less than half of what his opponent spent on the campaign, according to Transparency USA data.[53] Likewise, school-choice champions Ellen Troxclair and Carrie Isaac both defeated candidates who were endorsed by the Texas affiliate of Randi Weingarten's American Federation of Teachers.[54]

In all, eleven of fourteen Texas House of Representatives candidates endorsed by the pro-school-choice Texas Federation for Children PAC won their primary runoffs.[55] In nearly all these races, the losing candidates toed the party line on key issues such as abortion, gun rights, and taxes.[56] The primary issue where they diverged from their party platform—and their electoral base—was their opposition to school choice.[57]

Next door in Oklahoma, Republican opponents of school choice were feeling the heat—and I helped turn up the temperature. When Rep. Anthony Moore tweeted that he was a "hard pass" on the pending ESA legislation in February 2022, I called him out on being a fake Republican. He then deleted the tweet and blocked me—likely out of concern about how his constituents would take it.[58] Later that spring, when I was visiting the state capitol to advocate for school choice, Moore confronted me. It was a very awkward encounter at first, but soon I managed to engage Moore in dialogue. He repeated the usual union talking points against school choice—it was nothing I hadn't heard before, so I managed to refute all of them in person. By the end of our conversation, his opposition had softened, and he even said he would unblock me on Twitter. A year later, he voted in favor of universal school choice and even stood next to the Speaker when he presented the bill.

He wasn't the only one to have a change of heart. Rep. Rhonda Baker was a consistent opponent of school choice as the chair of the Oklahoma House Education Committee. But although she was an incumbent and had been endorsed by the teachers union, she faced a tough primary challenge. She won her primary, but by a razor-thin margin of sixty-nine votes. The following year, she presented the Speaker's universal school-choice bill on the floor. Obviously, the pressure worked. Sometimes you just need to get close to send a message.

But other Oklahoma Republicans had to learn the hard way. State Sen. Jake Merrick had signed AFC's education freedom pledge, but voted against the ESA bill in 2022.[59] Later that year, he was knocked out in the primary by a pro-school-choice challenger, Kristen Thompson, by a nearly ten-point margin. Likewise, in the hotly contested race for Oklahoma state superintendent of public instruction, pro-school-choice candidate Ryan Walters soundly defeated the union-backed opponent of school choice, April Grace.[60]

A similar dynamic played out in Kentucky, where an incumbent who led the opposition to school choice in the GOP caucus, Rep. Ed Massey, suffered a devastating primary defeat to school-choice champion Steve

Rawlings. Although he was significantly outspent, Rawlings garnered a whopping 69 percent of the vote.[61]

In the Tennessee Republican primary elections of 2022, ten candidates running for the state's House of Representatives were endorsed or funded by the teachers union. Nine of them lost their races. The teachers union endorsement proved a political kiss of death.

Meanwhile, support from school-choice groups proved politically profitable. Candidates endorsed by my employer's sister organization, the American Federation for Children Action Fund, overwhelmingly won their primaries or advanced to runoffs in states like Arkansas, Georgia, Idaho, Nebraska, North Carolina, South Carolina, Texas, and Utah.[62] Nationwide, 85 out of 115 GOP candidates backed by the AFC Action Fund and its affiliates won, as did eleven out of fifteen Democrats.

In 2022, Republican primary voters had a clear message for state lawmakers: Opposing parental rights in education was political suicide. That November, general election voters would deliver a similar message.

The Parents' Party Earns Voters' Trust and Support

American voters had long trusted Democrats more than Republicans on the issue of education. But if COVID taught parents anything, it was that the unions and their Democrat allies couldn't be trusted to keep schools open and keep politics out of the classroom. Two polls in 2020 captured the shift. Ironically, one was from a teachers union and the other was from a Democratic organization.

According to a survey of likely voters in battleground states commissioned by the American Federation of Teachers, 39 percent of respondents had more confidence in Republicans to deal with education issues versus 38 percent for Democrats.[63] Respondents said the number one problem with government schools was that "education has become too politicized."

In a classic case of projection, AFT president Randi Weingarten had repeatedly blamed Republicans for politicizing classrooms. But by a margin of 33 to 28 percent, respondents were more likely to say

Democrats were "more responsible for politicizing education (and making education too much a part of the culture war)" than Republicans. Even more were dissatisfied than satisfied with "the amount of say that parents have in what their children are taught." Voters were also substantially likelier to have a "great deal" or a "fair amount" of confidence in parent organizations (56%) and schoolteachers (62%) than teachers unions (44%). But the facts contained *in her own poll* didn't stop Weingarten from sharing the poll on social media, brazenly asserting that "extremist politicians are trying to drive a wedge between parents and teachers" while her union is "focused on investing in public schools and the essential knowledge and skills students need."[64]

The other poll was conducted in battleground congressional districts by Democrats for Education Reform (DFER). It found that Republicans were more trusted by voters on the issue of education by 3 points overall (47% to 44%), by 9 points with parents, and by 10 points with minority voters.[65] These results represent a seismic shift in support. As DFER's polling memo noted, "This represents a steep drop-off from before the pandemic, when Democrats enjoyed a double-digit advantage on education."[66] Indeed, a 2017 Gallup poll found that Democrats had a whopping nineteen-point advantage on education.[67] Now that lead had evaporated, squandered on putting pornographic books in kids' libraries and males in girls' locker rooms.

The trend was even starker among parents of school-age children. Although a poll in April 2022 had found only a three-point advantage for Republicans in congressional races overall, they boasted a whopping twenty-eight-point advantage with parents of children under the age of eighteen (60% to 32%).[68]

Even before the midterm elections, the left was starting to panic. The left-wing magazine *Mother Jones* detailed the rise of the Mama Bear voters in a breathless account titled, "The Most Powerful Moms in America Are the New Face of the Republican Party."[69] "So what will the Moms for Liberty do if they take over school boards?" the author asked rhetorically. "They mostly promise the obvious things, like fighting mask mandates and pressuring school libraries to remove books that they consider obscene. If you listen carefully, though, you may hear hints of a far more radical goal: getting rid of public schools altogether."[70]

That November, the voters' shift in trust on education manifested itself in the general election. Although the red wave that some had predicted had not materialized, there had been a *school-choice* wave. But don't take my word for it; shortly after the election, a left-wing activist and editor at the *New Yorker* lamented that supporters of education freedom and sanity had "fared depressingly well in the midterms."[71]

They weren't exaggerating. Of candidates supported by my employer's sister organization, the American Federation for Children Action Fund, and its affiliates, *76 percent* won their races.[72] And it wasn't because we only got involved in easy races. In fact, we targeted 69 incumbents—the toughest thing to do in politics—in state legislative races over their opposition to school choice. In 40 of the 69 races, the anti-school-choice incumbents were defeated. Likewise, just over half of the roughly five hundred school-board candidates endorsed by Moms for Liberty in 2022 won their races nationwide.[73]

In West Virginia, where legislators had gone all-in on universal education choice, the GOP expanded their supermajority in the House of Delegates from 78–22 to 88–12 and in the state senate from 23–11 to 30–4.[74] It's amazing to think that just a few years earlier, lawmakers were afraid that if they voted for school choice, voters would throw them out. Instead, voters rewarded them with a stronger majority.

Iowa Governor Kim Reynolds's wager on parent empowerment also paid off. Not only did she handily win reelection by a nearly twenty-point margin, the GOP expanded its majorities in the legislatures from 60–40 to 64–36 in the statehouse, and from 32–18 to 34–16 in the state senate.[75] Reynolds had promised voters that she would enact universal school choice if they reelected her alongside a willing legislature. Voters responded by giving her the legislative support to deliver on her promise.

Perhaps the biggest victory for parents in the 2022 midterms was in Florida, where Gov. Ron DeSantis won reelection by more than 19 points. In Miami-Dade, a county that favored Joe Biden by 7 points in 2020, DeSantis won by 11 points. About three-fourths of Miami-Dade students are enrolled in choice programs, but Democrat Charlie Crist foolishly went all-in for the public-school monopoly and picked the president of Miami's United Teachers of Dade as his running mate, while DeSantis held himself out as a champion of parents' rights and school choice. DeSantis outperformed Crist by 13 points with Latino voters, according to exit polls in a state where Biden had won the Latino vote by 7 in 2020. Notably, 38 percent of students using the state's largest private-school-choice program are Hispanic. DeSantis also had big coattails. Of the 30 school board candidates he endorsed, 24 won. Republicans also increased their majority in the Florida statehouse from 76–42 to 85–35 and in the state senate from 23–16 to 28–12.[76]

Pro-school-choice gubernatorial candidates nationwide had a great night. Govs. Chris Sununu of New Hampshire, Kevin Stitt of Oklahoma, Bill Lee of Tennessee, and Greg Abbott of Texas all blew out their opponents after making school choice a centerpiece of their campaigns.

Stitt faced a barrage of attacks from dark-money groups for his support for school choice, yet he won by nearly fourteen points—a margin larger than his 2018 win. As the *Oklahoman* newspaper noted, his Democratic opponent, Joy Hofmeister, "made opposition to vouchers a central part of her campaign, claiming it would be a 'rural school killer.'"[77] (You won't be shocked to learn that she attended private school.[78]) Ryan Walters, elected Oklahoma's superintendent of public instruction by more than thirteen points, said on election night that "we are going to do more than any other state in the country to empower parents."[79]

Even some Democrats apparently learned something from Glenn Youngkin's 2021 victory in Virginia. Josh Shapiro of Pennsylvania and Gov. J. B. Pritzker of Illinois both endorsed private-school-choice less than two months before the election and came out victorious. Gov. Kathy Hochul of New York also won after she publicly supported—for the first time—eliminating the cap on New York City charter schools. Their reversals on school choice were likely based on political expediency rather than conviction, but it doesn't really matter. As Milton Friedman once said, we can't count on electing the right people—we need to make it politically profitable for the *wrong people* to do the *right thing.*

If candidates for political office feel compelled to support school choice because it's what the voters demand, that's good news regardless of their motives. Voters just have to keep paying attention and hold them to account for their positions.

After the 2022 midterms, it's clear that for both parties, it is now becoming politically profitable to support education freedom. Opponents of school choice had long claimed that the issue was a political loser, and despite polling to the contrary, many in the establishment believed it. The 2022 election results dispelled that narrative.

School choice became a political winner because parents became a new special interest group. For far too long in K–12 education, the only special interest groups that commanded the attention of politicians represented the employees in the system, but now, the kids have a union of their own: their parents. And once a critical mass of parents got a taste of school choice, they fought hard to keep it.

The Parent Revolution is here to stay.

Chapter 8

THE SCHOOL-CHOICE TIDAL WAVE

> Prior to three years ago, I would have bet a lot of money you would have never seen this happen.
>
> —*Liz Cohen, Georgetown University*[1]

In Ernest Hemingway's *The Sun Also Rises*, one character asks another how he went bankrupt. "Two ways," the second man replied. "Gradually, then suddenly." Education choice had been expanding gradually for decades. In 2023, it expanded suddenly.

In 2020, parents woke up to the problems of government schooling. In 2021, they woke up as a political constituency. By 2022, *the Parent Revolution* began remaking one of the nation's two major political parties—and revolutionizing the nation's education system. "Fund students, not systems," became the battle cry of parents fighting to take back control of their children's education and was repeated by every politician who wanted to be their champions at the state capitol. But even optimistic advocates of school choice were amazed by the tidal wave unleashed in 2023. As Max Eden of the American Enterprise Institute put it in the *Washington Examiner*, the school-choice movement made "more progress in the first half of 2023 than it made in the preceding 23 years."[2]

The Red State Strategy was working. Now there was no stopping *the Parent Revolution.*

Iowa Leads the Year of Universal Choice

Gov. Kim Reynolds went all in on education choice in the 2022 GOP primary and general election and won big. In 2023, she doubled down.

Reynolds's education choice bill was no longer targeted to a few thousand students. Now her proposed education choice bill would allow *all* families to take their children's state-funded education dollars to the education providers of their choice.

On January 23, the Iowa legislature voted on Reynolds's bill. Republican legislators made it clear that it was their constituents' concerns about the ideology being pushed in the government school system. In an op-ed, Iowa state senator Adrian Dickey spelled it out: "The reason why school choice has the backing [of the Republican legislators is] due to the issues that have flooded our school: CRT, transgender bathrooms, pornographic books in the libraries, sexualization of our kids, drag shows in school, etc."[3]

On the floor of the Iowa House, Rep. Skyler Wheeler noted that parents became upset "when critical race theory got pushed on kids."[4] Sen. Jesse Green discussed hearing from constituents who had "enrolled their son into a small, local, rural public school... They believed that surely, the problems that urban schools face with woke ideology would not exist in their small-town environment. Unfortunately, they were wrong."[5] He continued:

> Iowans deserve to have their children educated without violating their values. In some schools, it is policy that individuals can use the public school bathroom that aligns with a person's gender identity rather than their undeniable biology. If we can't trust some of our public schools on biology in the bathroom, what makes us believe that we can trust those same schools on biology in the classroom?[6]

Rep. John Wills described several books in government schools around Iowa that discuss six- and eight-year-old children "having sexual experiences," noting that "both of those books are very explicit."[7] Senate President Amy Sinclair expressed a similar concern, asking: "What happens when a district's library and classrooms contain materials that are inappropriate for the age of students, and they violate a parent's right to direct that moral and educational upbringing of their child?"[8] The clear answer, in her view, was allowing families to take their public education dollars and choose a learning environment that aligned with their values.

Her colleagues agreed. The bill passed the Iowa House 55 to 45. Later that evening, the Senate passed it by a vote of 31 to 18. The Red State Strategy worked again.

Anticipating this historic victory, I had changed my travel plans during one of my busiest weeks of the year—National School Choice Week—to get to Des Moines. I ended up making it to the Iowa State Capitol shortly before the Senate became the second chamber to pass the bill. It was a momentous occasion that I'll never forget. Immediately after passage, I celebrated in the halls with legislative leadership, Lt. Gov. Adam Gregg, and, of course, the education freedom fighter herself, Kim Reynolds. We were ecstatic. "Reynolds cheered when Corey DeAngelis, a national school choice activist, appeared for a round of hugs and selfies," reported the *Des Moines Register*.[9]

As I reported to the *Des Moines Register* that night, "Iowa's now going to be a national leader on education freedom. And I'm happy that the governor, Kim Reynolds, has been a staunch supporter of parental rights in education, and this just cements that fact even further."[10] Reynolds signed the bill into law the following morning at the capitol at a glorious public signing event. I was invited to stand right by her alongside House and Senate leadership, including Speaker Pat Grassley and Senate president Amy Sinclair.

At least one person showed up to try to rain on our parade. During Reynolds's opening remarks, someone in the crowd yelled out, but their words were unintelligible. I wrote it off, figuring it was like just the ranting of some blue-haired Antifa nut. As it turns out, it was a state senator!

Senator Claire Celsi had been a staunch opponent of empowering families with school choice. It won't shock you to learn that she attended private school. When I had called her out on Twitter, she even tweeted at me: "I did go to a private school. That was my parents' choice. But they didn't ask taxpayers to pay for it."[11] She continued, "Enough is enough. Taxpayers shouldn't have to foot the bill for more than 500k students to go to private school." That's odd. Doesn't she know who foots the bill for those same students to go to government-run schools? Anyway, it seems she thinks only rich people should have school choice.

Celsi didn't stop beclowning herself at the capitol. She bragged on Twitter as if her pathetic screeching were a heroic act. "I had a word with Governor Reynolds this morning at her signing ceremony in the rotunda," she tweeted. "I yelled 'Nobody wants vouchers' loudly over the railing, then I waited a minute and yelled 'rural Iowa doesn't want vouchers.'"[12] Talk about "posting your Ls." She, a lone actor, screamed those absurdities at a sea of parents and children who obviously did want school choice—and at a governor who won her statewide election by nearly twenty points after campaigning heavily on education freedom. The unions are flailing. Choice and competition strike at the heart of monopoly.

A few days later, Gov. Reynolds celebrated the victory at the "Giving Parents a Voice" town hall hosted by Moms for Liberty.[13] The moms deserved a ton of credit for the win—as Iowa senator Brad Zaun told Fox News, "Groups like Moms for Liberty were down at the capitol nearly every day clamoring for school choice."[14]

They hadn't started as school-choice advocates. First, they just wanted their schools to reopen. Then they started noticing all the crazy things going on in the government schools once they *did* reopen. Samantha Fett, the Warren County chapter chair for Moms for Liberty, told Fox News how her group first got involved trying to remove pornographic books from elementary school libraries. "The public school administrators and school boards would just ignore us and hope we'd go away," she said.[15] After fighting with government school administrators over a host of issues, the moms realized that it was time to look elsewhere. "The frustration we had [with] the local level not making any progress, not getting any answers, and being pushed away, drove us to look for solutions outside the district system," said Fett.[16] School choice provided those solutions.

But that didn't mean abandoning the kids who were still attending government schools. At the town hall, Governor Reynolds also touted bills that would require schools to get parental permission before they start calling children by different names or pronouns—a hot-button issue after it had been revealed that some government schools in Iowa were "socially transitioning" children to different genders behind parents' backs. "It's sad that any of this actually needs to be written into law, but unfortunately that is where we're at," Reynolds said.[17]

When the education choice policy went into effect on May 31, there were more than a thousand applications in the first thirty minutes.[18] In the first nine days, there were more than fifteen thousand applications.[19] Within a month, the families of more than twenty-nine thousand students signed up.[20] It was finally happening!

And Iowa was just the beginning...

Utah Joins the Universal Club

It wasn't even February yet when state lawmakers enacted the Utah Fits All Scholarships, the second universal education choice program of 2023 and the fourth nationwide. Yet again, union overreach and parents' objections to woke ideology in the government schools were driving factors.

In chapter 4, I described how Utah parents were outraged at the radical ideology infecting the government school classrooms. But they didn't just get mad. They got organized. According to the Associated Press, Nichole Mason, a mother of five, "first became concerned when she learned administrators at her children's public school were allowing transgender students to use girls' bathrooms."[21] After switching schools, she grew frustrated with draconian masking mandates and other COVID craziness. But she didn't just complain—she cofounded the group Utah Parents United, which pushed back against the woke agenda in government schools and stormed the state capitol to advocate for school choice and parental rights in education.[22]

Utah Parents United advocated for legislation that would increase curricular transparency and parental involvement in the curriculum selection process. One bill would have required teachers to post learning materials and syllabi online for parents to review. Naturally, the unions opposed it. "This bill is insulting, burdensome and will not succeed in increasing transparency, but will certainly succeed in driving people from our profession," Heidi Matthews, president of the Utah Education Association, wrote to the committee.[23]

Another bill, sponsored by Utah Representative Lincoln Fillmore, a Republican, would require school boards to involve parents in the process of reviewing and selecting their school's curriculum.[24] The bill addressed the concerns of parents like Mason who felt shut out of the curriculum selection process and even had a hard time obtaining curricular materials to review. Mason had previously criticized the David School District for hiding its "anti-bias" curriculum from parents—the most they would let her see was a rough outline of the curriculum. "Wouldn't it be lovely if we allowed parents to see that before it was rolled out at a districtwide level?" Mason asked. "If we truly care about reinforcing principles in the home, wouldn't we want parents and taxpayers to see what was going on in the classroom before it happened?"[25]

That sounds reasonable enough, but the unions came out vociferously against it, too. "We've heard from teachers. The message has been loud and clear," Brad Asay, president of the Utah chapter of the American Federation of Teachers, told the legislative committee as he urged them to reject the bill. "They've had enough with the demands of a vocal minority. [. . .] Today teachers are taking a stand, and AFT stands with them."[26] In other words, parents should just shut up and trust the experts.

But parents no longer trusted the self-declared experts. A 2023 Gallup survey found that the public's confidence in government schools had fallen to just 26 percent, tied with 2014 for an all-time low.[27] Confidence was even lower among political independents at 24 percent. Even among

Democrats, fewer than half had any faith in the government schools. Among Republicans, confidence hit rock bottom at *just 9 percent.*

Utah families had good reason to distrust the government schools. That same week, an undercover sting video by Accuracy in Media had exposed numerous Utah government school administrators and union officials bragging about sneaking CRT and gender ideology into the classroom against the wishes of parents and state lawmakers. Michelle Love-Day, director of culture and diversity for the Jordan School District, boasted that the school had already "kind of gone around" restrictions on pushing radical ideology on students under the guise of "diversity, equity, and inclusion" training. "Whenever our team goes out we don't do an opt-out prior to. They just go out, meet the kids, work with them," Love-Day said. "And then we give a letter after they go out saying 'we were in your school and this is what they talked about.'"[28] Katie Ieremia, director of professional development of Salt Lake City Schools, was captured on video revealing that the American Federation of Teachers union has "a curriculum that they bring in" to the government schools through trainers "trained on social justice and NEA programs about that."[29]

State policymakers were not amused. "This is why so many people don't trust public education," commented Utah Representative Chris Stewart, a Republican. "And this is why nobody should be surprised that Utah gave parents the ability to choose with school [choice scholarships]."[30]

That same week, Utah Fits All Scholarship Act passed the statehouse by a vote of 54-20 and the senate 20 to 8. Describing his support for the education choice bill, Utah Rep. Ken Ivory, a Republican, said that "in recent years he's talked to parents with concerns about the books being taught in public schools" as well as onerous mask requirements, and believed that "parents should have a choice outside of that."[31]

As in West Virginia, the education choice bill also had a provision raising government-school teacher pay. That had been a priority of Gov. Spencer Cox, a Republican, and was likely to have passed anyway. But champions of parents made sure that it was tied to expanding educational opportunities for families. Teachers should be paid what they deserve, and parents deserve to choose the schools their children attend. It was a win-win compromise.

On January 28, 2023, Governor Cox signed the Utah Fits All Act into law along with a bill banning sex-change surgeries on children and placing a moratorium on the use of puberty blockers and cross-sex hormones on children.[32] The number of states with universal education choice had just doubled—and the 2023 legislative session was still just getting started…

Arkansas Makes Universal Choice a Trend

After President Biden's 2023 State of the Union Address, the Republican response was delivered by Arkansas Governor Sarah Huckabee Sanders. She took the opportunity to announce that her state would soon adopt "the most far-reaching, bold, conservative education reform in the country."[33] A day later, Sanders unveiled her "Arkansas LEARNS" initiative—Literacy, Empowerment, Accountability, Readiness, Networking, and School Safety—which she promised would ensure that schools would "educate, not indoctrinate our kids, and put students on a path to success."[34]

Sanders delivered. Her education reform package was the Red State Strategy in bill form. The core of the LEARNS Act was the Education Freedom Account program, which would work similar to ESAs in other states and would be available to *all* K–12 students after just three years. Among other things, the LEARNS Act would also raise the cap on the number of charter schools statewide, raise literacy standards, and raise teacher pay.[35] Teachers could even get bonuses if they performed well—but the bill also made it easier to fire teachers for poor performance. What a novel concept! The unions protect bad teachers because they pay dues like everyone else, but Governor Sanders thought that schools should be about children, not a jobs program for adults. Schools shouldn't be indoctrination centers, either, so LEARNS would prevent government schools from indoctrinating students in critical race theory.

The bill was well received by legislative leaders. "This bill includes everything I wanted," said Arkansas Senate President Bart Hester. "A lot of work has gone into this, and it will benefit parents and teachers in this state."[36] State Rep. Ryan Rose explained that he cosponsored the legislation because it would aid in "empowering parents and students in their education decisions and keeping woke politics out of our classrooms."[37]

The left went apoplectic. The official Twitter account of the Democratic Party of Arkansas posted a picture of the Republican legislators gathered at press conference announcing the Arkansas LEARNS initiative, calling them the "defund public schools caucus."[38] I couldn't help but call out the hypocrisy. "The chair of the Arkansas Democratic Party went to private school," I tweeted in response.[39] The fiscal effect on a government school of a child leaving that school is exactly the same whether they receive a scholarship or not. But with the left, it's always "choice for me, not for thee."

Of all the education choice bills in 2023, Arkansas LEARNS was the nearest and dearest to my heart because I had studied for my PhD at the University of Arkansas. I flew to Little Rock in January to help promote it, appearing onstage alongside Governor Sanders at a National School Choice Week event. When I was introduced as "Dr. Corey DeAngelis," I made sure to clarify: "I'm not a real doctor. I'm a 'Jill Biden' doctor." The crowd laughed, but someone in the room was not laughing: a journalist for the *Arkansas Times* who later whined that my leading children in a "fund students, not systems" cheer was "a little indoctrination-ish."[40] One wonders what she calls CRT and gender ideology in the government schools. She also called me a school-choice "evangelist"—a term I liked so much I started using it in my Twitter bio.

On March 2, the Arkansas House voted overwhelmingly—78 to 21—to pass the LEARNS Act. A few days later, the state senate passed it by a margin of 26 to 8. "Today we empower parents and fund students over systems," declared Arkansas Representative Keith Brooks. Upon signing the Arkansas LEARNS Act, a jubilant Governor Sanders proclaimed, "It is now the law of the land in my state to educate, not indoctrinate, empower parents, not government, and prepare students for a high paying job, not a lifetime in poverty."[41]

When the Education Freedom Accounts became available that summer, the families of more than 5,400 Arkansas students signed up.[42] The education choice tidal wave was becoming a tsunami.

Florida: The Fantastic Fourth

"It is time for Florida to fund students..." I called out to a crowd in Tallahassee, Florida, which finished the mantra by roaring back, "...not systems!" This has become a trend that my audiences from all across the country excitedly anticipate. Proponents of education freedom love when I show up in their state to provide air support—and they know it's a signal of even bigger things to come. Defenders of the status quo, of course, hate it. They can feel their control of other people's children slipping, and they can't stand it. We will win the war they waged on families once and for all.

This time, I was speaking at the annual dinner for Florida's premiere free market think tank—the James Madison Institute—and had the privilege to sit at a table with fantastic people in the education freedom movement, including former U.S. Secretary of Education Betsy DeVos and Florida House Speaker Paul Renner. It was January 2023, and the legislative session had just kicked off in the wake of massive GOP wins in the midterms. I was calling on Florida lawmakers to live up to their promise of being the Parents' Party.

A few days earlier, I had assembled a letter from more than thirty influencers and organizations calling on the Florida Legislature to immediately pass universal education savings accounts. Its signatories included, among others, Betsy DeVos, U.S. Representative Byron Donalds (R-FL), Chaya Raichik (Libs of TikTok), Christopher Rufo (Manhattan Institute), Karol Markowicz (Fox News and *New York Post*), Jason Bedrick, Lindsey Burke, and Jay P. Greene (Heritage Foundation), Max Eden and Robert Pondiscio (American Enterprise Institute), Nicole Neily (Parents Defending Education), the American Federation for Children, Americans for Prosperity, the American Legislative Exchange Council, the James Madison Institute, Heritage Action, Moms for Liberty, and more.[43] I sent the letter to Fox News, which became an exclusive that drove headlines. Republican legislators want extra assurance—they want to know the public has their back. This letter did just that.

The day after I spoke at the dinner, the Florida House Choice and Innovation Subcommittee passed a universal school-choice bill by a vote of 13 to 4, with every Republican voting in favor. The following day, *City & State Florida* reported the passage of the bill and credited me as its "winner of the week." They pointed out that "when House Speaker Paul Renner and others use phrases like 'education dollars belong to the student and not a system,' they echo the words of school choice evangelists such as DeAngelis."[44]

As I reiterated to the crowd, Florida has long been a national leader in school choice—a model for other states to follow. As it has expanded school choice, it has moved from the middle of the pack of states on the National Assessment of Educational Progress (commonly referred to as the Nation's Report Card) to the top, according to the Urban Institute's America's Gradebook, which controls for differences in student demographics across states.[45]

In fact, ten out of the eleven rigorous studies on the subject have found that private-school-choice competition has improved academic and behavioral outcomes in Florida public schools. Even government-run schools up their game in response to competition. The students who remain in public schools experience better test scores, less absenteeism, and fewer discipline problems. School choice is a rising tide that lifts all boats.

In late March, Gov. Ron DeSantis signed House Bill 1 into law. Sponsored by Rep. Kaylee Tuck and Sen. Corey Simon, and the priority of Speaker Renner, HB 1 expanded Florida's Family Empowerment Scholarship to universal eligibility, making Florida the fourth to enact universal choice in 2023 and the sixth to do so ever. All of the Sunshine State's 2.8 million K–12 students are now eligible for an ESA.

The legislation had moved easily through both Florida's House and Senate—with all Republicans voting in favor, along with four House Democrats. The school-choice bill passed the Florida House by a vote of 83 to 27 and the Senate 26 to 12.

Yet again, it was the Red State Strategy that carried the day. "When we talk about educational freedom, it is also about our values," explained Speaker Renner, who deplored "the craziness that happens in our K–12 schools, which we're combatting this year," and empathized with parents who "don't want [their] child to go to a school where their values are mocked and held up in derision."[46] Governor DeSantis even explicitly connected school choice to other efforts to combat wokeness and empower parents:

> We also did a parents bill of rights to make sure that parents are in charge of their kids' education. We just enacted universal school choice so you guys can send your kids to the school of your choice. And we made sure our school system is about educating our kids not indoctrinating our kids. We got rid of critical race theory. We got rid of gender ideology.[47]

In addition to expanding school choice to all Florida students and restricting CRT and gender ideology in the classroom, since 2019 DeSantis has eliminated Common Core, protected female athletes from having to compete against and shower with males, and helped parents take back control of school boards (twenty-four of the thirty school board candidates he endorsed won).[48] It was no wonder Florida took first place in the nation on the Heritage Foundation's inaugural Education Freedom Report Card.[49]

Even before going universal, Florida had more students participating in a school-choice program than any other state. A year earlier, Step Up for Students issued scholarships to about 184,000 students, plus nearly 60,000 scholarships for students with special needs. By the summer of 2023, Step Up issued more than 340,000 scholarships.[50]

Education freedom was on the march nationwide. But at the same time, the unions and their allies were plotting counteroffensives on multiple fronts. They were losing badly, and they knew it. But they weren't going down without a fight.

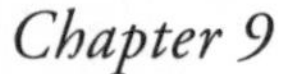

Chapter 9

THE GOVERNMENT SCHOOL EMPIRE STRIKES BACK

> This is propaganda. This is misinformation. This is the way in which wars start. This is the way in which hatred starts.
>
> —*Randi Weingarten, American Federation of Teachers, on parental rights legislation*[1]

Even as the Year of Universal Education Choice was delivering victory after victory for American families, the unions and their radical leftist allies were doing everything in their power to reverse them. Passing a bill isn't the end of the process. In politics, no victory is truly final. After a school-choice bill becomes law, the unions go on the attack in multiple venues—the legislature, the courts, the voting booth, and the court of public opinion.

The price of educational freedom is eternal vigilance.

Union Legislative Campaigns: Blocking and Reversing Wins

The Parents' Party didn't win everywhere. Even amid all the progress, in some states the unions managed to block legislation creating new education choice policies or expanding existing ones. In one case, the unions were even able to block legislative attempts to renew a scholarship program that was set to expire.

Wyoming came very close in 2023 to enacting universal education choice. Indeed, it all came down to one person: Wyoming's Republican House Speaker, Albert Sommers.

The Wyoming Freedom Scholarship Act would have created an ESA policy allowing all families in the state to take their children's taxpayer-funded education dollars to the education providers of their choosing. The bill passed the state's GOP-controlled Senate and had thirty-three cosponsors—a majority of the chamber—signed on from the Wyoming House. Considering more than half of the chamber cosponsored, the proposal clearly had the votes needed to pass the Wyoming House floor.

Wyoming was the "most Republican state" in 2023, according to Gallup polling and the Cook Partisan Voting Index.[2] School choice is on the Republican Party platform, and the GOP controlled more than *90 percent* of the seats in the Wyoming House, but Speaker Sommers still would not allow the bill to leave his drawer.

Sommers also blocked a parental rights bill that would have banned classroom instruction of sexual orientation and gender identity prior to fourth grade. Sommers told local reporters that he blocked the parental rights bill because it conflicted with his belief "in local control." But is there any control more local than *parents*? The Speaker further claimed that he blocked the Senate's school-choice bill because it was "identical to the one that already failed in [the House] Education Committee"—a committee that he had stacked with union-friendly opponents of school choice. These were clearly just convenient excuses to kill policies that were strongly supported by his own party and constituents.

But why? The most plausible explanation comes from the chair of the Wyoming Freedom Caucus, Rep. John Bear, who said, "I believe the biggest pressure [against the bill] is coming from the teachers union, of which [Speaker Sommers is] very supportive of."[3] Indeed, the Wyoming Education Association gave Rep. Albert Sommers a perfect score for the 2021 legislative session.

The unions also blocked school-choice progress in nearby Idaho. The Idaho Senate Education Committee started strong by passing a universal education choice policy, the Freedom in Education Act.[4] "Our education funding is meant for educating children, not for protecting a particular institution," argued Idaho Senator Brian Lenney.[5] But the bill soon ran into trouble in the full Senate, where it died despite having a 28–7 GOP supermajority. The Idaho Education Association crowed: "This is a significant win for public education."[6]

The Idaho Freedom Caucus blamed the "fearmongering about the possible demise of rural schools" by the unions and their allies for the failure. If school choice really destroyed rural government schools, then Arizona—the state with the longest-lived and most robust education choice policies in the nation—should be littered with the desiccated shells of rural schools. Instead, as a Heritage Foundation study found, rural schools in Arizona have significantly outperformed the national average gains in performance over the past fifteen years on the National Assessment of Educational Progress.[7] School choice is the rising tide that lifts all boats—even "boats" in rural areas.

The saddest case of 2023 was in Illinois.

In 2017, Republican Governor Bruce Rauner made a deal with the Democratic-controlled legislature to pass a budget that included a school-choice scholarship program for low-income students. But there was a catch: The Invest in Kids Scholarship Program was set to expire in 2022 unless the legislature voted to extend it—which it did, but only to 2023. That year, more than nine thousand students were benefiting from the scholarships.

But the unions don't care about the kids. They don't pay union dues. So they set about strong-arming politicians to oppose it.

When Illinois Governor J. B. Pritzker had first run for office, he sided with the unions against the scholarship program. As a candidate in August 2017, Pritzker publicly attacked the program, saying: "As governor, I will not support school vouchers and will work to do away with this program."[8] In April 2018, he said: "I'm opposed to that $75 million tax credit, that school voucher system." He added that "we should as soon as possible do away with it. What I oppose is taking money out of the public schools, and that's what happened here." (Naturally, Pritzker both attended and sent his children to posh private schools.[9])

This wasn't shocking, as the unions form an important part of the Democrat coalition. But when Pritzker took office, he quietly did an about-face and did not lift a finger to hurt the scholarship program, and even signed legislation to extend it. When he ran for reelection in 2022, he even endorsed school choice in response to a candidate survey. He answered yes to the question: "Do you support Illinois' tax credit scholarship program that provides financial support for students to attend private and parochial schools?"[10]

In a more detailed response, Governor Pritzker also noted that his "main focus with respect to K–12 education is ensuring that there is sufficient funding." He said that his budgets "have ultimately included the relatively small Invest in Kids Scholarship Program" because he had "assurance from the advocates" that they would "support increased public school funding."

This was exactly the sort of shift the Red State Strategy contemplated. Democrat candidates for office will, over time, shift toward support for school choice as they feel pressure to do so from the electorate.

But the unions can exert pressure, too. Unfortunately, at least for now, it seems that they still wield more power in Illinois than the rank-and-file Democratic parents and voters who support school choice. In 2023, the legislature failed to enact an expansion to the scholarship program before the legislative session ended. As the *Wall Street Journal* editorial board noted, "Democrats led by Illinois Senate President Don Harmon and House Speaker Emanuel Chris Welch tossed it aside in rank obeisance to the teachers unions."[11] Pritzker, for his part, did not appear to lift a finger to help the families benefitting from the scholarships. As this book goes to print, the scholarship program is slated for expiration.

If it does expire, most of those poor kids, deprived of their scholarships, will likely end up back in Chicago's government schools, where only one in ten black students can read on grade level and only one in twenty are proficient in math.[12] I guess that's what $30,000 per pupil gets you in Chicago![13] At least, that's what you get when the unions are running the show.

There is a lesson in this sad situation for supporters of school choice. Some argue that in the interests of fairness, equity, and social justice, choice policies should target low-income families and others most in need. But as Wilbur Cohen observed in a debate with Milton Friedman, programs for the poor make for poor programs. That's because low-income families lack the sort of political capital wielded by higher-income families. That's why welfare is often on the chopping block, but Social Security never is. Those who most want to help low-income families out of a sense of equity would do well to remember this lesson. The best way to help disadvantaged families is to align their political interests with those who have more political capital. Universal school-choice policies are much more politically sustainable for exactly that reason—yet they still help most of those low-income families who were the most choice deprived to begin with.

We saw a similar phenomenon play out in Pennsylvania. In September 2022, in the midst of a sometimes-close gubernatorial campaign, the commonwealth's then Attorney General Josh Shapiro quietly added language to his campaign website calling for "adding choices for parents and educational opportunity for students and funding lifeline scholarships like those approved in other states and introduced in Pennsylvania."[14] As Shapiro and his kids attended private schools, support for school choice would preempt accusations of hypocrisy. The issue was also popular among voters, with 77 percent of Pennsylvania parents of school-age children supporting ESAs in September 2022, according to Morning Consult.[15]

The Lifeline Scholarship bill was a proposed ESA policy that would give families with children assigned to failing public schools the power to reallocate their children's state education dollars. Republican state Representative Clint Owlett had introduced the bill, which passed the GOP-led Pennsylvania House in April 2022 by a narrow margin of 104–98, with only one Democrat in favor. The bill then passed the Senate Education Committee in June on a party-line 7–4 vote. The bill then stalled, as

Senate leadership expected a veto from then Governor Tom Wolf, a Democrat, who had vetoed other school-choice bills.

But once in office, Shapiro's spine softened. Although the Republican-controlled Pennsylvania Senate had passed a budget that included the Lifeline Scholarships, and although there was sufficient support in the Democrat-controlled House to pass the budget with the scholarships still included, Governor Shapiro promised to line-item veto the school-choice program. The governor blamed an impasse over the budget, but it was clear to everyone that he and Democrat House leadership were doing the will of their paymasters. Campaign finance records revealed that "in the 2022 election cycle, the Pennsylvania State Education Association's political action committee donated $775,000 to Shapiro's gubernatorial campaign" as well as "more than $1 million to Democratic legislative candidates."[16] Kids stuck in failing schools would just have to wait.

Lawfare Against Families

When school choice wins in the legislature, the unions almost always run to the courts. School-choice programs are batting more than .900 in state and federal courts thanks to public-interest law firms like the Institute for Justice and the Liberty Justice Center, but winning isn't always the point. Even when the unions know they'll eventually lose, it's in their interest to delay the implementation of school-choice policies for as long as possible. Forget the harm done to kids stuck in failing schools while waiting to get a scholarship, so long as it means the money is still flowing to the government schools.

After West Virginia adopted the universal Hope Scholarship program, the unions immediately sued the state to block its implementation. One of the plaintiffs was president of a county-level chapter of the state teachers union, and the law firm that filed the suit was "closely affiliated with and funded by teachers' unions."[17] Judges in West Virginia are elected, and the case was assigned to a judge, Joanna Tabi, who had been endorsed and funded by the teachers unions.[18] It will come as no surprise that the judge sided with the plaintiffs, declaring the ESAs unconstitutional and prohibiting the state from implementing the policy.

More than three thousand students had already signed up for ESAs before the judge's decision in the summer of 2022, expecting to be able to use them during the next academic year. Instead, they were left in limbo until the lawsuit was resolved.

According to the judge, the state constitution's requirement that the legislature provide "for a thorough and efficient system of free schools" means that it can pay for only public schools and no more. But a plain reading of the text finds no such limitation. The requirement to do *X* does not imply a restriction from doing *Y* and *Z* in addition to *X*.

West Virginia students were temporarily deprived of Hope, but not hope. State Attorney General Patrick Morrisey appealed the decision, which he called "legally incorrect." The West Virginia Supreme Court agreed. In early October, just two days after hearing oral arguments, the Mountain State's high court overturned the union judge's decision.[19]

Hope had been restored in West Virginia, but not every state was so fortunate. Sometimes, the bad guys do win, at least temporarily. In Kentucky, a union-backed group, the Council for Better Education, filed a lawsuit against the Education Opportunity Account policy the state had enacted in 2021. Kentucky's education choice policy was similar to ESAs in other states, albeit funded via private contributions to scholarship organizations. Donors would receive tax credits in return for their contributions. After a couple years of legal wrangling, the state supreme court issued its opinion, striking down the choice policy.

To reach its strained decision, the state supreme court adopted a fringe legal doctrine called "tax expenditure analysis" that has been rejected by the U.S. Supreme Court and numerous state supreme courts. Under tax expenditure analysis, your money can become the government's money even if it never entered the public treasury, so long as the government merely had a *claim* on your income, even if that claim was relinquished in the tax code. As the Kentucky Supreme Court ruled, the "money at issue cannot be characterized as simply private funds, rather it represents the tax liability that the taxpayer would otherwise owe but will have forgiven entirely or reduced."[20]

Taken to its logical conclusion, tax expenditure analysis treats any money you donate to a church for which you receive a tax deduction as the government's money, so all churches are essentially government funded. Recognizing the absurdity of this position, the U.S. Supreme Court held in *Arizona Christian School Tuition Organization v. Winn* (2011) that tax expenditure analysis "assumes that all income is government property," which is a "premise [that] finds no basis in standing jurisprudence." Rather, SCOTUS held that private citizens' money does not become the government's money until it has "come into the tax collector's hands."[21] Apparently the Kentucky Supreme Court thinks the tax collector's hands are already in your pockets.

But all is not lost. State lawmakers are pushing back with a proposed constitutional amendment. "Last year, the people of Kentucky elected the most pro-school choice General Assembly that has ever existed," said the amendment's sponsor, Kentucky Representative Josh Calloway, a Republican. "Time and again, they have spoken out loudly in support of more educational choice options."[22] Kentucky House Speaker David Osborne agreed, repeating a familiar refrain: "This House majority will fund students . . . not systems."[23] As this book goes to press, the legislature has not yet sent the amendment to Bluegrass State voters for approval.

Ballot Initiative Campaigns

Another tactic the unions use when they don't get their way in the state legislature is to turn to the voters via ballot referendums. This has been an effective tactic in several states because the unions can spend gobs of cash fearmongering that school choice is going to "destroy" the "local, neighborhood public schools that 90 percent of children attend." When one side is speaking to the voters' ideals and the other side speaks to their interests, the latter usually prevails over the former. That's why the unions have usually won ballot initiatives.

But that could change. In the past, the question before the voters was almost always about small voucher programs limited to specific populations, like students from low-income families. In other words, most voters were asked to vote to help someone else's child get a better education at the cost (according to the unions) of harming their own child's education at a government school. Even in Arizona, the ESA policy that made it to the ballot in 2018 was universal in terms of eligibility, but tightly capped so that only a tiny percentage of students could benefit. What's yet to be seen is what voters will do when asked to support or oppose a universal education choice policy.

Thus far, there doesn't seem to be much interest in even putting that question on the ballot. As described in chapter 7, Save Our Schools Arizona failed to obtain the requisite amount of signatures to refer the universal ESA expansion to the ballot in 2022. Likewise, the union-backed Citizens for Arkansas Public Education and Students failed to gather enough signatures in 2023 to refer Governor Sanders's Arkansas LEARNS initiative to the ballot.[24]

But at least one state is slated to vote in 2024 on whether to ratify the school-choice policy its legislature enacted. In Nebraska, the unicameral legislature passed the Opportunity Scholarships Act in 2023. It was the state's first school-choice program. "Our kids are our future, and we all believe that every Nebraska kid should have the opportunity to have their educational needs met, whether they live in Omaha or Scottsbluff," said Gov. Jim Pillen, a Republican, upon signing the law. "This law ensures that we are funding students, not systems."[25] But before it could go into effect, the scholarship law was challenged by a union-backed group called Support Our Schools.[26] (Hey, how about Support Our *Students*? Oh right, they want to fund systems, NOT students.)

It won't shock you to learn that the treasurer of Support Our Schools, which received more than $1 million from teachers unions in 2023, was the head of a local teachers union affiliate, Tim Royers.[27] That summer, I spoke with a local mom and activist named Clarice Jackson, who had confronted Royers over his opposition to school choice. In a video that went viral, she asked him: "Am I supposed to sit there and watch my daughter suffer...because you don't agree with somebody giving my daughter an opportunity scholarship?" He had no answers.[28]

The same union leader told local media that he was against school choice because some students "[don't] necessarily have an adult in their life who could advocate for them and move them through a system." Opponents of educational freedom think they know better than parents what's best for their own children.

Even before they had gathered enough signatures to put the Opportunity Scholarships on the ballot, Support Our Schools (SOS) began a disinformation campaign to trick voters into opposing it. For example, Jackson was out shopping when an SOS petitioner told her that the petition would give scholarships to low-income children, the exact opposite of its goal.[29] Another Nebraskan was told that "a really rich person could apply for the scholarship," again, exactly what the law's income restrictions do not allow. SOS has told others that the bill is a "giveaway to the rich" and takes money from public school funding, even though no such thing is the case.[30]

The fact that the unions know they need to lie to the voters to win tells you everything you need to know.

Smearing Parents

When all else fails, smear.

Remember that left-wing radical in Loudoun County, Virginia, who suggested having the Southern Poverty Law Center label parents' groups as "hate groups"? Well, apparently she wasn't the only one who thought weaponizing the SPLC's hate group list against parents was a good idea. In June 2023, the SPLC issued its "Year in Hate and Extremism" report, which included Moms for Liberty, Parents Defending Education, and several other parents' rights groups alongside neo-Nazis and the KKK in a list of "anti-government groups" and "hate groups."

"These groups were, in part, spurred by the right-wing backlash to COVID-19 public safety measures in schools," the SPLC report says. "But they have grown into an anti-student inclusion movement that targets any inclusive curriculum that contains discussions of race, discrimination and LGBTQ identities."[31] Well, that's *one way* to describe lesson plans that divide children into "oppressors" and "oppressed" based solely on their skin color and books that teach children how to engage in anal fisting.

The SPLC report warned that at "the forefront of this mobilization is Moms for Liberty, a Florida-based group with vast connections to the GOP that this year the SPLC designated as an extremist group." How can you tell you're dealing with hateful extremists when you see them? "They can be spotted at school board meetings across the country wearing shirts and carrying signs that declare, 'We do NOT CO-PARENT with the GOVERNMENT.'" *Quelle horreur!* Apparently, the only way to avoid being labeled an "anti-government extremist" by the SPLC is to embrace co-parenting with the government.

Why attack parents like this? The SPLC said the quiet part out loud when they noted the "vast connections to the GOP." In short, they attacked Moms for Liberty because they are *effective*. Out of the blue, they organized tens of thousands of angry parents, channeling their frustrations productively into winning elections in a way that made the Tea Party look like a tea party. Labeling them a "hate group" was a strategic move to tamp down on their effectiveness, making ordinary moms and dads less likely to get involved and forcing politicians to choose between shunning their support or being smeared as embracing a hate group.

It was a brilliantly evil strategy.

After receiving numerous threats, Moms for Liberty had to increase security at their annual conference. "The Southern Poverty Law Center has put a target on the back of every mom that wants to stand up and speak out on behalf of her child and we take that very seriously so we have invested in extra security," said Tina Descovich, a Florida school board member who co-founded Moms for Liberty, in an interview with the *Daily Signal*.[32] The group's other cofounder, Tiffany Justice, told the *Daily Signal* that the SPLC "gave people permission to treat us as subhuman," adding that the way critics were using the SPLC report helped "to whip people up into such a frenzy that they end up sending death threats to me and to the members and our children."[33]

Their website's contact page was barraged with vile attacks and threats, including one from a person using the name "Execute All-Nazis," who wrote, "Piece of s—— fascists like you deserve to be dragged against a wall and force-fed hot lead. Eat s—— and die."[34]

Just weeks after the SPLC report was published, the U.S. Department of Homeland Security announced that it was appointing new members to its Academic Partnership Council, which is charged with countering "the evolving and emerging threats to the homeland."[35] Among those new members was AFT's Randi Weingarten—the woman who cheered when the Biden administration labeled moms and dads "domestic terrorists." Now she was on a Homeland Security council that was supposed to improve "coordination and sharing of actionable threat and security-related information, including threats of violence as well as targeted violence and terrorism prevention."[36]

As Erika Sanzi of Parents Defending Education put it, "This is a major red flag—Randi is hyper-political and her current posture is very anti-parent. Her role in recent years has been defined by lies and failure, so in that sense, she'll be a perfect fit for the job."[37]

What do you think Weingarten will tell DHS? Well, just look what she says in public. In 2023, Weingarten used the SPLC to spear proponents of school choice as "racists" and "segregationists." "The same kind of roots that happened in the aftermath of *Brown v. Board*, those same words that you heard, in terms of wanting segregation, post–*Brown v. Board of Education*, those same words you hear today," Weingarten said in an interview when asked about the politics of schooling. "I was kind of gobsmacked when I was talking to Southern Poverty Law Center, and they showed me the same words: 'choice,' 'parental rights' and attempts to divide parents versus teachers, and at that point, it was white parents versus other parents. But it's the same kind of words."[38]

Never mind that the concept of school choice dates back to classical liberal thinkers of the seventeenth and eighteenth centuries like Adam Smith, Thomas Paine, and John Stuart Mill—long before *Brown v. Board of Education*.[39] And never mind that, as historian Phil Magness has documented, school-choice policies sped up racial integration while the teachers unions fought to preserve segregation.[40] And never mind that the term "freedom of choice" in education entered the political lexicon via "a voucher-supporting state senator and a voucher-supporting Catholic priest" who both vocally opposed segregation.[41] What's most distressing is that Weingarten is yet again in a position to collude with the government—just as she colluded over school closures during COVID—to put her organization's interests ahead of those of parents and students.

But this time, it's far more dangerous. In 2023, Washington state's attorney general worked with an "analyst" from SPLC to produce a report "urging the state to crack down on domestic terrorism."[42] Everyone wants the government to protect us from real domestic terrorists, like the people behind the Oklahoma City bombing. But can we trust the SPLC to determine who a "domestic terrorist" is when they can't distinguish between moms who refuse to "co-parent with the government" and the KKK?

Civil liberties attorneys have raised alarms. Kevin Snider, chief counsel at the Pacific Justice Institute, warned: "As a constitutional lawyer and member of the Washington State Bar Association, I believe this report poses a clear and present danger to the civil rights of those that law enforcement officials deem as holding 'anti-government ideologies' or who communicate 'online disinformation.'" Noting that the report "calls for family members to turn in 'someone they suspect may be on the path of radicalization,'" as well as "government funding of journalists to 'combat misinformation and disinformation,'" Snider concluded, "there can be little doubt that this report provides the building blocks for a police state."[43]

The enemies of education freedom and *the Parent Revolution* aren't smearing parents just for fun. It's a part of a long-term strategy that begins with delegitimization and could end with the iron fist of government cracking down on those who dare to dissent from left-wing orthodoxy.

Hypocrisy of the School-Choice Deniers

The people smearing ordinary moms and dads should take a break and look in the mirror. They say that people who live in glass houses shouldn't throw stones. Well, the school-choice deniers just can't help themselves.

By this point in the book, you've certainly noticed a pattern: The shrillest opponents of school choice often exercised school choice for their own children. What's more, many of these individuals benefited from private education themselves. Not long ago, CNN's Michael Smerconish pontificated on air, "Our children all went to a [private] school where the chapel service was a big part of their education. But here's the thing. We paid for that education." "Amen," chimed in his colleague Don Lemon. "Same with my parents. And that's how it should be."[44] This moment was merely another example of the unuttered yet prevailing mantra of the elite: *School choice for me, but not for thee.*

That's right. The very same people who bash ordinary parents as "racists" and "public school destroyers" for the sin of wanting the best education possible for their children are sending their own children to private school.

I made a name for myself by calling out these hypocrites on social media. In the Democrat primaries for the 2020 presidential election, *Education Week* asked all the candidates where they went to school and where they sent their kids to school. U.S. Senator Elizabeth Warren indicated that she attended public schools in Oklahoma. Oddly enough, however, she did not respond to the question about where she sent her kids to school. That was enough to tip me off.

Ordinary internet sleuthing didn't work, however. I couldn't find any indication of where Warren sent her children to school. This information was buried. After about a week or two, I used Ancestry.com to find the yearbook of Warren's son, Alex, who was then already forty-three years old. The website had only one yearbook for one year of his K–12 education—1987, when he was in fifth grade. The yearbook I uncovered revealed that Alex attended Kirby Hall, a private school in Austin, Texas. I blasted the revelation out on Twitter, wrote about it in the *New York*

Post, and conservative media had a field day. Days later, I exposed Senator Warren for lying on camera about where she sent her children to school. After a campaign event in Atlanta, a black grandmother, Sarah Carpenter, confronted Warren by saying, "I read that your children went to private schools." Warren quickly responded, "No, my children went to public schools."[45] That false denial also blew up and only added to the long list of lies spewed by Pocahontas.

I got into a Twitter spat with Bill Prady, cocreator of *The Big Bang Theory*. The Florida Board of Education held an emergency meeting to discuss private school vouchers for families who disagreed with mask mandates in their children's public schools. Prady attacked the school-choice proposal (which ultimately passed unanimously) with a now-deleted tweet saying that Florida was "combining the right-wing goal of eliminating public education with the right-wing goal of killing children to own the libs!" I shot back with a tweet saying, "You went to Cranbrook, that's a private school." I wasn't just making a polemical reference to *8 Mile*, the movie about the life of Eminem.[46] Get this. Prady himself actually went to Cranbrook,[47] a prestigious private school in the tony suburbs of Detroit whose annual tuition is $38,600.

Joe Biden attended and sent both of his sons to Archmere Academy in Claymont, Delaware, which costs more than $30,000 per year, yet he opposes school choice for other families.[48] Former House Speaker Nancy Pelosi went to the Institute of Notre Dame, a private school in Baltimore, and sent her son to Episcopal High School, a private boarding school in Virginia that now costs over $60,000 per year.[49] California Governor Gavin Newsom attended a private school in San Francisco and sends all four of his kids to private school. What's more, that private school reopened in 2020 during the pandemic while every nearby public school remained closed.[50]

Robert Reich, the left-wing internet pundit who served as secretary of labor under President Bill Clinton, opined in October 2023, "'School choice' sounds great, but it's a euphemism for defunding public schools and funneling the money to private, for-profit schools that don't have to accept all students, are not accountable for their curricula, and can use your tax dollars for religious indoctrination."[51] I guess that's one way to describe the private school he chose for his own son where tuition currently costs $50,000 a year.[52]

Former MSNBC politics commentator Keith Olbermann once attacked school choice by going after me on Twitter. "Don't worry," he opined, "if you're going to funnel public money into private religious brainwashing schools, the rest of the country will just stop recognizing Iowa high school degrees as sufficient for admission to universities and colleges." I responded by pointing out that *he* went to Hackley, a private, Ivy League prep school in New York that comes with a price tag of more than $60,000 a year. Olbermann should have stuck to sports punditry. It's no wonder he's been benched so many times since.

This hypocrisy ultimately seemed so widespread that its predictive quality earned a name: DeAngelis's Law. Garrett Watson, a senior policy analyst at Tax Foundation, defined it this way: "The zealousness of a person's actions and arguments against school choice and the probability they or their children went or currently go to a private educational institution are directly and proportionately related." *Timcast* news contributor Josie Glabach refers to it as "Corey's Razor."

Even top union leaders send their kids to private school. In September 2023, I uncovered that the Illinois Education Association's director of government relations, Sean Denney, sent his kids to private school.[53] A week earlier, the president of the Chicago Teachers Union and executive vice president of the American Federation of Teachers, Stacy Davis Gates, confirmed that she was sending her eldest son to a private school.[54]

In an interview with Chicago Magazine in 2022, Gates claimed: "I can't advocate on behalf of public education without it taking root in my own household."[55] At the time, she sent all three of her children to Chicago Public Schools. Well, that didn't last long!

Local journalists initially reported that MaxPreps, a website devoted to tracking high school sports, listed her son on the soccer team at De La Salle Institute, a private Catholic school boasting a 96 percent college attendance rate among its former students. Admins of a private Facebook group of Chicago Teachers Union members shortly thereafter mentioned that they had become aware of the news three weeks prior and that they "dislike the hypocrisy of CTU when they have gone after people who made the same choice."

It should go without saying, but Mrs. Gates is a fierce opponent of school choice, at least when it comes to other people's children. Just last year, she posted that "school choice was actually the choice of racists" and that school choice has "racist origins." The union she represents has consistently taken a hardline stance against private-school-choice programs.

When confronted with her hypocrisy, Gates argued that her decision to send her son to a private school "represents a stark statement about disinvestment in public schools." That flimsy defense is garbage, however, as these failure factories spend more than $29,000 per student per year, about twice as much as her son's private school tuition.

Gates issued a statement attempting to defend her hypocrisy. In it, she admits, "If you are a Black family living in a Black community, high-quality neighborhood schools have been the dream, not the reality." She goes on to say that the government schools are so bad that it ultimately "forced" her to choose a private school. She knows the Chicago Public School system is a complete dumpster fire that failed her son and so many others. Why should any kids, particularly ones from low-income families, be trapped in those failing institutions that are staffed by her union?

In her letter, Gates quadrupled down on her hypocrisy by saying that she and her union won't stop fighting against school choice for others. "We will continue to oppose siphoning public school resources off to private institutions through voucher programs," she said. She must realize that her decision to pull her own son out of his assigned government school diverts resources away from it just as much as a school-choice initiative allegedly does, as government schools are funded based on enrollment counts.

Gates is far from alone. Government school teachers are much more likely to enroll their own children in private school than the typical parent. According to a survey by *Education Next,* 20 percent of teachers with school-age children have sent one or more of their children to private school compared to only 13 percent of nonteachers.[56] What accounts for the difference? As Paul E. Peterson and Samuel Barrows of Harvard observed: "As insiders, teachers presumably know the truth about the level of education that is being provided."[57] A 2019 survey found that *fewer than half* of government school teachers *want* to send their children to a government school, while 53 percent would prefer to choose a private school or a charter school, or to homeschool.[58]

That's right. Even most government school teachers want school choice for their own children. That's one reason why the unions can slow down the spread of school choice, but there's nothing they can do to stop it.

Chapter 10

RETURN OF THE PARENTS' PARTY

> The day is coming when our K–12 policies will fully and appropriately respect the dignity of families to exercise autonomy in schooling. When that day comes, the unfulfilled, the disappointed, the mistreated, the misfit and the dreamer will seek better situations for themselves.
>
> —*Matthew Ladner, reimaginED, October 9, 2019*[1]

The union empire struck back, but soon the Parents' Party returned. The unions could slow *the Parent Revolution*, but they couldn't stop it.

By the middle of the 2023 legislative session, even the media started to notice the success of the Red State Strategy. "Republican lawmakers in over a dozen states have recently cited complaints about liberal ideology in public schools as a reason to support helping parents pay for private education," reported NBC News in March 2023.[2] "That shift in strategy has been hailed by organizations like the Heritage Foundation, a conservative think tank that helped spur parent protests." NBC added that the strategy "has helped cement funding for private schooling as a benchmark of Republican governance."[3] Likewise, the *New York Times* credited the "pandemic closures and classroom culture wars" for having "fueled the revival of the dormant school-choice movement."[4]

The Red State Strategy succeeded at making school choice a litmus test issue for Republicans. Now it was time to translate the GOP's support for choice into more legislative wins. It worked. The progress made expanding education freedom in 2023 dwarfed even the historic progress made in 2021. NBC even quoted me saying, "We're doing a lot of winning—I'm almost getting tired of winning so much because we're winning all across the country."[5]

But I was just kidding. I wasn't tired at all. I was just getting warmed up...

The Universal Choice Club Expands

In 2023, Gov. Kevin Stitt again pushed for universal school choice. "Every child deserves a quality education that fits their unique needs, regardless of economic status, or background," Governor Stitt declared in his State of the State Address, adding "Let's fund students, not systems."[6]

A year earlier, the Oklahoma House of Representatives blocked Governor Stitt's universal school-choice bill. But after the American Federation for Children Action Fund took a few scalps in the GOP primary, the legislature was singing a different tune. Rep. Rhonda Baker of the Oklahoma House Education Committee had opposed school choice in 2022, but a year later she presented Governor Stitt's bill on the House floor. Oklahoma House Speaker Charles McCall had also worked to block school choice, but after Governor Stitt made school choice a "centerpiece of his 2022 reelection campaign" and won by more than fourteen points, it was clear that he had a mandate from the voters.[7]

Even still, getting the bill over the finish line took grit and determination. After a few months of legislative wrangling, Governor Stitt had to veto several unrelated bills to pressure the legislature to reach a compromise. In May, the Oklahoma House and Senate reached an agreement on a refundable personal-use tax credit for education expenses available to the parents of all K–12 students in the Sooner State.

Oklahoma was the seventh state in the nation to enact a universal school-choice policy. A couple months later, Ohio would become the eighth.

In January, Ohio government schools were rocked by scandal when Accuracy in Media released undercover videos in which school officials admitted that they were lying to parents, policymakers, and the public about teaching critical race theory:

> In one instance, Matthew Boaz, the executive director of Diversity, Equity and Inclusion (DEI) in Upper Arlington, Ohio, was captured on video saying that "you can pass a bill that you can't teach CRT in the classroom, but if you didn't cover programming or you didn't cover extracurricular activities or something like that, that message might still get out. Oops. There will be a way."
>
> "There's more than one way to skin a cat," he said, adding that the school "absolutely" has conversations going around surrounding social justice, inclusion, and equity.
>
> "We have some parents that, you know, they don't fully understand [the curriculum]. So, you know, it's...when we 'trick them,' you know?" Hilary Staten, an administrative assistant in Groveport, Ohio, was caught saying. This was in regards to parents who are concerned about CRT in their children's curriculum.[8]

After the videos went viral, Ken Blackwell—a respected Ohio statesman who had served as mayor of Cincinnati, Ohio state treasurer, and Ohio secretary of state—penned an op-ed for the *Cincinnati Enquirer* calling for school choice as the solution. "Too many public school teachers and administrators think they should be free to teach students the secular religion of progressivism in the form of concepts such as CRT," Blackwell wrote. "That's one of the reasons school choice is so important, and so popular. [...] It gives [parents] an alternative to public school administrators who think and act like they have a right to mold young minds according to their own preferences and values, regardless of what parents want."[9]

The legislature agreed. In July, they passed a budget that expanded eligibility for the state's school voucher program to all K–12 students. Gov. Mike DeWine, a Republican, signed it immediately.

Local parent activists attributed the school-choice victory to parents losing faith in the government schools. "It was shocking to watch school employees from districts all across Ohio tell strangers that they would defy the law and lie to parents about the teaching of CRT," said Cathy Pultz, cochair of Protect Ohio Children, in response to the Accuracy in Media videos. "I believe parents are paying attention, and lawmakers are listening. Ohio's new budget extended school choice to all children, and that is a win for Ohio children."[10]

Runners-Up in the Year of Universal Education Choice

Several other states also expanded school choice in 2023. Most notably, Indiana expanded its Choice Scholarships policy to *nearly* every student in the state. Although the Republican-controlled state legislature did not make the scholarships universally available, they did raise the income threshold so that more than 95 percent of K–12 students would be eligible.

Meanwhile, South Carolina adopted a new ESA for students from low- and middle-income families. As in other states, the lawmakers advancing school choice did so in response to parental concerns over the radical ideology infecting the government school system. "There is a growing awareness that, in our traditional K–12 schools, it's not just reading, writing, and arithmetic anymore," said the bill's sponsor, state Senator Tom Davis, a Republican. "There's a social agenda layered into it. And I think those things are sort of driving this [school choice] movement. It's got resonance now."[11]

After years of trying, Nebraska passed a new tax-credit scholarship policy—the state's first school-choice policy. Although Nebraska's unicameral legislature has had majority support for school choice for some time, until 2023 it had lacked the supermajority necessary to overcome a filibuster. That year, the Opportunity Scholarships Act received thirty-three votes for cloture—exactly the number needed to prevail. The bill established a tax credit to encourage donations for private school scholarships up to about $7,000 a year to roughly 5,000 K–12 students in the state. Students in families below the federal poverty level would be a priority, as well as students with "exceptional needs," those who have been bullied, are in the foster system, are in military families, or have been denied the option to enroll their child in a public school district where they don't reside.

Although primarily supported by Republicans, the school-choice bill had the crucial support of three Democratic state senators who listened to their constituents instead of the teachers unions. Sens. Mike McDonnell, Terrell McKinney, and Justin Wayne cosponsored the bill and voted for its advancement. McKinney and Wayne gave powerful floor speeches in which they called colleagues out for sending their own kids to private schools while opposing school choice for others. The bill wouldn't have obtained enough votes for cloture had these senators not bucked their party's trend and stood for parents and children.[12] After its final passage, Gov. Jim Pillen, a Republican, quickly signed the bill into law. However, as noted in chapter 9, opponents gathered enough signatures to refer it to the ballot in 2024. Whether Nebraska children will get access to school choice in the near future remains to be seen.

Several states also expanded their existing choice policies. Alabama expanded its tax-credit scholarship policy while Montana, New Hampshire, and Tennessee expanded eligibility for their ESAs.[13] By the end of the summer of 2023, seven states had passed new school-choice policies, and eight states expanded existing ones. According to calculations by the Heritage Foundation, more than 10 million K–12 students nationwide were now eligible for school choice—the equivalent of about one in five American students.[14]

And the year wasn't even over...

The Red State Strategy Delivers North Carolina

"I'm declaring this a state of emergency because you need to know what's happening," announced North Carolina Governor Roy Cooper in May 2023. "If you care about public schools in North Carolina, it's time to take immediate action and tell them to stop the damage that will set back our schools for a generation."[15] What was the emergency? Was Cooper concerned about the historic low scores on the state test?[16] Was the governor going to take action to address the 24 percent spike in violence and crimes in North Carolina government schools?[17] Or maybe he was going to address the pornographic books found in government school libraries?[18]

If only!

Instead, Cooper declared an "emergency" over the Republicans' universal school-choice legislation. "They want to expand private school vouchers so that anyone—even a millionaire—can get taxpayer money for their children's private academy tuition," said Cooper breathlessly, as though millionaires were charged tuition at government schools.

(And yes, Cooper sent his own kid to private school.[19] Did you even have to ask?)

All thirty North Carolina Republican state senators signed on to a universal school choice bill that was introduced in March, giving them precisely the three-fifths supermajority needed to override Cooper's expected veto. But Cooper didn't declare an "emergency" at the time because, in the 120-member statehouse, Republicans were one seat short of the seventy-two-vote veto-override threshold. But that all changed in April when Rep. Tricia Cotham, a Democrat, announced her switch to the Republican Party over the issue of school choice.

"On issues like school choice, like charters, we have to evolve," Cotham, a former government-school teacher and principal, said in explaining her change of party. "One-size-fits-all in education is wrong for children."[20] Upon switching parties, she became the prime sponsor of the "Choose Your School, Choose Your Future" Act (HB 823) to expand North Carolina's Opportunity Scholarships to all K–12 students.

Cooper's proposed budget, by contrast, would have phased out the scholarships.

Cotham said that COVID made her realize the need for school choice, but her former party was virulently opposed to such reforms. While officially closed due to COVID, Durham Public Schools had infamously reopened some of its schools as "learning centers" that charged families $140 a week per child.[21] The dismal test scores further demonstrated just how badly the school shutdowns had affected student learning. Parents wanted more options, but her Democrat colleagues wouldn't hear it.

"The Democrat Party didn't really want to talk about children," said Cotham. "They had talking points from adults and adult organizations."[22] In 2022, the Wake County Democratic Party had even tweeted a cartoon comparing protesting parents to Q-Anon conspiracy theorists and neo-Confederates.[23] They later deleted it after an outpouring of criticism from parents. Cotham also criticized Democrat leaders for "villainiz[ing] anyone who has free thought, free judgment, has solutions and wants to get to work to better our state," adding, "If you don't do exactly what the Democrats want you to do, they will try to bully you. They will try to cast you aside."[24]

In May, I joined Cotham and North Carolina House Speaker Tim Moore at the lieutenant governor's mansion to promote school choice.[25] A few months later, the North Carolina legislature passed a budget that included the universal school-choice expansion, as well as bills to protect girls from having to compete against biological males, keep gender ideology out of the classroom, require parental notification before school staff address students by different names or pronouns, and restrict the use of cross-sex hormones and sex-change surgery on children.[26] With Cotham's support, the legislature was able to pass the budget, making North Carolina the ninth state to enact universal school choice, as well as override Governor Cooper's vetoes of all those bills, protecting kids from radical gender ideology.

The Fight for Education Freedom in the Lone Star State

Even more so than Arkansas, the fight to advance education freedom in Texas was nearest and dearest to my heart. I was raised in Texas, got my bachelor's and master's degrees at the University of Texas at San Antonio, and after a few years living in Washington, DC, I returned home to Texas with my wife to start a family.

The prospects of school choice in Texas had long been dim. For years, education-choice advocates have lamented the lack of schooling options in the red state. Proponents have been likened to Charlie Brown, optimistically believing that they'll finally kick the football, only to have Lucy pull it away at the last minute.

But this time felt different. Gov. Greg Abbott was a full-throated champion for universal education savings accounts (ESAs), declaring their introduction in 2023 to be an emergency item.[27] Lt. Gov. Dan Patrick had been a longtime advocate. There was palpable excitement in the halls of the state capitol. It was a top-eight Texas GOP legislative priority.[28] Parents were rallying in support.

Abbott put an impressive amount of political capital and grit into pushing for universal education choice. Neither rain, nor snow, nor legislator hypocrisy could keep Abbott off the school choice trail. Throughout 2023, the governor crisscrossed the Lone Star State extolling the virtues of education freedom, especially in the rural districts of legislators who were school-choice skeptics.

A year earlier, Abbott's commitment had been called into question. On April 19, 2022, someone sent me a video of Charles Foster Johnson, a left-wing activist who runs a union-funded outfit called Pastors for Texas Children, in which he said, "Even the governor is backing off. As soon as he went up to north Fort Worth and trucked out that parent choice thing, y'know, my phone was lighting up from rural House members saying, 'pastor, take a breath. Just got off the phone with [Governor Abbott]. He ain't gonna push a voucher bill.'"[29] I immediately asked Abbott about this publicly on Twitter. A few hours later, at 12:40 a.m. central time, Abbott tweeted a response:

1. I don't know who this person is.
2. I've never talked to this person.
3. He and I did not speak as he claims.[30]

As much as I appreciated that the governor had responded, his response was puzzling. I hadn't claimed that Abbott had talked to Johnson, and neither had Johnson. The video showed Johnson claiming that he had spoken with rural Republican legislators who had relayed what Abbott told them. In other words, Abbott was denying a claim that neither Johnson nor I had made.

Before I could reply, I heard from others that the governor really was on board for school choice. In any case, it was clear that I had gotten the governor's attention. After that, I made sure to inform the governor about a variety of issues in Texas's education system.

A few weeks later, Abbott spoke at an event in San Antonio focused on parental involvement in education. As the *Texas Scorecard* put it, "Just weeks after school-choice advocates expressed frustration over Gov. Greg Abbott's murky position on the issue, the Texas governor has announced he will support a proposal for school choice in the coming legislative session."[31] The article noted that although "Abbott had flirted with support for school choice since he first became governor in 2015, there had been no pressure from the governor on lawmakers to pass a school choice bill, and the issue faded for a few years." Now, Abbott and other state lawmakers were feeling the pressure. At the event, Abbott was emphatic in his support for education choice, telling the audience: "Empowering parents means giving them the choice to send their children to any public school, charter school, or private school with state funding following the student."[32]

Suddenly the prospects for school choice in Texas didn't look so dim.

In May 2022, I leaked evidence that a San Antonio superintendent pressured employees to vote for a nearly billion-dollar bond. Superintendents in Texas, as in many rural areas of red states, are even more formidable opponents of school choice than the teachers unions.[33] The *Texas Scorecard* credited me for breaking the story: "The official communications, exposed by Corey DeAngelis of the American Federation for Children, also showed the district was tracking which employees did and didn't vote in the election."[34] Governor Abbott said that what the superintendent did was "likely a crime," and that the Texas Education Agency would work with the Texas attorney general's office "to investigate and, if appropriate, prosecute this matter."[35]

In July, I had the opportunity to sit down with Governor Abbott one-on-one at his office in Austin.[36] I shared with him the benefits of school choice, including the research on its effectiveness and polling showing how popular it was nationally and especially in Texas. More than six in ten Texans supported school choice, according to a University of Houston poll published earlier that year—a figure that climbed to 78 percent for black Texans.[37] Sixty percent of respondents in rural Texas support school choice. Notably, a full 57 percent of Democratic respondents, and 78 percent of black Democrats, said they support school choice, too, as did 57 percent of Hispanic Democrats. Clearly, those officials who oppose education choice in Texas are out of step with most of their constituents.

The Texas Republican primary earlier that year confirmed the poll's findings. The primary included a nonbinding ballot proposition stating: "Texas parents and guardians should have the right to select schools, whether public or private, for their children, and the funding should follow the student." Texas GOP primary voters overwhelmingly supported it by a margin of 88 to 12 percent—up nine points since the question was last on the ballot, in 2018. Some of the most rural counties in Texas had the highest levels of support for school choice, including Culberson (97%), McMullen (90%), and Terrell (90%).[38]

Abbott assured me that he was a school-choice supporter. I believed him. And I intended to hold him to it.

After the 2022 legislative elections, the wind seemed to be in our sails. The Texas GOP listed school choice as a legislative priority, and the governor, the lieutenant governor, the state senate, and some key house members were on board. "Parents have truly woken up," said newly elected state Senator Mayes Middleton, who had served in the statehouse and was a longtime advocate for school choice. "You've seen in school boards—not just across the state, but across the country—where a lot [of parents] feel like their voice may not be heard, but at the end of the day, this is just giving them the tools." The major question was what the Texas House would do, where longtime critics of school choice, particularly from rural areas, still served as a significant stumbling block.

In January 2023, Governor Abbott explicitly endorsed a universal ESA at a Parent Empowerment Night event in Corpus Christi. "That will give all parents the ability to choose the best education option for their child," Abbott said.[39] A few weeks later, in his 2023 State of the State Address, Abbott spoke about parents who were "angry to learn that a woke agenda was being forced on" their children, and promised not only to "reform curriculum" and "get kids back to the basics of learning," but also to "empower parents" via a Parental Bill of Rights and education savings accounts, adding that "it's time to provide every parent with the ability to choose the best education option for their child."[40]

The following month, I noticed that the Texas House Democrats' Twitter account had tweeted a quote from Democrat state Representative Gina Hinojosa, who claimed that school choice would "drain money from Texas' already underfunded schools."[41] I replied that "the money doesn't belong to the government schools."[42] Amazingly, Representative Hinojosa then responded to me: "I know you don't live in Texas @DeAngelisCorey but what you disparagingly call 'government schools' are Texas public schools enshrined in our Texas constitution—as Texas as Friday night lights. You mind your California schools & we'll take care of our own."[43]

California? Sure, I was born in Sacramento, but my family moved to San Antonio when I was just four years old! Heck, my entire K–12 career was in Texas government schools. Twitter slapped Hinojosa's tweet with a Community Note: "Corey DeAngelis is a resident of Texas, has spent most of his life in Texas, and has two degrees from the University of Texas at San Antonio." I was accustomed to the school-choice deniers who couldn't debate the merits of the issue, but this ridiculous attempt to impeach my credibility was a first even for me.

In late March, I joined parents and education policy experts at a legislative hearing to testify in favor of the proposed universal ESA law.[44] Beforehand, I led a rally of parents at the Texas Public Policy Foundation's headquarters, after which we marched over to the state capitol. The hearing went into the wee hours of the night because there were so many parents in favor as well as union members and their allies in opposition.

Naturally, all three Democrats on the Texas senate education committee attended or sent their children to private schools, yet none of them stood up for giving other families that opportunity. Senator José Menéndez, a Catholic high school graduate, insisted repeatedly in the hearing that other families shouldn't have the same opportunities as he did.[45] Fortunately, his Republican colleagues didn't agree. The bill eventually cleared the committee.

In April, I testified before another legislative committee. This time, there was a familiar face across from me—Representative Hinojosa! I made sure to open by remarks by detailing my Texas bona fides. Afterward, a left-wing activist who drew cartoons for numerous Texas papers made a cartoon of me as a ventriloquist puppet sitting on former U.S. Secretary of Education Betsy DeVos's lap.[46] Yet again, a school-choice denier attacked the messenger when they couldn't handle the message. Hilariously, the cartoon spelled our names "Devon" and "Deanglis." He probably would have benefited from a private school education.

The unions' Democrat allies came out in full force against the bill. Texas House Minority Leader Trey Martinez Fischer—who had attended private school himself and, of course, sent his own children to private school—said in a cringeworthy video uploaded to Twitter: "If defunding education with vouchers is his [Governor Abbott's] dream, we're his nightmare."[47] Fischer had also said he'd "be the first one on the floor to use everything [he's] got to stop" the push for school choice.[48]

Not to be outdone, Democrat state Representative Armando Walle said that giving families options is "a fundamental threat to our democracy because it undermines the ability to pay for public schools."[49] As you probably guessed, he sent his kids to private schools.[50] The fiscal effect to his local government school of his decision was exactly the same as a family using a school-choice scholarship—did Walle believe his own schooling decisions were a "threat to democracy"?

Likewise, Beto O'Rourke, a serial Democrat candidate for high office in Texas and a staunch school-choice opponent, once called school choice a "ploy to funnel funds reserved for public education into private schools."[51] One wonders if he felt the same way when he chose not to enroll in public school ("depriving" that school of his tax dollars) and instead enroll in a tony private boarding school.

None of this is true, of course. A long list of rigorous empirical studies confirms that school choice improves academic outcomes, parent satisfaction with their child's schooling, student safety, tolerance of others, political participation, voluntarism, and a host of other indicators, all while saving money overall.[52] Most important, it enables families to select learning environments that align with their values.

Anti-school-choice hypocrites aren't exclusively Democrats. Republican Texas state Representative Travis Clardy sent his kids to private school—a fact that I revealed on Twitter—but consistently opposed school choice.[53] Libs of TikTok exposed that he is also funded by at least three teachers union groups.[54] By September, Clardy had already attracted a primary opponent who supported school choice and ultimately earned Governor Abbott's endorsement, Joanne Shofner, president of the Nacogdoches County Republican Women.[55]

Unfortunately, although the Texas Senate passed a universal ESA by a vote of 18–13, with only one Republican voting against it, the bill stalled in the Texas House. (At least eight of the twelve Democrats in the Texas Senate went to private school or sent their own kids to private school, yet all voted against school choice for others.)[56] The 2023 legislative session ended without any progress. But Abbott wasn't throwing in the towel just yet. In the fall, he called a special session for the legislature to consider another school-choice proposal.

Taking a page out of Iowa Governor Kim Reynolds's playbook, Abbott promised political consequences for Republican lawmakers who continued to block education freedom. "There's an easy way to get it done, and there's a hard way. We will take it either way—in a special session or after an election," he declared.[57]

Senator Ted Cruz backed him up. "Every two years, I sit down with my team and compile a spreadsheet, and I look at every vote the state legislature has taken on school choice," Cruz said at the Texas Tribune Festival in September.[58] "If you voted against choice, the chances of me supporting you are essentially zero. Odds are significant that I'm going to endorse your primary opponent and when I endorse, I don't do so gently."

Although the Texas Senate swiftly passed a universal education savings account early in the third special session, the Texas House did not vote on any school-choice bills before the October session concluded. Governor Abbott called the legislators back to Austin for a fourth special session in November 2023. The senate moved quickly in the fourth special session as well, handily passing their universal school-choice bill on November 9.[59]

The next day, the Texas House Select Committee on Educational Opportunity and Enrichment passed a universal school-choice bill—House Bill 1—by a vote of 10 to 4, strictly along party lines, with all Republicans voting in favor and all Democrats in opposition.[60] This was the first time a private-school-choice bill passed out of a Texas House education committee since 2005.

Although House Bill 1 cleared committee, a so-called Republican, Rep. John Raney, presented an amendment on the floor to strip school choice out of the legislation. The amendment to kill the bill's school choice provision passed the Texas House floor 84 to 63, with twenty-one "Republicans" joining all Democrats in opposition.[61] I later revealed that eighteen of those twenty-one Republicans were endorsed by the Texas state affiliate of the nation's largest teachers union (the NEA).[62] The "hard way" had just begun. Only sixteen of the Republicans who voted against school choice decided to run for reelection—and they all ended up with primary opponents in the March 2024 election.[63] Governor Abbott didn't waste any time, either. Before the conclusion of 2023,

Governor Abbott had already endorsed five of their challengers, and he also endorsed fifty-eight Republican incumbent legislators who voted for school choice.[64] As the *Wall Street Journal* editorial board put it in December 2023, "While the unions may have won this round, the battle to expand school choice in Texas isn't over."[65]

The Red State Strategy: Short-Term Hyperpartisan, Long-Term Bipartisan

Rep. Tricia Cotham of North Carolina wasn't the only state lawmaker nationwide to switch parties over school choice. Later in 2023, Georgia Democratic state Representative Mesha Mainor announced that she was switching to the GOP for similar reasons. Mainor had been the only Democrat to vote for a school-choice bill that ultimately died in the Georgia House that year after having passed the state senate along party lines. Democrat party leadership wasn't happy. "When I decided to stand up on behalf of disadvantaged children in support of school choice, my Democrat colleagues didn't stand by me," Mainor told Fox News.[66] Much worse than not standing with her, the party establishment made her a target, with some even promising a blank check to whomever would primary her.

"For far too long, the Democrat Party has gotten away with using and abusing the black community," said Mainor, who is black. If enough black voters changed their voting habits, it would spell the doom for the Democrats. A June 2023 poll from RealClear Opinion Research found that 66 percent of Democrats and 73 percent of black voters support school choice.[67] If the black community starts voting on the issue of school choice, as many black women did in Florida during the 2018 election, then Democrats will have to choose between keeping the unions happy or keeping a core constituency of their voting base.

The Red State Strategy is also starting the process of inducing blue states to adopt school choice. As I described in chapter 4, if we passed robust school-choice laws in enough red states, then we would normalize them. As citizens of those states became accustomed to more education freedom, voters in other states would start demanding school choice, too—either by lobbying their state lawmakers or leaving for states that had school-choice policies in place.

For example, in the fall of 2023, New York City Council members proposed a bill to study implementing a school-choice policy with the explicit goal of stopping the mass exodus of families fleeing from Gotham schools. "We have seen parents flee the [government] school system and seek alternatives that they might not be able to afford," said Councilmen Joe Borelli, a Republican, who cosponsored the bill along with Kalman Yeger, a Democrat, and six other members of the "Common Sense Caucus."[68] That fall, kindergarten enrollment was down a whopping 17 percent citywide, with some districts seeing enrollment fall more than 25 percent.[69] Over the past decade, NYC had lost about 20 percent of its K–12 student population. "What we've seen in the last few years is an abandonment of the city's school system by parents and children," said Yeger, who added that "parents need more options."[70]

The Red State Strategy is also supposed to induce elected Democrats to eventually embrace school choice. Again, as described in chapter 4, if the issue of school choice gave the Republicans a significant enough advantage in elections, then Democrats would eventually get tired of losing and tell the unions they weren't going to die on that hill anymore. We're already seeing this dynamic beginning to emerge, too.

"We've lost our advantage on education because I think that we've failed to fully acknowledge that choice resonates deeply with families and with voters," said the CEO of Democrats for Education Reform, Jorge Elorza, to *Politico* in September 2023.[71] "Neither the [Biden] administration, nor the left, has offered an alternative to the private school choice options that Republicans are offering," added Elorza, who is also the former mayor of Providence, Rhode Island. Although a critic of private school choice, Elorza implored his party to at least embrace more parental choice within the government school system or via charter schools. "What's going to happen if we don't as a party embrace choice is that, as polling shows us, we're going to lose voters to Republicans on this issue." Elorza pointed to polling showing that Republicans were tied with Democrats or beating them on the issue of education among voters in key swing states. "We're going to lose elections because of this issue. And policywise, we're going to end up with their version of choice—which is private school choice."[72]

As Nobel Laureate economist Milton Friedman famously said, "The way you solve things is by making it politically profitable for the wrong people to do the right things." Sooner or later, it won't just be party switchers like Representatives Cotham and Mainor embracing school choice, but choice-critical politicians in both parties realizing the political risks in continuing to oppose the wishes of parents.

Whether people like it or not, the Red State Strategy worked. And *the Parent Revolution* is not going to stop until we have school choice in all 50 states.

The MVP of The Year of Universal Education Choice

In 2023, America saw the biggest explosion of school-choice policy in our nation's history. As more and more states enacted universal education choice, the left started to panic. "It's really hard to overstate how different from any kind of previous legislation these programs are," fretted Liz Cohen, policy director for Georgetown University's FutureEd think tank, to Vox. "It's not income-tested; it's not about getting the lowest-income kids in the worst schools. Prior to three years ago, I would have bet a lot of money you would have never seen this happen."[73]

If I had to pick the MVP who did more than anyone else to make the Year of Universal Education Choice happen, it's a no-brainer: American Federation of Teachers president Randi Weingarten.

School-choice advocates had campaigned on the efficacy of school choice for years while well-funded and coordinated teachers unions, like Randi Weingarten's AFT, ignored their ideas and kept children in the same failing government schools. Proponents of educational freedom never gave up and continued to tout the empowerment of students and families, but until recently this fight remained an uphill battle.

The Red State Strategy worked, but only because Weingarten and her cronies overreached so badly. Soon they would come to regret it.

Through Zoom school, parents got a glimpse into the far left's radical education agenda. When concerned parents began questioning the education system they had entrusted to prioritize their children, they were met with more shutdowns, more masking, and no solutions. When parents objected to the atrocious misteaching of American history and explicit sexualization of children, the teachers unions and their allies doubled down. They demonized parents, called them Nazis and domestic terrorists, and told them that if they didn't like what government schools were doing, they should leave.

Parents listened. Millions left. Private school, charter school, and even homeschool enrollment skyrocketed. And the families who didn't have those options looked to legislation that would grant them that freedom. Thus, *the Parent Revolution* began.

I think Weingarten even knows that she's the one who woke the sleeping giant. For the last few years, she only rarely opens her posts on X (formerly Twitter) for comment. When she does, she's bombarded by parents pushing back against her radical agenda. In the fall of 2023, she explained why in a direct message to someone: "I will not open my replies," Weingarten explained. "DeAngelos [*sic*] tweeted at me thousands of times. Randi once again let everyone know that I'm over the target when she said at a conference in October 2023, "So if you listen to one thing that I say today, remember this name: Christopher Rufo. Rufo and DeAngelis. By the way, Corey DeAngelis tweets or posts at me. Like last year I think was— What was it, Asher, five thousand times last year?"[74] Apparently, Randi's digital director—who made over $200,000[75] in 2022—counted how many times I responded to her last year. That might just be about how many times she lied, so perhaps it is accurate. She just doesn't like being held accountable for her deception.

While the last few years have been painful for parents and students alike, education choice is finally becoming a reality for many families across the nation. Blinded by their agenda and failing to put kids first, the radical left is losing control over the minds of other people's children.

So, thank you, Randi Weingarten and the teachers unions, for showing America your true colors. We're freeing families from your depraved clutches once and for all, and there's nothing you can do about it.

CONCLUSION

THE PARENT REVOLUTION CONTINUES

> The condition upon which God hath given liberty to man is eternal vigilance.
>
> —*John Philpot Curran*

America's education system has reached a tipping point. The teachers unions and far-left radicals have abused their power by turning government schools into indoctrination centers, pushing their fundamentalist ideology on a captive audience of children. America's parents have risen up in response, standing athwart madness, yelling Stop.

Ordinary moms and dads don't want their children being told that some people are privileged and others are doomed solely due to their skin color. They don't want their children being told that there are an infinite number of genders. They don't want their daughters competing in sports against biological males, let alone sharing locker rooms and showers with them. They don't want their schools to secretly "socially transition" their children, calling them by different names and pronouns behind their parents' backs. Enough is enough.

The Parent Revolution is not a flash in the pan. There's no going back to the pre-COVID world in which radicals can hide from parents what they're doing in the classroom. But the job of parents is not done. Taking back a school board or passing a school choice bill are only first steps. The unions won't give up and neither can we. What follows are specific steps parents can take to protect their children from the left's radical ideology, as well as some policies that parents and activists should encourage policymakers to adopt to further that goal.

Exercising Voice: School Boards and State Legislatures

Parents must exercise their voices within the government school system. They should monitor their children's curriculum and extracurricular activities, ask their children questions about what's going on at school, listen to and speak out at school board meetings, and organize to elect proparent school board candidates and state lawmakers. Parents should get involved with groups like Moms for Liberty and Parents Defending Education to keep abreast of recent developments and to organize to change policies where and when necessary. Parents should also encourage state lawmakers and school board members to adopt state and local policies that will make schools and school boards more transparent and accountable to parents, and protect children's safety, dignity, privacy, and intellectual development.

Making School Boards Transparent and Accountable

Parents must continue to make their voices heard at school boards. But we also need policies that ensure school boards have a greater incentive to listen. As Max Eden of the American Enterprise Institute wrote, "If we want a public education system that caters to the cultural, policy, and pedagogical preferences of communities, then we should ensure that more citizens participate in local school board elections—and that they have a clear idea about what the candidates stand for."[1]

As discussed in detail in chapter 3, unions are able to capture school boards with the aid of various policies that make them less transparent and less accountable to parents and voters. By holding nonpartisan elections, voters have a harder time understanding whom they are voting for. And by holding off-cycle elections, voter turnout is suppressed. Nationwide, school board election turnout is generally between about 5 and 10 percent.[2] Both these policies make it easier for organized special interests, like the unions, to capture school boards. Currently, only about a dozen states hold on-cycle elections.[3]

Fortunately, the necessary fixes are apparent and simple: Hold school board elections at the same time as other statewide elections, and put the candidates' party affiliation on the ballot. Neither of these changes are silver bullets—voters will still need to do their due diligence—but both will markedly increase the school boards' level of transparency and accountability. Unions know this, which is why they oppose making any changes to the status quo. "Only the people that really are concerned about education are the ones who come out," said Buffalo Teachers Federation president Phil Rumore, who opposed a measure to move school board elections on-cycle.[4] "I'd rather have quality rather than quantity," he said. Of course, by "quality," he means "people who will vote how we tell them to."

Once parents have adequate representation on a given school board, it's important that the board have an appropriate sense of its mission and purpose. The Heritage Foundation developed a policy manual for school boards to use to "make transparent the policies and procedures our board and district staff will use to recognize a parent's role as their child's primary caregiver and develop policies that guard against the discrimination and harassment of students."[5] The manual informs school board members about the jurisprudence related to parental rights and the law, clearly defines key terms (e.g., "sex," "social transition," and "medical transition"), and offer model policies regarding parental rights, students' safety and privacy, academic transparency, parental consent regarding student medical care, sex education guidelines, sex-specific school activities, harassment policies, protection of student data, and more. Importantly, the manual also provides a model list of guiding principles for conducting the business of the school board:

Conclusion

1. Parents have the right to direct their children's education, including their moral and religious upbringing.
2. School officials will defer to parents' decisions regarding their children.
3. School officials will partner with parents concerning their child's education.
4. Parents have the right to know of any attempts to provide medical care, including counseling, mental health services, and any attempts to facilitate "social transitioning," to a minor-age child.
5. Parents have the right to make medical decisions for their children whether or not they are at school.
6. Parents have the right to be consulted and affirmatively asked for permission before their children are exposed to any school activity, exercise, or assignment that involves sex education, including sexual orientation, gender identity, contraceptives, abortion, or sexually explicit material.
7. Parents have the right to review the textbooks, curriculum, homework assignments, and other classroom work assigned to their children.
8. Parents have the right to speak during the public comment period of local school board meetings.
9. Children with disabilities that interfere with their learning have the right to receive special education services from this school district.
10. No student will be discriminated against on the basis of race, ethnicity, national origin, disability, religion, or biological sex by any employee or agent of this school district, and such discrimination will not be tolerated when engaged in by others on school property or during school activities and events.[6]

Even if a board adopts this or a similar list as their guiding principles, school board members and parents will still need to do their due diligence monitoring the policies the board considers in order to ensure that they conform to these principles. Nevertheless, adopting these guiding principles will make it easier to spot and block the adoption of anti-parent and anti-student policies.

Making Schools Transparent and Accountable

Too often, the radicals who have hijacked government schools and are abusing their role in the classroom to indoctrinate students are able to hide their activists from parents. Even when parents ask to see what their children are learning, schools often deny their requests or make them jump through numerous bureaucratic hoops—including forcing them to file public records requests for which the schools sometimes charge exorbitant fees. For example, in 2021, a Rhode Island school district demanded that a local mom, Nicole Solas, pay $74,000 when she asked to see the materials that the school would be teaching her child.[7] The National Education Association even sued to prevent her from being able to see the materials that the school wanted to show her child.[8] In Minnesota, a school district told parents in 2020 it would cost more than $900,000 to fulfill their request to see "information on the development of curriculum, conferences, or seminars for teachers and students related to 'equity and social justice topics often referred to as Critical Race Theory.'"[9] The lengths that schools will go to hide what they're doing from parents shows just how badly more sunlight is needed.

Every parent has a right to know what schools are telling their children. That's why we also need to adopt policies to make schools more transparent and accountable to parents. To that end, the Goldwater Institute developed the Academic Transparency Act, which would require that government schools and charter schools disclose on its website all lesson plans, learning materials, and teacher and staff training materials.[10] Such policies make it much easier to monitor what's going on in schools so that parents can take swift action to protect their children when something is awry. Sunlight is the best disinfectant.

Parents should also be consulted before schools ask their children intrusive questions in surveys. So-called social-emotional learning and school climate surveys are increasingly common and often ask children very personal or even inappropriate questions about their sexual activity, their gender identity, their mental and emotional well-being, and even suicide. As Erika Sanzi of Parents Defending Education has cautioned, "The surveys are usually electronic, meaning these data are easily stored and shared."[11] Federal law protects parents' right to opt their children out of such surveys, but often parents don't know they have a right to opt out or even that their children are being asked such questions at all. As Sanzi observes, the "opt out" notifications are "often found in a small bit of text in a 100-plus-page student handbook that parents are required to sign amid the flurry of back-to-school forms."[12] Instead of a weak "opt out" policy, such surveys should be "opt in," meaning that state policymakers should require that schools seek parents' explicit consent for such surveys in advance.

Ending Indoctrination and Protecting Students from Woke Ideology

Parents and policymakers should also be proactive to ensure that schools only adopt policies that put the best interests of students first. Here are just a few examples of policies that have been developed in recent years to protect children from the ravages of woke ideology.

The Women's Bill of Rights by Independent Women's Voice clearly defines what a woman is (paging Justice Ketanji Brown-Jackson!) and protects female-only sports and spaces, including bathrooms and locker rooms among other such spaces.[13] All too often, adults who should know better have put radical gender ideology before the safety, dignity, and privacy of young girls. For example, a high school in Vermont not only allowed a biological male into the girls' locker room, but also banned the girls' volleyball team from their own locker room when they had the temerity to object to undressing and showering alongside a male student.[14] Teenage and prepubescent girls should not have to shower or share changing facilities with biological males.

The Given Name Act by the Heritage Foundation requires that schools obtain written permission from parents before any teacher or other school official can call their children by different names (other than common diminutives) or pronouns.[15] In other words, the school wouldn't need permission to refer to Jonathan as John or Johnny, but they would need to talk to his parents before calling him Jenny and using she/her pronouns. This is particularly important because, as Parents Defending Education has documented, more than eighteen thousand government schools nationwide serving more than 10 million students have policies that "openly state that district personnel can or should keep a student's transgender status hidden from parents."[16]

The use of different names and pronouns is a key element of "social transition" from one gender identity to another, a process that is often followed by "chemical transition" (the use of puberty blockers and cross-sex hormones) and "surgical transition" (double mastectomies and sex-change surgeries). Ideologues have suggested that socially transitioning children without informing their parents is important to protect them from bullying or self-harm, but there is zero evidence that social transition actually achieves those goals. Meanwhile, as the Heritage Foundation notes, "Growing number of medical professionals now recommend 'watchful waiting' to allow parents and doctors to observe whether the experience of puberty leads to resolution of gender confusion, with some studies showing that the confusion naturally resolves itself in up to 90 percent of children."[17] Except in rare cases of documented abuse, parents must never be excluded from important decisions about their children's mental and emotional health and well-being.

The Protecting K–12 Students from Discrimination Act, also by the Heritage Foundation, ensures that government schools do not treat students differently on account of race or compel students—or teachers or other staff—to express ideas that they do not hold.[18] The law prohibits schools from compelling anyone to "adopt, affirm, adhere to, or profess ideas in violation of Title IV and Title VI of the Civil Rights Act of 1964," such as that some individuals or groups are "inherently superior or inferior," that anyone "should be adversely or advantageously treated on the basis of their race, ethnicity, color, or national origin," or that individuals bear "collective guilt" for past injustices committed by other members of the same race, ethnicity, color, or national origin.

This policy appropriately allows schools to continue to teach about past injustices without adopting the "critical race theory" lens that divides people into "oppressors" and "the oppressed" based solely on their skin color. It would also prevent schools engaging in classroom activities in which students are divided by race or hold events only for students of particular races.

The Education Licensure Certificate Act by the National Association of Scholars (NAS) would allow schools seeking to hire new teachers to bypass the education schools where teachers are indoctrinated in woke ideology before they ever set foot into a classroom. The proposed policy would create "a new, simplified education licensure pathway, which requires students to take a number of undergraduate courses focused on subject matter content, as well as a standardized test focused on subject matter content—and no other requirements, such as an undergraduate degree or an education major."[19] Research from the Brookings Institution has shown that there is no difference in performance between teachers who were traditionally certified versus those who were alternatively certified or not certified at all.[20] However, as NAS notes, the "radical education establishment...uses bureaucratic licensure requirements as a central tool to gain power over America's classrooms."[21] Significant reform of teacher licensure—or its repeal altogether—is necessary to expand the supply of nonwoke teachers.[22]

School boards and state lawmakers should also more closely monitor teacher trainers and consider defunding them altogether. As Rick Hess of the American Enterprise Institute has argued, the "lion's share of the blame [for woke indoctrination] should be reserved for the farrago of education-school faculty, diversity consultants, foundation-financed frauds, and bureaucrats who train our nation's teachers."[23] As Hess notes, the total amount spent on teacher training and professional development has been estimated at more than $18 billion annually nationwide, with more than $2 billion coming from the feds. These funds are being used as a jobs program for woke radicals to indoctrinate your children. Hess offers just a few examples:

> [In July 2021], the Loudoun County Public Schools in Virginia hired trainers from the "Equity Collaborative" to teach educators that they mustn't "profess color blindness" but instead need to accept that "addressing one's Whiteness (i.e., white privilege) is crucial for effective teaching." Teachers were taught that "fostering independence," "individual achievement," "individual thinking," and "self-expression" are racist hallmarks of "white individualism."
>
> Trainers in Seattle Public Schools taught teachers that the U.S. is a "race-based white-supremacist society," that our education system commits "spirit murder" against black children, and that white teachers must "bankrupt [their] privilege in acknowledgment of [their] thieved inheritance." In San Diego, trainers have taught educators that "Whiteness reproduces poverty, failing schools, high unemployment, school closings, and trauma for people of color."
>
> In Buffalo, N.Y., trainers designed a curriculum requiring schools to embrace "Black Lives Matter principles." Teachers were told they should promote "queer-affirming network[s] where heteronormative thinking no longer exists" and seek "the disruption of Western nuclear family dynamics." Kindergarten teachers were directed to discuss "racist police and state-sanctioned violence," and fifth-grade teachers to teach that a "school-to-grave pipeline" exists for black children.[24]

In *City Journal*, Max Eden documented how a group called Gender Spectrum, which he calls "arguably the most influential gender identity nonprofit in K–12 education," has infiltrated thousands of schools nationwide to push radical gender ideology via partnerships with the National Association of Secondary School Principals, the National PTA, the American School Counselors Association, and the School Superintendents Association, among others.[25] Gender Spectrum even published a report with the National Education Association and others titled

Schools in Transition in which they argued that schools should sometimes keep social gender transitions secret from parents, writing that "a school may choose not to bring the subject up if there is a concern that parents or caregivers may react negatively."[26] The report even details how schools could hide the social transition from parents by referring to a child by a certain name and pronoun in person while using a different name and pronoun in communications with the child's parents.[27] Gender Spectrum also has a training video titled *Intro to Neoidentities and Neopronouns* that teaches there are an infinite number of potential gender identities or pronouns, including—and I am not making this up—autismgender, rockgender, moongender, and foxgender as well as unpronounceable genders that can only be communicated via emojis.[28]

Do we really want our schools spending billions of dollars to teach our children that they can identify as a rock? If not, then school boards must do a better job of selecting and overseeing teacher trainers—and parents and voters must hold them accountable for doing so.

These policies would go a long way toward protecting children from the consequences of woke ideology. But we can't rely on policies alone. Policies like those listed above are important tools to help parents hold school officials and school boards accountable, but ultimately it's up to the parents to ensure that they are implemented and enforced. The price of liberty is eternal vigilance.

Striking at the Heart of the Problem: Banning Teachers Unions

Banning teachers unions sounds like a radical idea. But then again, not too long ago, funding students instead of systems sounded like a radical idea. In fact, less than a century ago, the notion that government employees should be allowed to collectively bargain was considered radical. In 1937, President Franklin Delano Roosevelt wrote a letter to the president of the National Federation of Federal Employees expressing his firm opposition to the notion:

> All Government employees should realize that the process of collective bargaining, as usually understood, cannot be transplanted

> into the public service... The very nature and purposes of Government make it impossible for administrative officials to represent fully or to bind the employer in mutual discussions with Government employee organizations. The employer is the whole people, who speak by means of laws enacted by their representatives in Congress.[29]

In the private sector, unions represent the interests of employees when they clash with the interests of the employer, but any excesses are moderated by a need to keep the firm competitive. Asking too much risks destroying the firm's competitive edge. But unlike a private firm in a market, the government has no competitors, and the employer is the entire populace, not a single employer or relatively small group of shareholders. Public sector unions, like teachers unions, are therefore acting as special interests negotiating against the public interest, with no market forces to moderate excesses.

As detailed in chapter 3, these problems are compounded when unions capture school board elections, essentially selecting the people who are supposed to represent the countervailing public interest. In the words of Terry Moe of Stanford University: "Teachers unions have more influence on the public schools than any other group in American society... Their massive memberships and awesome resources give them unrivaled power in the politics of education, allowing them to affect which policies are imposed on the schools by government—and to block reforms they don't like."[30]

Moe's research has shown that teachers unions have strong negative effects on government school performance—sacrificing students' academic interests for adults' financial interests.[31] A study by Michael Lovenheim and Alexander Willen of Cornell University found that "teacher collective bargaining reduces [male students' future] earnings by $149.6 billion in the US annually," amounting to a nearly 4 percent reduction in students' future annual earnings.[32]

Moreover, the unions even harm their own members, especially the most effective teachers. Unions have an incentive to pressure districts to hire more dues-paying teachers than to raise the wages of current employees, which has contributed to the stagnant wages teachers have suffered for decades. Moreover, unions typically oppose merit pay in favor of uniform step increases, which leads to "wage compression," which occurs "when the salaries of lower paid teachers are raised above the market rate, with the increase offset by reducing the pay of the most productive ones."[33]

It doesn't have to be this way. Indeed, in some states, it's not. According to the National Council on Teacher Quality, six states—Alabama, Arizona, Georgia, North Carolina, South Carolina, and Texas—currently ban teachers unions from collectively bargaining with government school districts.[34] Unions still operate in those states, and make their fair share of trouble, but without the ability to collectively bargain, their influence is significantly—and appropriately—curtailed. Other states would be wise to follow their lead.

For the sake of our children and our nation's future, it's time to end the unions' stranglehold over our nation's education system.

Exercising Choice: Universal Education Choice in All 50 States

The Parent Revolution has made tremendous strides in empowering families with education choice, but much work remains to be done. As this book goes to press, about a quarter of students nationwide are eligible for a private-school-choice program. That's a great start, but it's not enough. Parents must continue to reward politicians who support education choice, and punish those who do not.

The Republican Party's transformation into the Parents' Party is almost complete, but there are still some holdouts who must be replaced in GOP primaries. Over time, this development will also transform the Democratic Party. The more the GOP leans into parental rights as a political winner, the more it becomes politically disastrous for Democrats to oppose it. Perhaps counterintuitively, because politicians respond to power and not logic, bipartisan support for education choice in the long run can be achieved through hyperpartisanship in the short run.

The transformation has already begun. We've seen elected state lawmakers in Georgia and North Carolina flip from Democrat to Republican over the school-choice issue. We've also seen high-profile Democratic gubernatorial candidates in Illinois and Pennsylvania, who were both up in the polls, flip their education platforms to support school choice less than two months before the election. They might have been reading the tea leaves as opposed to having a true change of heart. But the reason doesn't really matter. That high-profile Democrats felt compelled to switch their stances on school choice right before the election is good news for parents.

We've seen this phenomenon play out before. Pell Grants and Medicaid, for example, were long opposed by Republicans until it simply became too politically disastrous to oppose the programs. When it comes to school choice, Republicans have an opportunity to flip the script. The lane is wide open to lead on a wildly popular issue among voters from all backgrounds. School choice is also the only "handout" that Republicans can offer while adhering to conservative principles. That's because it allows politicians to give money directly to voters while decreasing the size and scope of government. Republicans can win more votes here while forging a new and powerful single-issue group. Once parents get a taste of school choice, they fight tooth and nail to keep it.

Parents must continue to stand up for their kids and hold politicians accountable. Top-down reforms and school board races are absolutely steps in the right direction, but school choice is the very best way forward to fix the one-size-fits-all problem with our country's government-run school system. It is the only way to truly secure parental rights in education. Parents disagree about how they want their kids raised, and that's okay. These values-based disagreements mean that *choice* is the way forward.

Legislators will go bigger. While school-choice advocates have historically pushed an incremental approach, with initial program eligibility limited to disadvantaged populations (namely low-income and special needs kids and students assigned to failing schools) legislators will now seek to open the floodgates. Programs available to all families are much more popular than initiatives targeted to certain groups.

Allowing politically advantaged groups to benefit from the program is also a smart way to keep the policy protected for years to come. The same parents pushing back at school board meetings must be able to benefit from the programs or else they won't have as much of an interest in holding politicians accountable at the ballot box. And some conservatives might even view the program as welfare if it discriminates based on income.

Universal education choice is within reach. Indeed, it's already happening. Not long ago, the idea that we should fund students, not systems, was considered radical and fringe. The way government schools handled COVID made Americans rethink their commitment to a one-size-fits-all system of government schooling. Now nearly a dozen states offer universal education choice, and several more states appear ready to follow them.

And fortunately, it's all for the best of our children, our country, and our future.

ACKNOWLEDGMENTS

No book is the product of one person's efforts alone. There are many people to whom I am incredibly grateful, for without their guidance, friendship, encouragement, nurturing, and love, I would not be the person I am today, nor would this book be what it is.

I'm grateful for my closest advisors through my academic career—including Jay P. Greene, Robert Maranto, and Patrick J. Wolf—each of whom served on my doctoral dissertation committee at the Department of Education Reform at the University of Arkansas. A special thank-you goes to John D. Merrifield, my close mentor and economics professor during my bachelor's and master's studies at the University of Texas at San Antonio. Dr. Merrifield nudged me to pursue my PhD at the University of Arkansas, where my research on the benefits of school choice first thrust me into the national spotlight.

I'm grateful for my close-knit group of education freedom advocates—my best friends—who, with great foresight, devised the Red State Strategy long before the universal school-choice revolution ignited. That group includes Jason Bedrick, Lindsey Burke, Max Eden, Jay P. Greene, James Paul, Robert Pondiscio, Erika Sanzi, and Inez Stepman. A special thanks to Jason Bedrick for his invaluable assistance on the manuscript.

I'm grateful to my employer, the American Federation for Children, for giving me maximum autonomy to be the best advocate possible. The employees—the adults in the system—have had unions representing their interests all along. We represent the interests of the children and their families. The kids' union, if you will. Parents are winning the revolution with help from AFC's advocacy.

I'm grateful for my parents, Tom and Cheryl DeAngelis—my first and best teachers—who taught me the importance of a good education and character. They supported—and encouraged me—to pursue an education at a great magnet high school, Communications Arts, my first experience with school choice. That opportunity changed my life trajectory.

Most of all, I'm grateful for my wife, Miranda DeAngelis, for her steadfast support and unwavering love. I could not succeed in this fight without her by my side. I know she will be the best mother, and—soon—we will have the privilege of joining *the Parent Revolution* on the front lines, as parents, with all of you.

NOTES

INTRODUCTION: *THE PARENT REVOLUTION*

1 Robert Pondiscio (@rpondiscio), "An observation: No one in education policy, advocacy, or activism has ever lived rent-free in more heads at once than @DeAngelisCorey," X, September 13, 2023, 12:48 p.m., https://x.com/rpondiscio/status/1702001324362027348.

2 Paul Sacca, "Chicago Teachers Union Exec Says It Is Too Dangerous to Open Schools as She Vacations at Pool in the Caribbean," Blaze Media, January 2, 2021, https://www.theblaze.com/news/chicago-teachers-union-puerto-rico.

3 Robby Soave, "Chicago Teachers Union: 'The Push to Reopen Schools Is Rooted in Sexism, Racism, and Misogyny,'" *Reason*, Reason Foundation, December 6, 2020, https://reason.com/2020/12/06/chicago-teachers-union-reopen-schools-sexism-racism-misogyny/.

4 Elizabeth Elizalde, "Half of Americans Are Calling 2021 the 'Worst Year of Their Lives' So Far," OnePoll Research, December 22, 2021, https://www.onepoll.us/half-of-americans-are-calling-2021-the-worst-year-of-their-lives-so-far/.

5 Jason Bedrick, "The Year of Educational Choice Is Here," EdChoice, May 25, 2021, https://www.edchoice.org/engage/the-year-of-educational-choice-is-here/.

6 *Espinoza v. Montana* (Supreme Court of the United States, June 30, 2020).

7 John Clark, "McAuliffe: 'I Don't Think Parents Should Be Telling Schools What They Should Teach,'" MyStateline.com (Nexstar Media Group), September 29, 2021, https://www.mystateline.com/news/politics/mcauliffe-i-dont-think-parents-should-be-telling-schools-what-they-should-teach/.

8 Steven Allen Adams, "Divided West Virginia Supreme Court Rules Hope Scholarship Constitutional," *Intelligencer: Wheeling News Register*, October 7, 2022, https://www.theintelligencer.net/news/top-headlines/2022/10/divided-west-virginia-supreme-court-rules-hope-scholarship-constitutional/.

9 Andrew Wimer, "West Virginia Supreme Court Issues Full Ruling Upholding Hope Scholarship Program," Institute for Justice, November 17, 2022, https://ij.org/press-release/west-virginia-supreme-court-issues-full-ruling-upholding-hope-scholarship-program/.

CHAPTER 1: HOLDING AMERICA'S KIDS HOSTAGE

1 Corey A. DeAngelis (@DeAngelisCorey), "BREAKING: Randi Weingarten blames local NEA teachers union affiliates for keeping schools closed," X (formerly known as Twitter), November 6, 2021, 10:14 p.m., https://twitter.com/DeAngelisCorey/status/1457169474629554180.

2 Randi Weingarten, in "The Consequences of School Closures, Part 2: The President of the American Federation of Teachers, Ms. Randi Weingarten," House Oversight and Accountability Select Subcommittee on the Coronavirus Pandemic, April 26, 2023, https://www.congress.gov/event/118th-congress/house-event/115797?s=1&r=17.

3 Lexi Lonas, "House Republicans Grill Teachers Union Chief on Pandemic School Closures," *Hill*, April 26, 2023, https://thehill.com/homenews/education/3974073-house-republicans-grill-teachers-union-chief-on-pandemic-school-closures/.

4 Jason McGahan, "Exclusive: Cecily Myart-Cruz's Hostile Takeover of L.A.'s Public Schools," *Los Angeles Magazine*, August 26, 2021, https://www.lamag.com/citythinkblog/cecily-myart-cruz-teachers-union/.

5 Sarah D. Sparks, "Two Decades of Progress, Nearly Gone: National Math, Reading Scores Hit Historic Lows," Student Achievement, *Education Week*, October 24, 2022, https://www.edweek.org/leadership/two-decades-of-progress-nearly-gone-national-math-reading-scores-hit-historic-lows/2022/10.

6 Ibid.

7 Jake Bryant et al., "Halftime for the K–12 stimulus: How are districts faring?," McKinsey & Company, November 2, 2022, https://www.mckinsey.com/industries/education/our-insights/halftime-for-the-k-12-stimulus-how-are-districts-faring; National Center for Education Statistics, "Digest of Education Statistics, 2013," Table 203.20 Institute of Education Sciences, October 18, 2022, https://nces.ed.gov/programs/digest/d13/tables/dt13_203.20.asp.

8 Kevin Mahnken, "NAEP Scores 'Flashing Red' After a Lost Generation of Learning for 13-Year-Olds," *The 74*, June 21, 2023, https://www.the74million.org/article/naep-scores-flashing-red-after-a-lost-generation-of-learning-for-13-year-olds/.

9 National Assessment of Educational Progress, "Mathematics and Reading Scores of Fourth- and Eighth-Graders Declined in Most States During Pandemic,

Nation's Report Card Shows," press release, October 24, 2022, https://www.nationsreportcard.gov/mathematics/supportive_files/2022_rm_press_release.docx.

10 Ibid.

11 Emma Dorn et al., "COVID-19 and Education: The Lingering Effects of Unfinished Learning," McKinsey & Company, July 27, 2021, https://www.mckinsey.com/industries/education/our-insights/covid-19-and-education-the-lingering-effects-of-unfinished-learning.

12 Ibid.

13 Ibid.

14 "A Nation at Risk: The Imperative for Educational Reform," National Commission on Excellence in Education, The Reagan Foundation, 1983, https://www.reaganfoundation.org/media/130020/a-nation-at-risk-report.pdf.

15 Michelle Goldberg, "Opinion: We Desperately Need Schools to Get Back to Normal," *New York Times*, December 17, 2021, https://www.nytimes.com/2021/12/17/opinion/randi-weingarten-schools.html.

16 Randi Weingarten, in "The Consequences of School Closures, Part 2: The President of the American Federation of Teachers, Ms. Randi Weingarten," House Oversight and Accountability Select Subcommittee on the Coronavirus Pandemic, April 26, 2023, https://www.congress.gov/event/118th-congress/house-event/115797?s=1&r=17.

17 Virginia Myers, "Weingarten Sets the Record Straight over School Reopening," American Federation of Teachers, April 27, 2023, https://www.aft.org/news/weingarten-sets-record-straight-over-school-reopening.

18 Laura Baker and *Education Week* Staff, "Forever Changed: A Timeline of How COVID Upended Schools," School & District Management, *Education Week*, April 5, 2022, https://www.edweek.org/leadership/forever-changed-a-timeline-of-how-covid-upended-schools/2022/04.

19 Education Week, "Map: Coronavirus and School Closures in 2019–2020," *Education Week*, March 6, 2020, https://www.edweek.org/leadership/map-coronavirus-and-school-closures-in-2019-2020/2020/03.

20 Nicole Chavez and Artemis Moshtaghian, "48 States Have Ordered or Recommended That Schools Don't Reopen This Academic Year," CNN, May 7, 2020, https://www.cnn.com/2020/04/18/us/schools-closed-coronavirus/index.html.

21 Corey DeAngelis, "How Pennsylvania Is Discouraging Education During the Coronavirus Crisis: Opinion," *PennLive*, April 16, 2020, https://www.pennlive.com/opinion/2020/04/how-pennsylvania-is-discouraging-education-during-the-coronavirus-crisis-opinion.html.

22 Michael B. Henderson et al., "What American Families Experienced When Covid-19 Closed Their Schools," *Education Next*, July 8, 2020, https://www.educationnext.org/what-american-families-experienced-when-covid-19-closed-their-schools/.

23 Bridget Loft, "Continuous Learning Plans," Arlington Public Schools, April 9, 2020, Wayback Machine archived webpage, https://web.archive.org/web/20200503140558/https://www.apsva.us/post/continuous-learning-plans/.

24 "Common Sense Media–SurveyMonkey Poll: How Teens Are Coping and Connecting in the Time of the Coronavirus," Common Sense Media, 2020, Wayback Machine archived webpage, https://web.archive.org/web/20200414103223/https://www.commonsensemedia.org/sites/default/files/uploads/pdfs/2020_surveymonkey-key-findings-toplines-teens-and-coronavirus.pdf.

25 Robin Lake et al., "Required Teachers to Deliver Instruction This Spring. They Mustn't Be Left on Their Own Again in the Fall," *The 74*, June 16, 2020, https://www.the74million.org/article/analysis-just-1-in-3-districts-required-teachers-to-deliver-instruction-this-spring-they-mustnt-be-left-on-their-own-again-in-the-fall/.

26 Michael B. Henderson et al., "What American Families Experienced When Covid-19 Closed Their Schools," *Education Next*, July 8, 2020, https://www.educationnext.org/what-american-families-experienced-when-covid-19-closed-their-schools/.

27 Paul DiPerna, Andrew D. Catt, and Michael Shaw, "Public Opinion on COVID-19 and K–12 Education," EdChoice, June 2, 2020, https://www.edchoice.org/wp-content/uploads/2020/07/UPDATED-07-2020-SIA-slide-deck-ONE-1.pdf.

28 Jeffrey M. Jones, "Parents Slightly Favor Full-Time, In-Person School This Fall," Gallup, June 18, 2020, https://news.gallup.com/poll/312674/parents-slightly-favor-full-time-person-school-fall.aspx.

29 Yael Halon, "Teachers Union Leader Insists Schools Will Need More Funding to Reopen on Time amid Pandemic," Fox News, July 2, 2020, https://www.foxnews.com/media/randi-weingarten-aft-schools-reopening-coronavirus-pandemic.

30 Rebecca R. Skinner et al., "CARES Act Education Stabilization Fund: Background and Analysis," Congressional Research Service, August 6, 2020, https://crsreports.congress.gov/product/pdf/R/R46378.

31 Stacey Childress, "Gallup: Parents Give Schools Low Marks on Reopening Plans. What Happens Next?," *Forbes*, August 16, 2020, https://www.forbes.com/sites/staceychildress/2020/08/16/parents-give-schools-low-marks-on-reopening-plans-what-happens-next/.

32 "School Districts' Reopening Plans: A Snapshot," *Education Week*, July

15, 2020, https://www.edweek.org/leadership/school-districts-reopening-plans-a-snapshot/2020/07/.

33 "Common Sense Media–SurveyMonkey Poll: How Teens Are Coping and Connecting in the Time of the Coronavirus," Common Sense Media, 2020, Wayback Machine archived webpage, https://web.archive.org/web/20200414103223/https://www.commonsensemedia.org/sites/default/files/uploads/pdfs/2020_surveymonkey-key-findings-toplines-teens-and-coronavirus.pdf.

34 Bethany Mandel, "'Remote Learning' Is a Disaster, and Terrible for Children," *New York Post*, September 16, 2020, http://nypost.com/2020/09/16/remote-learning-is-a-disaster-and-terrible-for-children/.

35 Stacy Greenhut, "Report: 12-Year-Old Plays with Nerf Gun in Virtual Class, School Calls Cops," WKMG, September 8, 2020, https://www.clickorlando.com/news/local/2020/09/08/report-12-year-old-plays-with-nerf-gun-in-virtual-class-school-calls-cops/.

36 Corey A. DeAngelis, "Are Public School Systems Leaving Families out to Dry?," Institute for Family Studies, October 6, 2020, https://ifstudies.org/blog/are-public-school-systems-leaving-families-out-to-dry/.

37 Chris Butler, "Rutherford County Schools Tell Parents Not to Monitor Their Child's Virtual Classrooms," *Tennessee Star*, August 15, 2020, https://tennesseestar.com/news/rutherford-county-schools-tell-parents-not-to-monitor-their-childs-virtual-classrooms/cbutler/2020/08/15/.

38 Hristina Byrnes, "Reopening Schools amid COVID-19: A Mix of In-Person Attendance, Remote Learning and Hybrid Plans," *USA Today*, August 3, 2020, https://www.usatoday.com/story/money/2020/08/03/every-states-plan-to-reopen-schools-in-the-fall/112599652/.

39 Eliza Shapiro and Juliana Kim, "'Remote Learning Is Not Working': Shutdown Hurts Children, Parents Say," *New York Times*, November 19, 2020, https://www.nytimes.com/2020/11/19/nyregion/schools-closing.html.

40 Ibid.

41 Ibid.

42 Lindsey Burke, "Schools Use Empty Classes for Expensive Day Care, and Parents Are Charged Twice. This Needs to End," *Daily Signal*, August 20, 2020, https://www.dailysignal.com/2020/08/20/districts-are-using-empty-schools-as-expensive-day-cares-and-taxpaying-parents-are-being-charged-twice-this-needs-to-end/.

43 Bill Miston, "'Can't Shut Down Our Lives': Mequon-Thiensville Parents Protest, Calling for In-Person Learning This Fall," FOX 6 Now Milwaukee, August 23, 2020, https://www.fox6now.com/news/cant-shut-down-our-lives-mequon-thiensville-parents-protest-calling-for-in-person-learning-this-fall.

44 Claire Cain Miller, "In the Same Towns, Private Schools Are Reopening While Public Schools Are Not," The Upshot, *New York Times*, July 16, 2020, https://www.nytimes.com/2020/07/16/upshot/coronavirus-school-reopening-private-public-gap.html.

45 Katie Reilly, "Public Schools Will Struggle Even More as Parents Move Kids to Private Ones During the Pandemic," *Time*, August 31, 2020, https://time.com/5885106/school-reopening-coronavirus/.

46 Jessica Dickler, "Families Jump to Private Schools as Coronavirus Drags On," CNBC, November 8, 2020, https://www.cnbc.com/2020/11/08/coronavirus-why-families-are-jumping-to-private-schools.html.

47 "Running Towards the Danger: Early Learnings from Catholic Schools in the Midst of the Pandemic," *NCEA Talk*, October 27, 2020, https://nceatalk.org/2020/10/running-towards-the-danger-early-learnings-from-catholic-schools-in-the-midst-of-the-pandemic/.

48 Jack Brammer and Daniel Desrochers, "U.S. Supreme Court Declines to Block Beshear's Order Shutting Kentucky Schools," *Lexington Herald Leader*, December 17, 2020, https://www.kentucky.com/news/coronavirus/article247649375.html.

49 Corey DeAngelis and Christos Makridis, "Are School Reopening Decisions Related to Union Influence?," *Social Science Quarterly* 102, no. 5 (September 2021), https://onlinelibrary.wiley.com/doi/abs/10.1111/ssqu.12955.

50 Corey A. DeAngelis, "School Reopenings Linked to Union Influence and Politics, Not Safety," *Reason*, Reason Foundation, August 19, 2020, https://reason.com/2020/08/19/school-reopenings-linked-to-union-influence-and-politics-not-safety/.

51 Michael T. Hartney and Leslie K. Finger, "Politics, Markets, and Pandemics: Public Education's Response to COVID-19," *EdWorkingPapers*, October 2020, https://doi.org/10.26300/8ff8-3945.

52 Matt Grossmann et al., "All States Close but Red Districts Reopen: The Politics of In-Person Schooling During the COVID-19 Pandemic," *Educational Researcher* 50, no. 9 (September 24, 2021): 0013189X2110488, https://doi.org/10.3102/0013189x211048840.

53 "AFT President Randi Weingarten Says Educators Remain Confused over CDC Guidance on School Reopening, Nothing Is Off the Table for Teachers If Schools Aren't Safe," American Federation of Teachers, press release, July 24, 2020, https://www.aft.org/press-release/aft-president-randi-weingarten-says-educators-remain-confused-over-cdc.

54 "News Release: Joint Statement from San Diego Unified, Los Angeles Unified School Districts Regarding Online Start to School Year," San Diego

Unified, Los Angeles Unified School Districts, press release, July 15, 2020, Wayback Machine archived webpage, https://web.archive.org/web/20200715020026/https://www.sandiegounified.org/newscenter/node/2285.

55 Michael Burke, "LA Unified, Teachers' Union Reach Agreement over Distance Learning Guidelines," *EdSource*, April 9, 2020, https://edsource.org/2020/la-unified-teachers-union-reach-agreement-over-distance-learning-guidelines/628559.

56 "UTLA Recommends Keeping LAUSD School Campuses Closed; Refocus on Robust Distance Learning Practices for Fall," UTLA, press release, July 9, 2020, Wayback Machine archived webpage, https://web.archive.org/web/20200714115414/https://www.utla.net/news/utla-recommends-keeping-school-campuses-closed/.

57 Ibid.

58 *The Same Storm, but Different Boats: The Safe and Equitable Conditions for Starting LAUSD in 2020–21*, UTLA, July 2020, Wayback Machine archived webpage, https://web.archive.org/web/20200714115414/https://www.utla.net/sites/default/files/samestormdiffboats_final.pdf.

59 "About," Demand Safe Schools, Wayback Machine archived webpage, https://web.archive.org/web/20200806124519/https://www.demandsafeschools.org/about/.

60 "Demands," Demand Safe Schools, Wayback Machine archived webpage, https://web.archive.org/web/20200806154505/https://www.demandsafeschools.org/demands/.

61 Howard Blume and Laura Newberry, "California Teacher Unions Fight Calls to Reopen Schools," *Los Angeles Times*, October 16, 2020, https://www.latimes.com/california/story/2020-10-16/state-teacher-unions-push-back-against-calls-to-reopen-k-12-campuses-parents-divided.

62 Emily Oster, "Emily Oster: School Infection Rates Are Low Even in Areas with High COVID-19 Rates, According to Data on 550,000 US Students," *Insider*, October 12, 2020, https://www.insider.com/emily-oster-school-infections-low-in-areas-with-rampant-coronavirus-2020-10.

63 Emma Dorn et al., "COVID-19 and Learning Loss—Disparities Grow and Students Need Help," McKinsey & Company, December 8, 2020, https://www.mckinsey.com/industries/public-sector/our-insights/covid-19-and-learning-loss-disparities-grow-and-students-need-help.

64 Ibid.

65 "California Parent Poll: Fall 2020," The Education Trust—West, October 2020, https://west.edtrust.org/california-parent-poll-october-2020/.

66 Esmeralda Fabián Romero, "L.A. Parents in Desperate Straits with Distance Learning Say It's Time for the Most Vulnerable Students to Be Back in School,"

The 74, October 30, 2020, https://www.the74million.org/article/l-a-parents-in-desperate-straits-with-distance-learning-say-its-time-for-the-most-vulnerable-students-to-be-back-in-school/.

67 Paul Blest, "Teachers Are Making Their Own Gravestones and Coffins to Protest Going back to School," *Vice*, August 4, 2020, https://www.vice.com/en/article/y3zxp5/teachers-are-making-their-own-gravestones-and-coffins-to-protest-going-back-to-school.

68 Corey DeAngelis, "Charlie Crist Goes All in for Teachers Unions," Opinion, *Wall Street Journal*, August 28, 2022, https://www.wsj.com/articles/charles-crist-goes-all-in-for-teachers-unions-karla-hernandez-mats-american-federation-of-teachers-virginia-youngkin-desantis-closure-choice-weingarten-governor-running-mate-11661687436; Daniel Arkin, "Florida's Largest Teachers Union Sues State over Reopening Schools," NBC News, July 20, 2020, https://www.nbcnews.com/news/us-news/florida-s-largest-teachers-union-files-suit-against-state-over-n1234382; Haley Victory Smith, "DC Teachers Line Up Fake Body Bags Outside School System Offices to Protest Potential Return to Classroom," *Washington Examiner*, July 28, 2020, https://www.washingtonexaminer.com/news/dc-teachers-line-up-fake-body-bags-outside-school-system-offices-to-protest-potential-return-to-classroom; Karen Cuen and Rebecca Friedrichs, "Teachers Want to Teach, Marxist Unions Want to Blackmail," *Washington Times*, August 10, 2020, https://www.washingtontimes.com/news/2020/aug/10/teachers-want-to-teach-marxist-unions-want-to-blac/.

69 Noelani Bonifacio, "Disservice to Teachers Evident in Chicago Union's Tweet," RealClearEducation, September 18, 2020, https://www.realcleareducation.com/articles/2020/09/18/disservice_to_teachers_evident_in_chicago_unions_tweet_110472.html; Joseph A. Wulfsohn, "Chicago Teachers Union Panned for Music Video Using Interpretive Dance to Demand 'Safe' Return to Schools," Fox News, January 27, 2021, Wayback Machine archived webpage, https://web.archive.org/web/20210127201828/https://www.foxnews.com/media/chicago-teachers-union-panned-for-video-demanding-safe-return-to-schools-through-interpretive-dance/.

70 Emma Camp, "Chicago Teachers Union Boss Sends Son to Private School," *Reason*, September 2023, https://reason.com/2023/09/19/chicago-teachers-union-boss-sends-son-to-private-school/.

71 Lily Altavena, "J.O. Combs District Cancels School on Tuesday, Wednesday as Teacher Sick-out Continues," *Arizona Republic*, August 17, 2020, https://www.azcentral.com/story/news/local/arizona-education/2020/08/17/j-o-combs-unified-school-district-remain-closed-after-teacher-sick-out/3387214001/; Katie Reilly, "Arizona Teachers Waged a Sickout over Coronavirus Concerns, and Organizers

Say Other School Districts Could Be Next," *Time*, August 18, 2020, https://time.com/5880630/arizona-teachers-sickout-coronavirus/; Andrew DeMillo, "Little Rock Schools Close for 2 Days over Teacher Sick Calls," Associated Press, February 10, 2020, https://apnews.com/3862fa4d103ff83bed06f5af84fa8966; Mike Elk, "Utah Teachers Organize 'Sickout' Strikes—Striking Wash Fruit Workers Unionize—Atlantic City Teachers Strike—OSHA Under Biden: A Preview," *Payday Report*, November 16, 2020, https://paydayreport.com/utah-teachers-organize-sickout-strikes-striking-wash-fruit-workers-unionize-atlantic-city-teachers-strike-osha-under-biden-a-preview/; Richard Luscombe, "New York City Teachers Threaten Mass 'Sickout' as Schools Stay Open amid Coronavirus," World News, *Guardian*, March 15, 2020, https://www.theguardian.com/world/2020/mar/15/new-york-city-coronavirus-schools-teachers; Caroline Reinwald, "Kenosha Teachers Union Calls Situation 'Dangerous and Untenable,'" WISN, September 21, 2020, https://www.wisn.com/article/kenosha-teachers-union-calls-current-teaching-situation-dangerous-and-untenable/34103246; Brakkton Booker, "Teachers Union OKs Strikes If Schools Reopen Without Safety Measures in Place," NPR, July 28, 2020, https://www.npr.org/sections/coronavirus-live-updates/2020/07/28/896265783/teachers-union-oks-strikes-if-schools-reopen-without-safety-measures-in-place.

72 Jon Levine, "Powerful Teachers Union Influenced CDC on School Reopenings, Emails Show," *New York Post*, May 1, 2021, https://nypost.com/2021/05/01/teachers-union-collaborated-with-cdc-on-school-reopening-emails/.

73 Ibid.

74 "AFT's Weingarten on CDC's Schools Reopening Guidelines," American Federation of Teachers, press release, February 12, 2021, https://www.aft.org/press-release/afts-weingarten-cdcs-schools-reopening-guidelines.

75 Victor Nava, "AFT Boss Randi Weingarten Questioned Language in School Reopening Plan in Chummy Exchange with CDC Chief, Texts Show," *New York Post*, June 2, 2023, https://nypost.com/2023/06/02/texts-reveal-exchange-between-cdc-director-teachers-union-boss-before-school-reopening-memo/.

76 Deidre McPhillips, "Nearly All US Kids Live in Red Zones Under New CDC School Guidance," CNN, February 15, 2021, https://www.cnn.com/2021/02/12/health/us-kids-red-zones-cdc-school-guidelines/index.html.

77 "Jake Tapper Presses CDC Director on Reopening Schools," CNN, video, February 14, 2021, https://www.cnn.com/videos/health/2021/02/14/cdc-director-rochelle-walensky-reopening-schools-tapper-sotu-vpx.cnn.

78 Joe Schoffstall, "White House Considered Teachers Unions' Labor Disputes Before Releasing Reopening Guidance, Emails Show," Fox News, December 17, 2021, https://www.foxnews.com/politics/white-house-teachers-unions-labor-disputes-school-reopening-guidance-emails.

79 Ibid.

80 Ibid.

81 Corey A. DeAngelis, "School Reopenings Linked to Union Influence and Politics, Not Safety," *Reason*, Reason Foundation, August 19, 2020, https://reason.com/2020/08/19/school-reopenings-linked-to-union-influence-and-politics-not-safety/.

82 Corey A. DeAngelis and Christos A. Makridis, "Are School Reopening Decisions Related to Funding? Evidence from over 12,000 Districts During the COVID-19 Pandemic," *Journal of School Choice* 16, no. 3 (June 2022): 454–476, https://www.tandfonline.com/doi/abs/10.1080/15582159.2022.2077164/.

83 Marguerite Roza and Katie Silberstein, "Financial Turmoil: Open or Remote? What It Means for School District Budgets," Edunomics Lab, Georgetown University, March 3, 2021, https://edunomicslab.org/wp-content/uploads/2021/03/Financial-Turmoil-Webinar-Mar3.pdf.

CHAPTER 2: THE SLEEPING GIANT AWAKENS

1 John Mooney, "Parents Organize 'Rally to Open Schools' Outside Scotch Plains–Fanwood BOE Offices on Mon, Nov. 16," *TAPinto Scotch Plains/Fanwood*, November 15, 2020, https://www.tapinto.net/towns/scotch-plains-slash-fanwood/sections/education/articles/parents-organize-rally-to-open-schools-outside-scotch-plains-fanwood-boe-offices-on-mon-nov-16.

2 Jeff Hudson, "School Board Ponders Reopening as Parents Keep Up Pressure," *Davis Enterprise*, February 6, 2021, https://www.davisenterprise.com/news/school-board-ponders-reopening-as-parents-keep-up-pressure/article_e7582abf-38fb-58ba-b0f5-a50d0a1799c9.html.

3 Ibid.

4 Emily Gilbert, "Parents to School Board: Fully Open Schools," *Whidbey News-Times*, March 12, 2021, https://www.whidbeynewstimes.com/news/parents-to-school-board-fully-open-schools/.

5 Emily Gilbert, "Schools Chief Leaving Oak Harbor for New Job," *Whidbey News-Times*, April 2, 2021, https://www.whidbeynewstimes.com/news/schools-chief-leaving-oak-harbor-for-new-job/.

6 Charles Flesher, "'We Are Leaving a Lot of Kids Behind': Des Moines Parents, Students Ask District to Reopen Schools," *Des Moines Register*, September 14, 2020, https://www.desmoinesregister.com/story/news/education/2020/09/14/des-moines-public-schools-parents-students-ask-district-open-school-buildings-online-hybrid-classes/5799807002/.

7 Ibid.

8 Ian Richardson, "Gov. Kim Reynolds: Iowa Schools Must Conduct at Least Half of Instruction In-Person," *Des Moines Register*, July 17, 2020, https:

//www.desmoinesregister.com/story/news/politics/2020/07/17/iowa-schools-education-governor-kim-reynolds-in-person-learning-return-online-covid-coronavirus/5443853002/.

9 Philip Joens, "Judge Denies Des Moines Public Schools' Injunction Request; District Says Classes Will Stay Online," *Des Moines Register*, September 8, 2020, https://www.desmoinesregister.com/story/news/2020/09/08/des-moines-public-schools-dmps-injunction-denied-judge-must-hold-in-person-classes-covid-coronavirus/5743788002/.

10 "ICCSD and ISEA Dropping Lawsuit Against Governor Reynolds and Iowa Department of Education," KWWL, November 25, 2020, https://www.kwwl.com/coronavirus/iccsd-and-isea-dropping-lawsuit-against-governor-reynolds-and-iowa-department-of-education/article_0076610d-088b-593e-9ab7-3a9073459354.html.

11 Philip Joens, "Judge Denies Des Moines Public Schools' Injunction Request; District Says Classes Will Stay Online," *Des Moines Register*, September 8, 2020, https://www.desmoinesregister.com/story/news/2020/09/08/des-moines-public-schools-dmps-injunction-denied-judge-must-hold-in-person-classes-covid-coronavirus/5743788002/.

12 Charles Flesher, "Des Moines Public Schools Is Ready to Hold In-Person Classes Again. The First Students Will Return in Two Weeks.," *Des Moines Register*, October 1, 2020, https://www.desmoinesregister.com/story/news/education/2020/09/30/des-moines-public-schools-reopen-schools-starting-october-in-person-online-hybrid-covid-coronavirus/5873648002/.

13 Jeff Tavss, "Families Sue Herbert, SLC School District over Closed Schools," FOX 13 News Utah (KSTU), December 14, 2020, https://www.fox13now.com/news/local-news/families-sue-herbert-slc-school-district-over-closed-schools.

14 Courtney Tanner, "Salt Lake City Parents Lose Their Legal Fight to Reopen Schools. But Not for the Reasons You Might Think.," *Salt Lake Tribune*, January 28, 2021, https://www.sltrib.com/news/education/2021/01/29/salt-lake-city-parents/.

15 Nina Agrawal, "California Is Failing to Provide Free and Equal Education to All During Pandemic, Suit Alleges," *Los Angeles Times*, December 1, 2020, https://www.latimes.com/california/story/2020-12-01/parents-community-groups-sue-state-education-officials-over-inadequate-distance-learning.

16 Melissa Gomez, "California Supreme Court Rejects Petition to Force LAUSD to Partially Reopen for In-Person Classes," *Los Angeles Times*, January 21, 2021, https://www.latimes.com/california/story/2021-01-21/lausd-schools-reopening-lawsuit.

17 Alejandro Lazo, "San Francisco Parents Work to Recall School Board Members amid Reopening Controversy," *Wall Street Journal*, February 28, 2021, https://www.wsj.com/articles/san-francisco-parents-work-to-recall-school-board-members-amid-reopening-controversy-11614531601.

18 Stella Chan and Amanda Jackson, "San Francisco School Board Votes to Rename 44 Schools, Including Abraham Lincoln and George Washington High Schools," CNN, January 27, 2021, https://www.cnn.com/2021/01/27/us/san-francisco-school-name-changes-trnd/index.html.

19 Isaac Chotiner, "How San Francisco Renamed Its Schools," *New Yorker*, February 6, 2021, https://www.newyorker.com/news/q-and-a/how-san-francisco-renamed-its-schools.

20 Thomas Fuller, "It's Liberals Vs. Liberals in San Francisco After Schools Erase Contested Names," *New York Times*, January 28, 2020, https://www.nytimes.com/2021/01/28/us/san-francisco-school-name-debate.html.

21 Stella Chan and Amanda Jackson, "San Francisco School Board Votes to Rename 44 Schools, Including Abraham Lincoln and George Washington High Schools," CNN, January 27, 2021, https://www.cnn.com/2021/01/27/us/san-francisco-school-name-changes-trnd/index.html.

22 Alejandro Lazo, "San Francisco Parents Work to Recall School Board Members amid Reopening Controversy," *Wall Street Journal*, February 28, 2021, https://www.wsj.com/articles/san-francisco-parents-work-to-recall-school-board-members-amid-reopening-controversy-11614531601.

23 Jocelyn Gecker, "San Francisco Recalls 3 Members of City's School Board," Associated Press, February 16, 2022, https://apnews.com/article/san-francisco-school-board-elections-d22ee9c5175904885d41e149775102a5.

24 "School Board Recalls," 2021 data, Ballotpedia, https://ballotpedia.org/School_board_recalls#2021; "School Board Recalls," 2022 data, Ballotpedia, https://ballotpedia.org/School_board_recalls#2022/.

25 "School Board Recalls," 2019 data, Ballotpedia, https://ballotpedia.org/School_board_recalls#2019.

26 Robby Soave, "Chicago Teachers Union: 'The Push to Reopen Schools Is Rooted in Sexism, Racism, and Misogyny,'" *Reason*, Reason Foundation, December 6, 2020, https://reason.com/2020/12/06/chicago-teachers-union-reopen-schools-sexism-racism-misogyny/.

27 Benjamin Fearnow, "Teacher Says Parents Who Want Schools Reopened Reflect White Supremacy," *Newsweek*, March 29, 2021, https://www.newsweek.com/teacher-calls-parents-who-want-schools-reopened-white-supremacists-debate-rages-1579590.

28 Mackenzie Mays, "LA Teachers Union Slams California Schools Plan as 'Propagating Structural Racism,'" *Politico*, March 2, 2021, https://www.politico.com/states/california/story/2021/03/02/la-teachers-union-slams-state-plan-as-propagating-structural-racism-1366367/.

29 Marc Levy, "'No Confidence' Voted for School District Officials; Educators

Want Say in Hiring Next Superintendent," *Cambridge Day*, January 22, 2021, https://www.cambridgeday.com/2021/01/22/no-confidence-voted-for-school-district-officials-educators-want-say-in-hiring-next-superintendent/; Matt Welch, "Teachers Unions Use Accusations of Racism to Oppose School Reopening," *Reason*, Reason Foundation, January 27, 2021, https://reason.com/2021/01/27/teachers-unions-use-accusations-of-racism-to-oppose-school-reopening/.

30 Cameron Probert, "100+ Teachers Support Union President's 'White Privilege' Remarks on Reopening Schools," *Tri-City Herald*, January 26, 2021, https://www.tri-cityherald.com/news/local/education/article248754040.html.

31 Valerie Strauss, "The Racist Effects of School Reopening During the Pandemic—by a Teacher," perspective, *Washington Post*, July 23, 2020, https://www.washingtonpost.com/education/2020/07/23/racist-effects-school-reopening-during-pandemic-by-teacher/.

32 Mike Friedberg, "Will We Let 'Nice White Parents' Kill Black and Brown Families?," *Chicago Unheard*, January 24, 2021, https://chicagounheard.org/blog/will-we-let-nice-white-parents-kill-black-and-brown-families/.

33 Yana Kunichoff, "Chicago Says Most of Its Teachers and Staff Should Return to Campus for 4th Quarter," *Chalkbeat Chicago*, March 24, 2021, https://chicago.chalkbeat.org/2021/3/24/22349516/chicago-asks-most-teachers-to-return-to-campus/.

34 Gabrielle LaMarr LeMee and Cassie Walker Burke, "Data: How Many Students Are Returning to Your Chicago School?," *Chalkbeat Chicago*, March 1, 2021, https://chicago.chalkbeat.org/2021/3/1/22307733/data-how-many-chicago-students-returning-school-in-person-remote-learning-per-school-enrollment/.

35 Mike Friedberg, "Will We Let 'Nice White Parents' Kill Black and Brown Families?," *Chicago Unheard*, January 24, 2021, https://chicagounheard.org/blog/will-we-let-nice-white-parents-kill-black-and-brown-families/.

36 Emma Dorn et al., "COVID-19 and Education: The Lingering Effects of Unfinished Learning," McKinsey & Company, July 27, 2021, https://www.mckinsey.com/industries/education/our-insights/covid-19-and-education-the-lingering-effects-of-unfinished-learning.

37 Allie Griffin, "California Teachers Union Spied on Parents Who Wanted Schools to Reopen During COVID: Emails," *New York Post*, September 7, 2022, https://nypost.com/2022/09/06/california-teachers-union-spied-on-parents-who-wanted-schools-to-reopen-during-covid-emails/.

38 KTVU Staff, "Berkeley Teachers Union President Defends Sending Daughter to In-Person Preschool," KTVU Fox 2, March 1, 2021, https://www.ktvu.com/news/berkeley-teachers-union-president-defends-sending-daughter-to-in-person-preschool.

39 National Education Association, CES Center for Enterprise Strategy, "Opposition Report: Pandemic Pods," September 2020, *Wall Street Journal*, https://www.wsj.com/public/resources/documents/Prenda.pdf.

40 "The Proliferation of Pandemic Pods, Micro-Schools, and Home Education," National Education Association, Wayback Machine archived webpage, https://web.archive.org/web/20201019204727/https://educatingthroughcrisis.org/wp-content/uploads/2020/08/Pandemic-Pods-Report.pdf.

41 Elliot Kaufman, "the Teachers Union's Tiny New Enemy," Opinion, *Wall Street Journal*, October 14, 2020, https://www.wsj.com/articles/the-teachers-unions-tiny-new-enemy-11602709305.

42 Ibid.

43 Jeremy Duda, "Microschools on the Rise in Arizona, with COVID Providing Added Boost," *Arizona Mirror*, July 28, 2020, https://www.azmirror.com/2020/07/28/microschools-on-the-rise-in-arizona-with-covid-providing-added-boost/.

44 Paul Sacca, "Chicago Teachers Union Exec Says It Is Too Dangerous to Open Schools as She Vacations at Pool in the Caribbean," Blaze Media, January 2, 2021, https://www.theblaze.com/news/chicago-teachers-union-puerto-rico.

45 Jessica Dickler, "Families Jump to Private Schools as Coronavirus Drags On," CNBC, November 8, 2020, https://www.cnbc.com/2020/11/08/coronavirus-why-families-are-jumping-to-private-schools.html.

46 Ibid.

47 Ibid.

48 Kathleen Porter-Magee, "Amid the Pandemic, Progress in Catholic Schools," *Wall Street Journal*, October 27, 2022, https://www.wsj.com/articles/amid-the-pandemic-progress-in-catholic-schools-partnership-naep-report-card-math-reading-public-charter-black-hispanic-11666902117.

49 Associated Press, "Enrollment Drops in School District That Includes Las Vegas," ABC 13 Las Vegas News KTNV, September 16, 2020, https://www.ktnv.com/news/enrollment-drops-in-school-district-that-includes-las-vegas/; Emilee Speck, "Thousands of Unregistered Orange County Students Will Not Result in Layoffs This Semester, Superintendent Says," WKMG, September 4, 2020, http://www.clickorlando.com/news/local/2020/09/04/thousands-of-unregistered-orange-county-students-will-not-result-in-layoffs-this-semester-superintendent-says/.

50 Bethany Blankley, "Texas Homeschool Coalition: 400 Percent Increase in Parents Withdrawing Students from Public Schools," *Corridor News*, September 15, 2020, http://smcorridornews.com/texas-homeschool-coalition-400-percent-increase-in-parents-withdrawing-students-from-public-schools/.

51 Kalyn Belsha et al., "Across U.S., States See Public School Enrollment Dip as

Virus Disrupts Education," *Chalkbeat,* December 22, 2020, https://www.chalkbeat.org/2020/12/22/22193775/states-public-school-enrollment-decline-covid.

52 Carter Evans, "Public Schools Have Seen a Massive Drop in Enrollment Since the Start of the Pandemic," CBS News, August 25, 2021, https://www.cbsnews.com/news/public-schools-enrollment-drop-pandemic/.

53 Post Editorial Board, "City Department of Education Is Trying to Hide the True Drop in Public-School Enrollment," editorial, *New York Post,* November 1, 2021, https://nypost.com/2021/11/01/nyc-doe-trying-to-hide-the-true-drop-in-public-school-enrollment/.

54 Christos Makridis, Clara Piano, and Corey DeAngelis, "The Effects of School Closures on Mental Health: Evidence from the Covid-19 Pandemic," Social Science Research Network, January 10, 2022, https://doi.org/10.2139/ssrn.4001953.

55 Steven Duvall, "Homeschooling Continues to Grow in 2021," Home School Legal Defense Association, July 7, 2021, https://hslda.org/post/homeschooling-continues-to-grow-in-2021.

56 Tareena Musaddiq et al., "The Pandemic's Effect on Demand for Public Schools, Homeschooling, and Private Schools," *Journal of Public Economics* 212 (August 2022): no. 104710, https://doi.org/10.1016/j.jpubeco.2022.104710.

57 Benjamin Scafidi, Roger Tutterow, and Damian Kavanagh, "This Time Really Is Different: The Effect of COVID-19 on Independent K–12 School Enrollments," *Journal of School Choice* 15, no. 3 (2021): 305–330, https://doi.org/10.1080/15582159.2021.1944722.

58 Julie Bosman, "The Board Voted to Keep Schools Closed. Parents Revolted.," *New York Times,* January 21, 2021, https://www.nytimes.com/2021/01/21/us/coronavirus-schools-wisconsin.html.

59 Michael T. Hartney and Leslie K. Finger, "Politics, Markets, and Pandemics: Public Education's Response to COVID-19," *EdWorkingPapers,* October 2020, https://doi.org/10.26300/8ff8-3945.

60 Matthew Reichbach, "A 'Pause' on In-Person K–12 Teaching Until at Least Labor Day," NM Political Report, July 23, 2020, https://nmpoliticalreport.com/2020/07/23/a-pause-on-in-person-instruction-until-at-least-labor-day/.

61 Cedar Attanasio, "New Mexico Releases Plan for Reopening Public Schools," *Las Cruces Sun News,* June 23, 2020, https://www.lcsun-news.com/story/news/education/2020/06/23/covid-19-coronavirus-new-mexico-public-school-reopen-plan-rules/3244219001/.

62 Simon Romero, Giulia McDonnell Nieto del Rio, and Patricia Mazzei, "If Public Schools Are Closed, Should Private Schools Have to Follow?," *New York Times,* August 5, 2020, https://www.nytimes.com/2020/08/05/us/schools-reopening-private-public.html.

63 Tyler Waldman, "Gov. Hogan Overrules Montgomery County, Says Schools, Systems Can Decide Whether to Open," WBAL NewsRadio 1090 and FM 101.5, August 3, 2020, https://www.wbal.com/article/472343/188/gov-hogan-overrules-montgomery-county-says-schools-systems-can-decide-whether-to-open.

64 Governor Larry Hogan (@GovLarryHogan), "I have issued an amended emergency order ensuring that local schools and school systems retain the primary authority to determine when to safely reopen their facilities," X (formerly known as Twitter), August 3, 2020, 12:54 p.m., https://twitter.com/GovLarryHogan/status/1290330304830246912/photo/1.

65 "New Order Released to Block In-Person Classes at Non-Public Schools in Montgomery County," WBAL NewsRadio 1090 and FM 101.5, August 6, 2020, https://www.wbal.com/article/472817/188/new-order-released-to-block-in-person-classes-at-non-public-schools-in-montgomery-county.

66 Ashley McGuire, "If Public Schools Are Closed, Should Private Schools Have to Follow?," RealClearEducation, August 14, 2020, https://www.realcleareducation.com/articles/2020/08/14/if_public_schools_are_closed_should_private_schools_have_to_follow_110451.html.

67 Simon Romero, Giulia McDonnell Nieto del Rio, and Patricia Mazzei, "If Public Schools Are Closed, Should Private Schools Have to Follow?," *New York Times*, August 5, 2020, https://www.nytimes.com/2020/08/05/us/schools-reopening-private-public.html.

68 Ibid.

69 Ibid.

70 Ashley McGuire, "If Public Schools Are Closed, Should Private Schools Have to Follow?," RealClearEducation, August 14, 2020, https://www.realcleareducation.com/articles/2020/08/14/if_public_schools_are_closed_should_private_schools_have_to_follow_110451.html.

71 Walter Olson, "Maryland Governor Reverses County's Decree Against Private School Reopening," Cato Institute, August 4, 2020, https://www.cato.org/blog/maryland-governor-reverses-countys-decree-against-private-school-reopening.

CHAPTER 3: PUBLIC SCHOOLS ARE GOVERNMENT SCHOOLS

1 John Taylor Gatto, "I Quit, I Think," Education Revolution, Alternative Education Resource Organization, October 7, 2011, https://www.educationrevolution.org/blog/i-quit-i-think/. This article originally appeared in the *Wall Street Journal* on July 25, 1991.

2 The White House, "Remarks by President Trump in State of the Union Address," February 4, 2020, https://trumpwhitehouse.archives.gov/briefings-statements/remarks-president-trump-state-union-address-3/.

3 See, for example: Valerie Strauss, "In State of the Union, Trump Makes Clear His Aversion to Public Schools," *Washington Post*, February 5, 2020, https://www.washingtonpost.com/education/2020/02/05/state-union-trump-makes-clear-his-aversion-public-schools/.

4 E.g., the group Public Funds Public Schools, which claims that "public schools" are "open to all children." "Home," (Public Funds Public Schools, 2023), https://pfps.org/.; See also: Mark Lieberman, "What Does It Actually Mean for Schools to Be Public?," *Education Week*, August 31, 2023, https://www.edweek.org/leadership/what-does-it-actually-mean-for-schools-to-be-public/2023/08.

5 See, for example: Office of the Attorney General for the District of Columbia, "AG Racine Sues Six Maryland Parents for Residency Fraud at D.C. Schools, Seeks Nearly $700K in Unpaid Tuition and Damages," press release, December 12, 2018, https://oag.dc.gov/release/ag-racine-sues-six-maryland-parents-residency; Kyle Spencer, "Can You Steal an Education?," The Hechinger Report, May 18, 2015, https://hechingerreport.org/can-you-steal-an-education/; Daniel Tepfer, "Tanya McDowell Sentenced to 5 Years in Prison," *Connecticut Post*, March 28, 2012, https://www.ctpost.com/news/article/Tanya-McDowell-sentenced-to-5-years-in-prison-3437974.php; Keri D. Ingraham, "'Public' Schools That Aren't Public," Opinion, *Wall Street Journal*, August 8, 2023, https://www.wsj.com/articles/public-schools-that-arent-public-school-choice-zip-codes-k-12-f4d4b4d5.

6 "Ohio Mom Kelley Williams-Bolar Jailed for Sending Kids to Better School District," ABC News, January 25, 2011, https://abcnews.go.com/US/ohio-mom-jailed-sending-kids-school-district/story?id=12763654.

7 Tim DeRoche, Hailly T. N. Korman, and Harold Hinds, "When Good Parents Go to Jail," Available to All, August 2023, https://availabletoall.org/report-when-good-parents-go-to-jail/.

8 Emily Parker, "50-State Review," Education Commission of the States, March 2016, https://www.ecs.org/wp-content/uploads/2016-Constitutional-obligations-for-public-education-1.pdf.

9 Justice Jerome Powell, Court opinion, "*San Antonio Independent School District v. Rodriguez*, 411 U.S. 1 (1973)," March 21, 1973, Justia Law, https://supreme.justia.com/cases/federal/us/411/1/#tab-opinion-1950218.

10 Tyler Cowen, "Public Goods," Econlib, 2018, https://www.econlib.org/library/Enc/PublicGoods.html.

11 Milton Friedman, "The Role of Government in Education," EdChoice, 1982, https://www.edchoice.org/who-we-are/our-legacy/articles/the-role-of-government-in-education/.

12 Ibid.

13 "School Choice Bibliography," EdChoice, June 7, 2023, https://www.edchoice.org/school-choice-bibliography/.

14 See, for example: Jason Bedrick, "The Folly of Overregulating School Choice," *Education Next*, January 5, 2016, https://www.educationnext.org/the-folly-of-overregulating-school-choice/; Jason Bedrick, "On Regulating School Choice: A Response to Critics," *Education Next*, January 14, 2016, https://www.educationnext.org/on-regulating-school-choice-a-response-to-critics/.

15 Corey A. DeAngelis and Lindsey Burke, "Unintended Consequences of Regulating Private School Choice Programs: A Review of the Evidence," in *Regulation and Economic Opportunity: Blueprints for Reform*, ed. Adam Hoffer and Todd Nesbit (Logan, UT: The Center for Growth and Opportunity at Utah State University, 2020), https://www.thecgo.org/books/regulation-and-economic-opportunity-blueprints-for-reform/unintended-consequences-of-regulating-private-school-choice-programs-a-review-of-the-evidence/.

16 Valerie Strauss, "Why It Matters Who Governs America's Public Schools," perspective, *Washington Post*, November 4, 2018, https://www.washingtonpost.com/education/2018/11/04/why-it-matters-who-governs-americas-public-schools/.

17 Patrick J. Wolf, PhD, "The Civic Effects of School Choice," EdChoice, September 9, 2020, https://www.edchoice.org/wp-content/uploads/2020/0/The-Civic-Effects-of-School-Choice-Patrick-Wolf.pdf.

18 EIA Communiqué, Educational Intelligence Agency, May 10, 1999 (?).

19 Corey A. DeAngelis and Patrick J. Wolf, "Private School Choice and Character: More Evidence from Milwaukee," *Journal of Private Enterprise* 35, no. 3 (2020): 13–48, http://journal.apee.org/index.php/Parte3_2020_Journal_of_Private_Enterprise_Vol_35_No_3_Fall.

20 Mancur Olson, *The Logic of Collective Action: Public Goods and the Theory of Groups*, second printing (Cambridge, MA: Harvard University Press, 1971), https://doi.org/10.2307/j.ctvjsf3ts.

21 Michael Hartney, "It's Time to Eliminate 'Off-Cycle' School Board Elections," Brookings Institution, February 26, 2016, https://www.brookings.edu/blog/brown-center-chalkboard/2016/02/26/make-education-politics-great-again-eliminate-off-cycle-school-board-elections/.

22 Samuel Wonacott, "State Law in Four States Requires Partisan Labels for School Board Elections," *Ballotpedia News*, October 3, 2022, https://news.ballotpedia.org/2022/10/03/state-law-in-four-states-requires-partisan-labels-for-school-board-elections/.

23 Terry M. Moe, *Special Interest: Teachers Unions and America's Public Schools* (Washington, DC: Brookings Institution Press, 2011), 113.

24 Michael T. Hartney, "Still the Ones to Beat: Teachers' Unions and School Board Elections," Manhattan Institute, October 2022, https://media4.manhattan-institute.org/sites/default/files/still-the-ones-to-beat-teachers-unions-and-school-board-elections.pdf.

25 Ibid.

26 "American Federation of Teachers Profile: Recipients," OpenSecrets, Center for Responsive Politics, March 20, 2023, https://www.opensecrets.org/orgs/american-federation-of-teachers/recipients?id=D000000083.

27 "Teachers Unions: Long-Term Contribution Trends," OpenSecrets, https://www.opensecrets.org/industries/totals.php?ind=L1300.

28 Ronn Blitzer, "Teachers Union Spends More on Dem Causes Than Its Own Members, Analysis Finds," Fox News, April 7, 2022, https://www.foxnews.com/politics/teachers-union-spending-democratic-causes-its-own-members-analysis.

29 Author's calculations based on data from the National Center of Education Statistics, Table 236.55, https://nces.ed.gov/programs/digest/d22/tables/dt22_236.55.asp.

30 Author's calculations based on data from the National Center of Education Statistics, Table 211.50, https://nces.ed.gov/programs/digest/d22/tables/dt22_211.50.asp.

31 Nat Malkus and R. J. Martin, "NEA Embraces the Woke Agenda—but Votes Down 'Student Learning,'" American Enterprise Institute, July 11, 2019, https://www.aei.org/education/k-12-schooling/nea-embraces-the-woke-agenda-but-votes-down-student-learning/.

32 Hanna Panreck, "Colorado Teachers Union Leader Reportedly Rallied Against Charter School: 'A Further Decrease in Enrollment,'" Fox News, June 3, 2022, https://www.foxnews.com/media/colorado-teachers-union-leader-email-charter-school.

33 "2020 NEA Policy Playbook for Congress and the Biden-Harris Administration," National Education Association, November 12, 2020, https://www.nea.org/resource-library/2020-nea-policy-playbook-congress-and-biden-harris-administration.

34 Inez Stepman (@InezFeltscher), "Shorter teachers' union: we will close the schools and keep your money, how dare you try to find alternatives for your children!," X (formerly known as Twitter), November 19, 2020, 9:49 a.m., https://twitter.com/InezFeltscher/status/1329436607586463751.

CHAPTER 4: THE SCHOOL WARS: OUR CHILDREN, OUR CHOICE

1 Lindsay Kornick, "'Parents, Do You Agree?' Biden Alarms with Assertion There's 'No Such Thing as Someone Else's Child,'" Fox News, April 25, 2023, https://www.foxnews.com/media/parents-agree-biden-alarms-assertion-no-thing-someone-elses-child.

2 Houston Keene, "Michigan Democrats Criticized After Dismissing Parents' Role in Public Education," Fox News, January 17, 2022, https://www.foxnews.com/politics/michigan-democrats-criticized-dismissing-parents-role-public-education.

3 Linda Jacobson, "With Some Parents Mad over Issues from School Closures to Critical Race Theory, Leaders Fear Impact on Fall Enrollment," *The 74*, July 15, 2021, https://www.the74million.org/with-some-parents-mad-over-issues-from-school-closures-to-critical-race-theory-leaders-fear-impact-on-fall-enrollment/.

4 Ibid.

5 Jonathan Butcher and Mike Gonzalez, "Critical Race Theory, the New Intolerance, and Its Grip on America," Heritage Foundation, December 7, 2020, https://www.heritage.org/civil-rights/report/critical-race-theory-the-new-intolerance-and-its-grip-america.

6 Marina Watts, "In Smithsonian Race Guidelines, Rational Thinking and Hard Work Are White Values," *Newsweek*, July 17, 2020, https://www.newsweek.com/smithsonian-race-guidelines-rational-thinking-hard-work-are-white-values-1518333.

7 Ibid.

8 Derrick A. Bell, "Who's Afraid of Critical Race Theory?," *University of Illinois Law Review* 893 (1995): 899, https://heinonline.org/HOL/LandingPage?handle=hein.journals/unilllr1995&div=40&id=&page=.

9 Richard Delgado and Jean Stefancic, *Critical Race Theory: An Introduction*, second edition (New York: New York University Press, 2012), p. 3, https://www.jstor.org/stable/j.ctt9qg9h2.

10 Derrick A. Bell, "Who's Afraid of Critical Race Theory?," *University of Illinois Law Review* 893 (1995): 902, https://heinonline.org/HOL/LandingPage?handle=hein.journals/unilllr1995&div=40&id=&page=.

11 Jonathan Butcher and Mike Gonzalez, "Critical Race Theory, the New Intolerance, and Its Grip on America," Heritage Foundation, December 7, 2020, https://www.heritage.org/civil-rights/report/critical-race-theory-the-new-intolerance-and-its-grip-america.

12 Richard Delgado and Jean Stefancic, *Critical Race Theory: An Introduction*, second edition (New York: New York University Press, 2012), pp. 28–29, https://www.jstor.org/stable/j.ctt9qg9h2.

13 Phil McCausland, "Teaching Critical Race Theory Isn't Happening in Classrooms, Teachers Say in Survey," NBC News, July 1, 2021, https://www.nbcnews.com/news/us-news/teaching-critical-race-theory-isn-t-happening-classrooms-teachers-say-n1272945.

14 "Schools Not Teaching Race Theory, Some Want to Ban It Anyway," Associated Press, July 14, 2021, https://apnews.com/article/education-race-and-ethnicity-a6d37d7c273bab67acafc830215b2dac.

15 Zach Goldberg and Eric Kaufmann, "Yes, Critical Race Theory Is Being Taught in Schools," *City Journal*, October 20, 2022, https://www.city-journal.org/article/yes-critical-race-theory-is-being-taught-in-schools.

16 Robby Soave, "Is Critical Race Theory Taught in K–12 Schools? The NEA Says Yes, and That It Should Be.," *Reason*, Reason Foundation, July 6, 2021, https://reason.com/2021/07/06/critical-race-theory-nea-taught-in-schools/.

17 Corey A. DeAngelis (@DeAngelisCorey), "The nation's largest teachers union approved a $127k measure to publicize information on CRT," X (formerly known as Twitter), July 6, 2021, 10:20 a.m., https://twitter.com/DeAngelisCorey/status/1412416254263107591; Nat Malkus and R. J. Martin, "NEA Embraces the Woke Agenda—but Votes Down 'Student Learning,'" American Enterprise Institute, July 11, 2019, https://www.aei.org/education/k-12-schooling/nea-embraces-the-woke-agenda-but-votes-down-student-learning/.

18 Brittany Bernstein, "Nation's Largest Teachers' Union to Conduct Opposition Research on CRT Opponents," *National Review*, July 2, 2021, https://www.nationalreview.com/news/nations-largest-teachers-union-to-conduct-opposition-research-on-crt-opponents/.

19 Robby Soave, "Is Critical Race Theory Taught in K–12 Schools? The NEA Says Yes, and That It Should Be.," *Reason*, Reason Foundation, July 6, 2021, https://reason.com/2021/07/06/critical-race-theory-nea-taught-in-schools/.

20 "Parent Testimonials of Critical Race Theory Being Taught in Utah Schools," Utah Parents United, https://www.utahparentsunited.org/crt.html.

21 Leslie M. Harris, "I Helped Fact-Check the 1619 Project. The *Times* Ignored Me.," *Politico Magazine*, March 6, 2020, https://www.politico.com/news/magazine/2020/03/06/1619-project-new-york-times-mistake-122248; "*New York Times* Quietly Edits '1619 Project' after Conservative Pushback," Heritage Impact, Heritage Foundation, September 26, 2020, https://www.heritage.org/american-founders/impact/new-york-times-quietly-edits-1619-project-after-conservative-pushback; Timothy Sandefur, "The 1619 Project: An Autopsy," Cato Institute, October 27, 2020, https://www.cato.org/commentary/1619-project-autopsy; Phillip W. Magness, "The 1619 Project Unrepentantly Pushes Junk History," *Reason*, Reason Foundation, March 29, 2022, https://reason.com/2022/03/29/the-1619-project-unrepentantly-pushes-junk-history/; Marybeth Gasman, "What History Professors Really Think about 'the 1619 Project,'" *Forbes*, June 3, 2021, https://www.forbes.com/sites/marybethgasman/2021/06/03/what-history-professors-really-think-about-the-1619-project/.

22 "Parent Testimonials of Critical Race Theory Being Taught in Utah Schools," Utah Parents United, https://www.utahparentsunited.org/crt.html.

23 Ibid.

24 Eesha Pendharkar, "Pride Flags and Black Lives Matter Signs in the Classroom: Supportive Symbols or Propaganda?," Equity & Diversity, *Education Week*, January 25, 2022, https://www.edweek.org/leadership/pride-flags-and-black-live-matters-signs-in-the-classroom-supportive-symbols-or-propaganda/2022/01.

25 "Vision for Black Lives," The Movement for Black Lives, https://m4bl.org/policy-platforms/; Mike Gonzalez, "The Agenda of Black Lives Matter Is Far Different from the Slogan," Heritage Foundation, July 3, 2020, https://www.heritage.org/progressivism/commentary/the-agenda-black-lives-matter-far-different-the-slogan; Mark Moore, "BLM Leader: If Change Doesn't Happen, Then 'We Will Burn Down This System,'" *New York Post*, June 25, 2020, https://nypost.com/2020/06/25/blm-leader-if-change-doesnt-happen-we-will-burn-down-this-system/; "BLM Demands," Black Lives Matter, https://blacklivesmatter.com/blm-demands/.

26 Jay W. Richards, PhD, "What Is Gender Ideology?," Heritage Foundation, July 7, 2023, https://www.heritage.org/gender/commentary/what-gender-ideology.

27 Pronouns List, https://pronounslist.com/.

28 Elizabeth Harrington, "'Gender Unicorn' for Kids Lets Them Color in Their 'Gender Identity,'" *Washington Free Beacon*, August 12, 2016, https://freebeacon.com/culture/gender-unicorn-kids-lets-color-gender-identity/.

29 Erika Stanish, "State Rep. Aaron Bernstine Looking into 'Gender Unicorn' Taught to Education Students," CBS News Pittsburgh, April 13, 2022, https://www.cbsnews.com/pittsburgh/news/state-rep-aaron-bernstine-gender-unicorn/.

30 For these and other outrageous examples, see the appendix of the following report, beginning on page 9: Jay P. Greene, Max Eden, and Madison Marino, "The Book Ban Mirage" Education Freedom Institute, 2023, https://www.efinstitute.org/wp-content/uploads/2023/07/EFI-Book_Ban_Mirage.pdf.

31 Blaze TV, "Dad STUNS School Board When He Reads Aloud DISGUSTING Book from Library," YouTube, video, October 24, 2022, https://www.youtube.com/watch?v=bFKdRjsRHEI.

32 Cyera Williams, "Groups Rally Ahead of Elizabethtown Board of Education Vote for Controversial Book," Fox 43, October 25, 2022, https://www.fox43.com/article/news/education/elizabethtown-board-of-education-me-earl-and-the-dying-girl/521-dc9ceee0-c0aa-444b-8295-37a3ee9160f6; Ashley Stalnecker, "Elizabethtown Area School Board Votes to Keep 'Me and Earl and the Dying Girl' on Library Shelves," *Lancaster Online*, October 25, 2022, https://lancasteronline.com/news/local/elizabethtown-area-school-board-votes-to-keep-me-and-earl-and-the-dying-girl-on/article_3a4498a2-54d0-11ed-aa96-efeb87c8472d.html.

33 Jay P. Greene, Max Eden, and Madison Marino, "The Book Ban Mirage," Education Freedom Institute, 2023, https://www.efinstitute.org/wp-content/uploads/2023/07/EFI-Book_Ban_Mirage.pdf.

34 Nicole Carr and Lucas Waldron, "How School Board Meetings Became Flashpoints for Anger and Chaos Across the Country," ProPublica, July 19, 2023, https://projects.propublica.org/school-board-meetings-flashpoints-for-anger-chaos/.

35 Bailey Gallion, "Moms for Liberty Sues Brevard School Board, Saying

Speech Rules Discriminate by View," *Florida Today*, November 8, 2021, https://www.floridatoday.com/story/news/education/2021/11/08/moms-liberty-brevard-sues-school-board-over-first-amendment-rights/6337527001/.

36 Tiffany Justice and Tina Descovich, "Opinion: What 'School Board Moms' Really Want—and Why Candidates Ignore Us at Their Peril," *Washington Post*, November 8, 2021, https://www.washingtonpost.com/opinions/2021/11/08/moms-for-liberty-education-elections/.

37 Bailey Gallion, "Moms for Liberty Sues Brevard School Board, Saying Speech Rules Discriminate by View," *Florida Today*, November 8, 2021, https://www.floridatoday.com/story/news/education/2021/11/08/moms-liberty-brevard-sues-school-board-over-first-amendment-rights/6337527001/.

38 Edward Graham, "Who Is Behind the Attacks on Educators and Public Schools?," NEAToday, National Education Association, December 14, 2021, https://www.nea.org/nea-today/all-news-articles/who-behind-attacks-educators-and-public-schools.

39 Ibid.

40 Rebecca S. Pringle, "NEA's Letter to Social Media Companies," National Education Association, October 8, 2021, https://www.nea.org/about-nea/leaders/president/from-our-president/neas-letter-social-media-companies.

41 Nicole Solas, "Calling Us Terrorists Wasn't Enough: NSBA Wanted Military to Crack Down on Concerned Parents," *Daily Signal*, May 25, 2022, https://www.dailysignal.com/2022/05/25/calling-us-terrorists-wasnt-enough-nsba-wanted-military-to-crack-down-on-concerned-parents/; "National School Boards Association Letter to Biden," September 29, 2021, Document Cloud, https://www.documentcloud.org/documents/21094557-national-school-boards-association-letter-to-biden.

42 Ben Zeisloft, "NSBA's First Draft of 'Domestic Terrorism' Letter Called for Feds to Sic 'Army National Guard and Its Military Police' on Parents, Independent Review Shows," Daily Wire, May 23, 2022, https://www.dailywire.com/news/nsbas-first-draft-of-domestic-terrorism-letter-called-for-feds-to-sic-army-national-guard-and-its-military-police-on-parents-independent-review-shows.

43 U.S. Department of Justice, Office of Public Affairs, "Justice Department Addresses Violent Threats Against School Officials and Teachers," press release, October 4, 2021, https://www.justice.gov/opa/pr/justice-department-addresses-violent-threats-against-school-officials-and-teachers; Tim Pearce, "DOJ, FBI Investigating 'Disturbing Spike' in 'Harassment,' 'Threats' Against School Administrators," Daily Wire, October 5, 2021, https://www.dailywire.com/news/doj-fbi-investigating-disturbing-spike-in-harassment-threats-against-school-administrators.

44 Brandon Gillespie, "White House indicates people making 'violent antisemitic threats' not classified as 'domestic terrorists,'" Fox News, October 31, 2023, https://www.foxnews.com/politics/white-house-indicates-people-making-violent-antisemitic-threats-classified-domestic-terrorists.

45 The Editorial Board, "About Those Domestic-Terrorist Parents," Opinion, *Wall Street Journal*, October 26, 2021, https://www.wsj.com/articles/about-those-domestic-terrorists-national-school-boards-association-merrick-garland-memo-fbi-11635285900.

46 "US House Judiciary Republicans: DOJ Labeled Dozens of Parents as Terrorist Threats," House Judiciary Committee, press release, May 20, 2022, https://judiciary.house.gov/media/press-releases/us-house-judiciary-republicans-doj-labeled-dozens-of-parents-as-terrorist.

47 Tim Pearce, "17 State AGs Condemn DOJ Targeting School Board Meetings: Trying to 'Chill Lawful Dissent by Parents,'" Daily Wire, October 18, 2021, https://www.dailywire.com/news/17-state-ags-condemn-doj-targeting-school-board-meetings-trying-to-chill-lawful-dissent-by-parents.

48 Chuck Ross, "White House Knew About Letter That Compared Parents to Domestic Terrorists," *Washington Free Beacon*, October 21, 2021, https://freebeacon.com/campus/white-house-knew-about-letter-that-compared-parents-to-domestic-terrorists/; "Full NSBA Letter to Biden Administration and Department of Justice Memo," Parents Defending Education, press release, November 29, 2021, https://defendinged.org/press-releases/full-nsba-letter-to-biden-administration-and-department-of-justice-memo/.

49 Jarrett Stepman, "'No Legitimate Basis' for DOJ Targeting of Protesting Parents, House Panel's Report Concludes," *Daily Signal*, March 22, 2023, https://www.dailysignal.com/2023/03/22/house-panels-report-details-how-doj-was-used-target-protesting-parents/; "A 'Manufactured' Issue and 'Misapplied' Priorities: Subpoenaed Documents Show No Legitimate Basis for the Attorney General's Anti-parent Memo: Interim Staff Report of the Committee on the Judiciary and the Select Subcommittee on the Weaponization of the Federal Government," U.S. House of Representatives, Committee on the Judiciary and the Select Subcommittee on the Weaponization of the Federal Government, 2023, https://judiciary.house.gov/sites/evo-subsites/republicans-judiciary.house.gov/files/evo-media-document/2023-03-21-school-board-documents-interim-report.pdf.

50 Ashe Schow, "NSBA Apologizes for Letter Describing Potential Domestic Terrorism at School Board Meetings," Daily Wire, October 23, 2021, https://www.dailywire.com/news/nsba-apologizes-for-letter-describing-potential-domestic-terrorism-at-school-board-meetings.

51 Zachary Faria, "National School Board Group Bleeding Membership and Money After Comparing Parents to Terrorists," Restoring America, *Washington*

Examiner, December 8, 2021, https://www.washingtonexaminer.com/restoring-america/community-family/national-school-board-group-bleeding-membership-and-money-after-comparing-parents-to-terrorists.

52 Bradley Thomas, "Antonio Gramsci: the Godfather of Cultural Marxism," FEE Stories, Foundation for Economic Education, March 31, 2019, https://fee.org/articles/antonio-gramsci-the-godfather-of-cultural-marxism/.

53 Rachel Reese, "Exit, Voice, and Incentives: An Institutional Analysis of Urban Public School Districts," George Mason University, Mercatus Center, September 2015.

54 Ian Kingsbury and Jason Bedrick, "Why American Jews Should Embrace Education Choice," Jewish Policy Center, March 30, 2021, https://www.jewishpolicycenter.org/2021/03/30/why-american-jews-should-embrace-education-choice/.

55 Albert O. Hirschman, "Exit, Voice, and Revolution," *Harvard University Press Blog*, December 14, 2012, https://harvardpress.typepad.com/hup_publicity/2012/12/exit-voice-and-revolution-albert-o-hirschman.html.

56 Bedrick has provided this analysis in a number of presentations over the years but has never published it. He graciously allowed me to include it here.

57 Jennifer Wagner, "Blame the Left: Who Needs Bipartisanship Anyway?," EdChoice, Medium, November 5, 2019, https://medium.com/educationchoice/blame-the-left-who-needs-bipartisanship-anyway-f75d08c81155.

58 Jay P. Greene and Frederick M. Hess, "America's Students Flounder While Education Reformers Virtue Signal," *National Review*, November 5, 2019, https://www.nationalreview.com/2019/11/school-reform-struggles-virtue-signaling-ignores-student-performance-stagnation/.

59 Ibid.

60 Robert Pondiscio, "The Left's Drive to Push Conservatives out of Education Reform," The Thomas B. Fordham Institute, May 26, 2016, https://fordhaminstitute.org/national/commentary/lefts-drive-push-conservatives-out-education-reform; Justin Cohen, "An Open Letter," Justin Cohen (website), May 26, 2016, http://www.justinccohen.com/blog/2016/5/26/an-open-letter; Jay P. Greene, "Stacey Childress Misses the Point," *Jay P. Greene's Blog*, May 27, 2016, https://jaypgreene.com/2016/05/27/stacey-childress-misses-the-point/; Eric Kalenze, "The Pondiscio Kerfuffle Pt 1: Good Luck with That, Reform Bubble," A Total Ed Case, May 30, 2016, https://erickalenze.wordpress.com/2016/05/30/the-pondiscio-kerfuffle-pt-1-good-luck-with-that-reform-bubble/; Erika Sanzi, "Pondiscio Raises Important and Fair Questions," Good School Hunting, May 27, 2016, Wayback Machine archived webpage, https://web.archive.org/web/20160529091307/http://goodschoolhunting.org/2016/05/pondiscio-raises-important-fair-questions.html; Elizabeth Green, "Does Black Lives Matter Belong in Education Reform? A Private Debate Bursts

into Public View," Chalkbeat, June 1, 2016, https://www.chalkbeat.org/2016/5/27/21098692/does-black-lives-matter-belong-in-education-reform-a-private-debate-bursts-into-public-view.

61 Jay P. Greene and Frederick M. Hess, "America's Students Flounder While Education Reformers Virtue Signal," *National Review*, November 5, 2019, https://www.nationalreview.com/2019/11/school-reform-struggles-virtue-signaling-ignores-student-performance-stagnation/.

62 Jay P. Greene, PhD, and Jason Bedrick, "What's Behind the Recent Surge in School-Choice Victories," Heritage Foundation, February 7, 2023, https://www.heritage.org/education/commentary/whats-behind-the-recent-surge-school-choice-victories.

CHAPTER 5: A NEW HOPE FOR PARENTS IN WEST VIRGINIA

1 "podcastED: SUFS President Doug Tuthill Interviews West Virginia Sen. Patricia Rucker," ReimaginED, podcast, September 1, 2021, https://www.reimaginedonline.org/2021/09/podcasted-sufs-president-doug-tuthill-interviews-west-virginia-sen-patricia-rucker/.

2 See, for example, Corey A. DeAngelis and Christos A. Makridis, "School Isn't Closed for Lack of Money," Opinion, *Wall Street Journal*, March 9, 2021, https://www.wsj.com/articles/school-isnt-closed-for-lack-of-money-11615332385; Jason Bedrick and Corey A. DeAngelis, "Parents Know Better than Standardized Tests," Opinion, *Wall Street Journal*, August 28, 2019, https://www.wsj.com/articles/parents-know-better-than-standardized-tests-11567033335.

3 Andrew Prokop, "The Conservative Push for 'School Choice' Has Had Its Most Successful Year Ever," Vox, August 7, 2023, https://www.vox.com/politics/23689496/school-choice-education-savings-accounts-american-federation-children.

4 Rachel M. Cohen, "School Choice and Charter Proponents Target Public Education in Key States," *Capital & Main*, May 25, 2021, https://capitalandmain.com/school-choice-and-charter-proponents-target-public-education-in-key-states-0525.

5 Karolina Buczek, "Gov. Beshear Vetoes Two Controversial Education Bills," LEX 18 News (WLEX), March 24, 2021, https://www.lex18.com/news/covering-kentucky/gov-beshear-vetoes-two-controversial-education-bills.

6 Corey A. DeAngelis (@DeAngelisCorey), "Governor Beshear: 'I am a proud product of public education. A proud graduate of Kentucky's public schools. My commitment to public education runs deep,'" X (formerly known as Twitter), March 29, 2021, 5:01 p.m., https://twitter.com/DeAngelisCorey/status/1376640565203247106.

7 Jason Bedrick, "The Year of Educational Choice Is Here," Engage by EdChoice, May 25, 2021, https://www.edchoice.org/engage/the-year-of-educational-choice-is-here/.

8 Jay P. Greene and James D. Paul, "Does School Choice Need Bipartisan Support? An Empirical Analysis of the Legislative Record," American Enterprise Institute, September 22, 2021, https://www.aei.org/research-products/report/does-school-choice-need-bipartisan-support-an-empirical-analysis-of-the-legislative-record/.

9 Kris Maher, "West Virginia Teachers Go on Statewide Strike," *Wall Street Journal*, February 22, 2018, https://www.wsj.com/articles/west-virginia-teachers-go-on-statewide-strike-1519309185.

10 Ibid.

11 Gloria Guzman, "New Data Show Income Increased in 14 States and 10 of the Largest Metros," U.S. Census Bureau, September 26, 2019, https://www.census.gov/library/stories/2019/09/us-median-household-income-up-in-2018-from-2017.html.

12 Amir Vera, "Why Are West Virginia Teachers on Strike? Take a Look at Their Salaries," CNN, February 27, 2018, https://www.cnn.com/2018/02/27/health/west-virginia-teachers-salaries-trnd/index.html.

13 Ben Scafidi, "Priorities of State and Local Governments from 1994 to 2022: K–12 Public Schools Have Been the Major Employment Priority," EdChoice, August 2023, https://www.edchoice.org/wp-content/uploads/2023/08/08-23-Staffing-Surge-Priorities.pdf.

14 Editorial Board, "West Virginia Teachers Give a Lesson in Union Power," Opinion, *New York Times*, March 2, 2018, https://www.nytimes.com/2018/03/02/opinion/west-virginia-unions-teachers.html.

15 "AFT's Weingarten on Settlement of West Virginia Teachers' Strike," American Federation of Teachers, press release, February 28, 2018, https://www.aft.org/press-release/afts-weingarten-settlement-west-virginia-teachers-strike.

16 Scott Heins, "As West Virginia Strike Winds Down, Angry Teachers Look to Bolster Progressives in Elections," *Intercept*, March 7, 2018, https://theintercept.com/2018/03/07/west-virginia-teacher-strike-midterm-elections/.

17 Dave Mistich, "Outside Groups Spent Big in West Virginia in 2018, but Public Filings Don't Show the Full Picture," West Virginia Public Broadcasting, November 22, 2018, https://wvpublic.org/outside-groups-spent-big-in-west-virginia-in-2018-but-public-filings-dont-show-the-full-picture/.

18 "West Virginia House of Delegates Elections, 2018," Post-election analysis, Ballotpedia, https://ballotpedia.org/West_Virginia_House_of_Delegates_elections,_2018.

19 Daniel Davis, "Native Venezuelan, Now Proud American, Warns of 'Fruits of Socialism,'" *Daily Signal*, December 11, 2019, https://www.dailysignal.com/2019/12/11/native-venezuelan-now-proud-american-warns-of-fruits-of-socialism/.

20 Ibid.

21 Gerald Robinson, Cara Candal, and Patricia Puertas Rucker, "WV State Sen. Patricia Puertas Rucker on Universal School Choice," *The Learning Curve* no. 88, podcast, Ricochet, May 25, 2022, https://ricochet.com/podcast/the-learning-curve/wv-state-sen-patricia-puertas-rucker-on-universal-school-choice/.

22 Ibid.

23 Michael Erb, "Wood County AFT Gathers to Discuss Education Bill," *Parkersburg News and Sentinel*, February 5, 2019, https://www.newsandsentinel.com/news/local-news/2019/02/wood-county-aft-gathers-to-discuss-education-bill/.

24 There was also an ESA on the books in Nevada, but due to a lawsuit it never became operational. Eventually the state supreme court determined that everything about Nevada's ESA was constitutional, but that the legislature had funded it improperly. Before the legislature fixed the funding mechanism, the Democrats took over. The ESA policy languished on the books for several years, with zero dollars allocated and zero students served, before the Democrats repealed it altogether. "THE ABCs of SCHOOL CHOICE" (EdChoice, 2019), https://www.edchoice.org/wp-content/uploads/2019/01/The-ABCs-of-School-Choice-2019-Edition.pdf.

25 Jason Bedrick and Michael Q. McShane, "West Virginia and Kentucky Lead 2021's Educational Choice Wave," Opinion, *Newsweek*, April 20, 2021, https://www.newsweek.com/west-virginia-kentucky-lead-2021s-educational-choice-wave-opinion-1584795.

26 Associated Press, "West Virginia Teachers to Strike Again over Education Bill," *Guardian*, February 19, 2019, https://www.theguardian.com/us-news/2019/feb/19/west-virginia-teachers-strike-education-bill.

27 WTAP, WSAZ, and Associated Press, "Update: W.Va. Teacher Strike Officially Over," WTAP, January 30, 2019, https://www.wtap.com/content/news/West-Virginia-Senate-takes-up-education-bill-505086371.html.

28 Daniel Davis, "Native Venezuelan, Now Proud American, Warns of 'Fruits of Socialism,'" *Daily Signal*, December 11, 2019, https://www.dailysignal.com/2019/12/11/native-venezuelan-now-proud-american-warns-of-fruits-of-socialism/.

29 Brian Bergstrom, "School Employees Strike to Protest Bill That Could Strip Funding from Public Schools," *My Buckhannon*, February 19, 2019, https://www.mybuckhannon.com/teachers-strike-to-protest-bill-that-could-strip-funding-from-public-schools/.

30 "West Virginia Senate Passes Student Success Act on 18–15 Vote," *Wetzel Chronicle*, June 5, 2019, https://www.wetzelchronicle.com/news/local-headlines/2019/06/05/west-virginia-senate-passes-student-success-act-on-18-15-vote/.

31 "Authorized Charter Schools," West Virginia Professional Charter School Board, https://wvcharters.org/schools.

32 Matthew Umstead, "More than $300K Spent in West Virginia Senate Race," *Herald-Mail Media*, October 13, 2020, https://www.heraldmailmedia.com/story/news/local/2020/10/13/more-than-300k-spent-in-west-virginia-senate-race/115810928/.

33 Dave Mistich, "West Virginia Senate Passes Anti-Strike Bill, Teacher Unions Call It Retaliation," West Virginia Public Broadcasting, February 22, 2021, https://wvpublic.org/west-virginia-senate-passes-anti-strike-bill-teacher-unions-call-it-retaliation/.

34 Steven Allen Adams, "Education Reform Advocates Make Another Attempt at Education Savings Accounts," *Weirton Daily Times*, February 10, 2021, https://www.weirtondailytimes.com/news/local-news/2021/02/education-reform-advocates-make-another-attempt-at-education-savings-accounts/.

35 Ibid.; Jason Bedrick, "The Secret Ingredient Behind the Year of Educational Choice," American Enterprise Institute, December 6, 2021, https://www.aei.org/research-products/report/the-secret-ingredient-behind-the-year-of-educational-choice/.

36 Steven Allen Adams, "Education Reform Advocates Make Another Attempt at Education Savings Accounts," *Weirton Daily Times*, February 10, 2021, https://www.weirtondailytimes.com/news/local-news/2021/02/education-reform-advocates-make-another-attempt-at-education-savings-accounts/.

37 Jayme Metzgar, "Once Held Hostage by Teachers' Unions, West Virginia Just Passed the Nation's Broadest School Choice Law," *Federalist*, March 25, 2021, https://thefederalist.com/2021/03/25/once-held-hostage-by-teachers-unions-west-virginia-just-passed-sweeping-school-choice-legislation/.

38 Camille Walsh, "Case Study: How the Cardinal Institute Built Coalitions to Pass the Most Expansive School Choice Program in the Country," State Policy Network, August 4, 2021, https://spn.org/articles/case-study-cardinal-institute-school-choice/.

39 Jason Bedrick and Ed Tarnowski, "Who's Afraid of School Choice?: Examining the Validity and Intensity of Predictions by School Choice Opponents," EdChoice, December 2021, https://www.edchoice.org/wp-content/uploads/2021/11/Whos-Afraid-of-School-Choice-by-Jason-Bedrick-and-Ed-Tarnowski.pdf.

40 Ibid.

41 Ibid.

42 Liz McCormick, "Hope Scholarship Bill Nears End of Legislative Journey," West Virginia Public Broadcasting, March 18, 2021, https://wvpublic.org/hope-scholarship-bill-nears-end-of-legislative-journey/.

43 Steven Allen Adams, "Education Savings Account Bill Gets OK from West Virginia Senate," *Parkersburg News and Sentinel*, March 18, 2021, https://www.newsandsentinel.com/news/local-news/2021/03/education-savings-account-bill-gets-ok-from-west-virginia-senate/.

44 West Virginia Senate Republicans, "Sen. Patricia Rucker on Senate's Passage of HOPE Scholarship Bill: Sen. Patricia Rucker Talks About the Senate's Passage of the HOPE Scholarship Bill (HB 2013), Which Creates Education Savings Accounts That Will Provide…," Facebook, March 18, 2021, https://www.facebook.com/wvsenategop/videos/294802732082245/.

CHAPTER 6: RISE OF THE PARENTS' PARTY

1 John Clark, "McAuliffe: 'I Don't Think Parents Should Be Telling Schools What They Should Teach,'" MyStateline.com, Nexstar Media Group, September 29, 2021, https://www.mystateline.com/news/politics/mcauliffe-i-dont-think-parents-should-be-telling-schools-what-they-should-teach/.

2 Virginia Allen, "How Parents' Battle over Critical Race Theory Swung Virginia's Election for Youngkin," *Daily Signal*, December 9, 2021, https://www.dailysignal.com/2021/12/09/how-parents-battle-over-critical-race-theory-swung-virginias-election-for-youngkin/.

3 Colleen Grablick, "Loudoun County Schools Are At The Center Of Virginia's Elections," WAMU, American University Radio, October 26, 2021, https://wamu.org/story/21/10/26/loudoun-county-in-virginia-governors-race-culture-wars-2/; U.S. District Court, Eastern District of Virginia, *Patti Hildago Menders et al. v. Loudoun County School Board*, complaint, https://ljc-assets.s3.amazonaws.com/2021/06/2021-06-02-Menders-v-Loudoun-County-School-Board_Complaint.pdf.

4 Minyvonne Burke, "Pronoun Policy Debate Leads to Chaos at Virginia School Board Meeting," NBC News, June 23, 2021, https://www.nbcnews.com/feature/nbc-out/pronoun-policy-debate-leads-chaos-virginia-school-board-meeting-n1272134.

5 Drew Wilder, Jackie Bensen, and Andrea Swalec, "'The Meeting Has Degenerated': 1 Arrest, 1 Injury at Loudoun Schools Meeting on Equity," NBC4 Washington, June 22, 2021, https://www.nbcwashington.com/news/local/northern-virginia/loudoun-school-board-transgender-student-policy-race-equity/2708185/.

6 Ibid.

7 Ibid.

8 Minyvonne Burke, "Pronoun Policy Debate Leads to Chaos at Virginia School Board Meeting," NBC News, June 23, 2021, https://www.nbcnews.com/feature/nbc-out/pronoun-policy-debate-leads-chaos-virginia-school-board-meeting-n1272134.

9 Hannah Natanson and Tom Jackman, "Loudoun School Board Cuts Short Public Comment During Unruly Meeting; One Arrested," *Washington Post*, June 23, 2021, https://www.washingtonpost.com/local/education/loudoun-school-board-closes-meeting/2021/06/22/30493128-d3ad-11eb-9f29-e9e6c9e843c6_story.html.

10 Sudiksha Kochi, "Glenn Youngkin Pardons Father Arrested at School Board Meeting After His Daughter Was Sexually Assaulted," *USA Today*, September 11, 2023, https://www.usatoday.com/story/news/politics/2023/09/11/glenn-youngkin-pardon-scott-smith/70821236007/.

11 Viola M. Garcia, EdD, and Chip Slaven, Esq., "Re: Federal Assistance to Stop Threats and Acts of Violence Against Public Schoolchildren, Public School Board Members, and Other Public School District Officials and Educators," letter from the National School Boards Association to President Joseph R. Biden, National School Boards Association, September 29, 2021, Wayback Machine archived webpage, https://web.archive.org/web/20211001001553/https://nsba.org/-/media/NSBA/File/nsba-letter-to-president-biden-concerning-threats-to-public-schools-and-school-board-members-92921.pdf.

12 Luke Rosiak, "Loudoun County Schools Tried to Conceal Sexual Assault against Daughter in Bathroom, Father Says," Daily Wire, https://www.dailywire.com/news/loudoun-county-schools-tried-to-conceal-sexual-assault-against-daughter-in-bathroom-father-says.

13 "Report of the Special Grand Jury on the Investigation of Loudoun County Public Schools," Circuit Court of Loudoun County, December 2022.

14 Ibid., p. 3.

15 Luke Rosiak, "Loudoun County Schools Tried to Conceal Sexual Assault Against Daughter in Bathroom, Father Says," Daily Wire, https://www.dailywire.com/news/loudoun-county-schools-tried-to-conceal-sexual-assault-against-daughter-in-bathroom-father-says.

16 "Report of the Special Grand Jury on the Investigation of Loudoun County Public Schools," Circuit Court of Loudoun County, December 2022, p. 8.

17 Luke Rosiak, "Loudoun County Schools Tried to Conceal Sexual Assault Against Daughter in Bathroom, Father Says," Daily Wire, https://www.dailywire.com/news/loudoun-county-schools-tried-to-conceal-sexual-assault-against-daughter-in-bathroom-father-says.

18 Caitlynn Peetz, "How a Virginia District 'Failed at Every Juncture' to Prevent Sexual Assault," School Climate & Safety, *Education Week*, December 9, 2022, https://www.edweek.org/leadership/how-a-virginia-district-failed-at-every-juncture-to-prevent-sexual-assault/2022/12; Lee Brown, "Teen Sentenced for Sex Attacks That Sparked Political Firestorm in Loudoun County," *New York Post*, January 13, 2022, https://nypost.com/2022/01/13/teen-sentenced-for-sex-attacks-that-sparked-loudoun-county-protests/.

19 Luke Rosiak, "Loudoun County Schools Tried to Conceal Sexual Assault Against Daughter in Bathroom, Father Says," Daily Wire, https://www.dailywire.com/news/loudoun-county-schools-tried-to-conceal-sexual-assault-against-daughter-in-bathroom-father-says.

20 Caitlynn Peetz, "How a Virginia District 'Failed at Every Juncture' to Prevent Sexual Assault," School Climate & Safety, *Education Week*, December 9, 2022, https://www.edweek.org/leadership/how-a-virginia-district-failed-at-every-juncture-to-prevent-sexual-assault/2022/12; "Report of the Special Grand Jury on the Investigation of Loudoun County Public Schools," Circuit Court of Loudoun County, December 2022.

21 Times-Mirror Staff, "Updated: Beth Barts Resigns from Loudoun County School Board," *Loudoun Times-Mirror*, October 15, 2021, https://www.loudountimes.com/news/updated-beth-barts-resigns-from-loudoun-county-school-board/article_c689594a-2de6-11ec-a4f3-4f2185b5c58a.html.

22 Matthew Torres, "Loudoun County School Board Member Steps Down amid Scrutiny from Parents, Community Groups," WUSA 9, October 15, 2021, https://www.wusa9.com/article/news/local/virginia/lcps-board-member-resigns-amid-scrutiny-from-parents-and-community-groups/65-ba6d1ade-ae5c-4511-b5f4-4fd580fd3122.

23 Tyler Kingkade, "In Wealthy Loudoun County, Parents Face Threats in Battle over Equity in Schools," NBC News, June 1, 2021, https://www.nbcnews.com/news/us-news/wealthy-loudoun-county-virginia-parents-face-threats-battle-over-equity-n1269162.

24 Luke Rosiak, "Loudoun County Schools Tried to Conceal Sexual Assault Against Daughter in Bathroom, Father Says," Daily Wire, https://www.dailywire.com/news/loudoun-county-schools-tried-to-conceal-sexual-assault-against-daughter-in-bathroom-father-says.

25 Times-Mirror Staff, "Updated: Beth Barts Resigns from Loudoun County School Board," *Loudoun Times-Mirror*, October 15, 2021, https://www.loudountimes.com/news/updated-beth-barts-resigns-from-loudoun-county-school-board/article_c689594a-2de6-11ec-a4f3-4f2185b5c58a.html.

26 Ibid.

27 "Report of the Special Grand Jury on the Investigation of Loudoun County Public Schools," Circuit Court of Loudoun County, December 2022, https://www.loudoun.gov/SpecialGrandJury.

28 Tavleen Tarrant, "A Virginia Superintendent Is Fired After a State Report into Handling of Sexual Assaults at School Is Issued," CNN, December 8, 2022, https://amp.cnn.com/cnn/2022/12/08/us/virginia-school-superintendent-fired-report-sexual-assaults/index.html.

29 "Report of the Special Grand Jury on the Investigation of Loudoun County Public Schools," Circuit Court of Loudoun County, December 2022, https://www.loudoun.gov/SpecialGrandJury, p. 3.

30 "GOP Gains in Governor's Race," Monmouth University, Polling Institute, October 20, 2021, https://www.monmouth.edu/polling-institute/reports/monmouthpoll_va_102021/.

31 Joshua Jamerson and Aaron Zitner, "Critical Race Theory Becomes Key to GOP Campaign Strategy in Virginia," Politics, *Wall Street Journal*, July 26, 2021, https://www.wsj.com/articles/virginia-campaign-will-test-whether-critical-race-theory-moves-voters-11627304401.

32 Matthew Continetti, "The Politics of Parental Revolt," *National Review*, October 16, 2021, https://www.nationalreview.com/2021/10/the-politics-of-parental-revolt/.

33 Kabir Khanna et al., "CBS News Poll: Vaccine and Economy Fights Driving Tight Virginia Governor's Race," CBS News, October 13, 2021, https://www.cbsnews.com/news/virginia-governor-race-vaccine-economy-opinion-poll/.

34 John Clark, "McAuliffe: 'I Don't Think Parents Should Be Telling Schools What They Should Teach,'" MyStateline.com, Nexstar Media Group, September 29, 2021, https://www.mystateline.com/news/politics/mcauliffe-i-dont-think-parents-should-be-telling-schools-what-they-should-teach/.

35 Ian Schwartz, "VA Gov. Candidate McAuliffe: 'I Don't Think Parents Should Be Telling Schools What They Should Teach,'" RealClearPolitics, September 28, 2021, https://www.realclearpolitics.com/video/2021/09/28/va_gov_candidate_mcauliffe_i_dont_think_parents_should_be_telling_schools_what_they_should_teach.html.

36 Glenn Youngkin (@GlennYoungkin), "Glenn Youngkin: 'I believe parents should be in charge of their kids' education,'" X (formerly known as Twitter), September 28, 2021, 9:13 p.m., https://twitter.com/GlennYoungkin/status/1443021016838647818.

37 Charlie McCarthy, "Trafalgar Poll: Virginia Race in Dead Heat with Youngkin Edge," Newsmax, October 15, 2021, https://www.newsmax.com/us/virginia-governor-election-youngkin/2021/10/15/id/1040646/; "Virginia Governor

General Election Survey," The Trafalgar Group, October 2021, https://drive.google.com/file/d/1gbDpNxQzRPhP4QbgfClwGvcP-ZdboNt0/view.

38 "GOP Gains in Governor's Race," Monmouth University, Polling Institute, October 20, 2021, https://www.monmouth.edu/polling-institute/reports/monmouthpoll_va_102021/.

39 Victoria Balara, "Fox News Poll: Schools, Economy Driving Close Virginia Governor's Race," Fox News, October 14, 2021, https://www.foxnews.com/official-polls/schools-economy-driving-close-virginia-governors-race.

40 Charles Creitz, "Terry McAuliffe's Comment 'Not to Let Parents' Choose Curriculum Was His 'Deplorables' Moment: McDowell," Fox News, September 29, 2021, https://www.foxnews.com/media/terry-mcauliffe-not-let-parents-choose-curriculum-deplorables.

41 Brandon Jarvis (@Jaaavis), "'That's why I want you to hear this from me, Glenn Youngkin is taking my words out of context,' @TerryMcAuliffe says in a new ad," X (formerly known as Twitter), October 18, 2021, 4:37 p.m., https://twitter.com/Jaaavis/status/1450199344863399939.

42 Chris Cillizza (@chriscillizza), "This strategic decision suggests the Youngkin ads on education are hurting Terry," X (formerly known as Twitter), October 18, 2021, 5:59 p.m., Wayback Machine archived webpage, https://web.archive.org/web/20211019005930/https://twitter.com/ChrisCillizza/status/1450265267876007938.

43 Glenn Youngkin, "7 Times Terry McAuliffe Confirmed He Thinks Parents Should Have No Say in Their Child's Education," YouTube, video, October 18, 2021, https://www.youtube.com/watch?v=gfSQOPm_qmg.

44 Terry Jeffrey, "Terry McAuliffe Did Not Go to Government Schools," Townhall, October 6, 2021, https://townhall.com/columnists/terryjeffrey/2021/10/06/terry-mcauliffe-did-not-go-to-government-schools-n2597010; Jim Geraghty, "Another Anti-Voucher Democrat, with Kids in the Best Private School," *National Review*, April 26, 2013, https://www.nationalreview.com/the-campaign-spot/another-anti-voucher-democrat-kids-best-private-school-jim-geraghty/.

45 Louis Llovio, "McAuliffe Vetoes Three Education Bills, Including School-Choice Legislation," *Richmond Times-Dispatch*, April 5, 2016, https://richmond.com/news/local/mcauliffe-vetos-three-education-bills-including-school-choice-legislation/article_18c4ab60-2bf0-51c6-a654-5d2a93d3e1a4.html; Elizabeth Tyree, "Gov. McAuliffe Vetoes Six Pieces of Legislation Concerning Public Schools," WSET ABC13 News, March 23, 2017, https://wset.com/news/at-the-capitol/gov-mcauliffe-vetoes-six-pieces-of-legislation-concerning-public-schools.

46 Corey A. DeAngelis (@DeAngelisCorey), "Terry McAuliffe on school choice: 'I will never allow that as governor.' He exclusively attended private schools and sent

his kids to private schools," X (formerly known as Twitter), October 14, 2021, 12:48 p.m., https://twitter.com/DeAngelisCorey/status/1448692213718867972; Corey A. DeAngelis, "Democrats' Teachable Moment," Cato Institute, October 15, 2021, https://www.cato.org/commentary/democrats-teachable-moment.

47 Houston Keene, "Biden to Campaign for McAuliffe, Who Received $650K from Teachers' Unions Promoting Critical Race Theory," Fox News, July 23, 2021, https://www.foxnews.com/politics/biden-mcauliffe-campaign-northern-virginia-critical-race-theory-teachers-unions; "Terry McAuliffe: Top Donors," The Virginia Public Access Project, https://www.vpap.org/candidates/11897/top_donors/.

48 "Terry McAuliffe: Donors by Occupation: Labor—Public Employees," The Virginia Public Access Project, https://www.vpap.org/candidates/11897/donors_per_industry/146?start_year=all&end_year=all&contrib_type=all.

49 Julia Manchester, "Top Teachers Union Rolls Out Ad in Support of McAuliffe in Virginia," *Hill*, October 17, 2021, https://thehill.com/homenews/campaign/577122-top-teachers-union-rolls-out-ad-in-support-of-mcauliffe-in-virginia; Joshua Rhett Miller, "Critics Blast Randi Weingarten–Terry McAuliffe Rally," *New York Post*, November 2, 2021, https://nypost.com/2021/11/02/critics-blast-randi-weingarten-terry-mcauliffe-rally/.

50 "New Poll: Voters Overwhelmingly Reject Elected Officials Who Are School Choice Hypocrites," American Federation for Children, press release, June 28, 2022, https://www.federationforchildren.org/new-poll-voters-overwhelmingly-reject-elected-officials-who-are-school-choice-hypocrites/; David N. Bass, "Poll: Voters Reject Hypocritical Politicians on School Choice," *Carolina Journal*, October 4, 2021, https://www.carolinajournal.com/news-article/poll-voters-reject-hypocritical-politicians-on-school-choice/.

51 James Gordon, "Virginia Democratic Candidate Terry McAuliffe Is Slammed for Hypocrisy After Praising Virginia's Public Schools—Despite Privately Educating Four of His Kids: Governor's Race Goes to the Wire," Daily Mail.com, November 1, 2021, https://www.dailymail.co.uk/news/article-10151011/Terry-McAuliffe-slammed-hypocrisy-praising-Virginias-public-schools-four-kids-private.html; Ronn Blitzer, "McAuliffe References Raising 5 Children in Virginia in Touting Public Schools—4 Went to Private," Fox News, October 31, 2021, https://www.foxnews.com/politics/mcauliffe-references-raising-5-children-in-virginia-in-touting-public-schools-4-went-to-private.

52 "*Meet the Press*—October 31, 2021," NBC News, transcript, October 31, 2021, https://www.nbcnews.com/meet-the-press/news/meet-press-october-31-2021-n1282808.

53 Scott Clement, Emily Guskin, and Madison Dong, "Exit Poll Results from the 2021 Election for Virginia Governor," *Washington Post*, November 3, 2021, https://www.washingtonpost.com/elections/interactive/2021/exit-polls-virginia-governor/.

54 "Virginia Governor's Race," Echelon Insights, 2021 election data, https://echeloninsights.com/in-the-news/vagov/; Brent Buchanan, "Cygnal Poll: Youngkin Tied; Generic Republican +1," Cygnal, October 24, 2021, http://www.cygn.al/cygnal-poll-youngkin-tied/.

55 Fox News Staff, "Hilton Rips Dems, Media for Blaming VA Election Loss on 'Racism': 'They're Doubling Down on Hate and Division,'" Fox News, November 8, 2021, https://www.foxnews.com/media/hilton-rips-dems-for-blaming-va-election-loss-on-racism-theyre-doubling-down-on-hate-and-division; The Editorial Board, "The Big 'Racist' Fail in Virginia," Opinion, *Wall Street Journal*, November 3, 2021, https://www.wsj.com/articles/virginia-governor-election-glenn-youngkin-race-11635979212.

56 Brandon Gillespie, "CNN Reporter Repeats Questionable Claim That Critical Race Theory Is Not Being Taught in Virginia Schools," Fox News, November 3, 2021, https://www.foxnews.com/media/cnn-eva-mckend-claims-critical-race-theory-not-taught-virginia-schools.

57 Brandon Gillespie, "Rick Scott Clashes with CNN over the Teaching of Critical Race Theory: 'Parents Aren't Dumb,'" Fox News, November 8, 2021, https://www.foxnews.com/media/rick-scott-clashes-cnn-teaching-critical-race-theory-parents.

58 Brenda L. Townsend Walker, PhD, JD, "Legal Implications of School Discipline: 'CRED' (Culturally-Responsive and Equitable Discipline)," Commonwealth of Virginia, Department of Education, September 22, 2015, Wayback Machine archived webpage, https://web.archive.org/web/20161002014407/www.doe.virginia.gov/support/virginia_tiered_system_supports/resources/2015_fall_institute/Legal_implications_of_discipline.pdf; Andrew Mark Miller, "Virginia Dept. of Education Website Promotes CRT Despite McAuliffe Claims It's 'Never Been Taught' There," Fox News, October 30, 2021, https://www.foxnews.com/politics/virginia-dept-of-education-website-promotes-crt-despite-mcauliffe-claims-its-never-been-taught-there.

59 "American Views 2022: Part 2 Trust Media and Democracy," Knight Foundation, February 15, 2023, https://knightfoundation.org/reports/american-views-2023-part-2/.

60 Education Freedom Pledge, accessed September 28, 2023, https://www.edfreedompledge.com/.

CHAPTER 7: THE KIDS GET THEIR OWN UNION

1 Kiera Butler, "The Most Powerful Moms in America Are the New Face of the Republican Party," *Mother Jones*, August 22, 2022, https://www.motherjones.com/politics/2022/08/the-most-powerful-moms-in-america-are-the-new-face-of-the-republican-party/.

2 Jonathan Butcher and Jason Bedrick, "Schooling Satisfaction: Arizona Parents' Opinions on Using Education Savings Accounts," EdChoice, October 2013, https://www.edchoice.org/wp-content/uploads/2013/10/SCHOOLING-SATISFACTION-Arizona-Parents-Opinions-on-Using-Education-Savings-Accounts-NEW.pdf.

3 Doug Ducey (@dougducey), "When parents have more choices, kids win. Looking forward to signing #SB1431 tonight. #AZboundless," X (formerly known as Twitter), April 6, 2017, 9:48 p.m., https://twitter.com/DougDucey/status/850163418615095296.

4 E. J. Montini, "Montini: More Bad News for School Voucher Scammers," Opinion, *Arizona Republic*, February 15, 2017, https://www.azcentral.com/story/opinion/op-ed/ej-montini/2017/02/15/montini-school-choice-vouchers-arizona-legislature/97934204/.

5 Yvonne Wingett Sanchez and Rob O'Dell, "Delivery of 111K Signatures Puts Arizona School-Voucher Expansion on Hold," *Arizona Republic*, August 8, 2017, https://www.azcentral.com/story/news/politics/arizona-education/2017/08/08/arizona-school-voucher-expansion-law-signatures-ballot/547143001/.

6 "Arizona Proposition 305, Expansion of Empowerment Scholarship Accounts Referendum (2018)," Ballotpedia, https://ballotpedia.org/Arizona_Proposition_305,_Expansion_of_Empowerment_Scholarship_Accounts_Referendum_(2018).

7 Associated Press, "Arizona Proposition 305 Fails, Blocking Expansion of School Vouchers for Families," ABC15 Arizona (KNXV), November 7, 2018, https://www.abc15.com/news/state/arizona-proposition-305-fails-reducing-school-vouchers-available-to-families.

8 Jenny Clark to Corey A. DeAngelis, email, September 12, 2023.

9 Loretta Hunnicutt, "Military Family Denied ESA by Arizona Department of Education," Arizona Daily Independent, July 1, 2019, https://arizonadailyindependent.com/2019/06/30/military-family-denied-esa-by-arizona-department-of-education/.

10 Dillon Rosenblatt, "Bill Allows 10 Navajo Nation Students to Use Arizona Vouchers across State Lines | Arizona Capitol Times," *Arizona Capitol Times*, May 22, 2019, https://azcapitoltimes.com/news/2019/05/21/bill-allows-10-navajo-nation-students-to-use-arizona-vouchers-across-state-lines/.

11 Robert Enlow, Jason Bedrick, and Lauren Hodge, "Ep. 159: The Monthly Debrief—January Looking to February 2020," podcast, EdChoice, February 12, 2020.

12 Jason Bedrick and Matt Beienburg, "Fact: ESAs Help Native American Families," *In Defense of Liberty Blog*, Goldwater Institute, February 27, 2020, https://www.goldwaterinstitute.org/fact-esas-help-native-american-families/.

13 Ibid.

14 Ibid.

15 Laurie Roberts, "A Voter Drive to Block Arizona's Leaders from Expanding School Vouchers (Again)? Yes, Please," Opinion, *Arizona Republic*, February 26, 2020, https://www.azcentral.com/story/opinion/op-ed/laurieroberts/2020/02/26/save-our-schools-act-block-arizona-school-vouchers-again/4881213002/.

16 "Arizona Limits on Private Education Vouchers Initiative (2020)," Ballotpedia, https://ballotpedia.org/Arizona_Limits_on_Private_Education_Vouchers_Initiative_(2020).

17 "Residents of Arizona Think Education Is Headed . . . ," EdChoice, April 21, 2021, Wayback Machine archived webpage, https://web.archive.org/web/20210422000532/https://edchoice.morningconsultintelligence.com/reports/arizona.pdf.

18 Matthew Ladner, "The State That Created the Most New Schools Is Also the One Where Students Learned More than Anywhere Else," *Education Next*, October 5, 2021, https://www.educationnext.org/state-that-created-the-most-new-schools-is-also-the-one-where-students-learned-more-than-anywhere-else-arizona/.

19 Rob O'Dell, "Arizona Senate Passes Huge School Voucher Expansion, 2 Years After Voters Said No," *Arizona Republic*, February 15, 2021, https://www.azcentral.com/story/news/politics/arizona-education/2021/02/15/arizona-senate-passes-sb-1452-huge-expansion-school-vouchers/6757482002/.

20 Ibid.

21 "Arizona School Choice Hypocrisy Map," Education Freedom Institute, February 5, 2020, https://www.efinstitute.org/maps/school-choice-hypocrisy-map/arizona/.

22 Rob O'Dell, "Arizona Senate Passes Huge School Voucher Expansion, 2 Years after Voters Said No," The Arizona Republic, February 15, 2021, https://www.azcentral.com/story/news/politics/arizona-education/2021/02/15/arizona-senate-passes-sb-1452-huge-expansion-school-vouchers/6757482002/.

23 Mary Jo Pitzl and Andrew Oxford, "With Contentious Voucher Vote, Legislature Ends Its Annual Session as Ducey Signs $13B Budget," *Arizona Republic*, June 30, 2021, https://www.azcentral.com/story/news/politics/legislature/2021/06/30/arizona-budget-legislature-adjourns-sine-die-after-long-session/7818496002/.

24 "Arizona School Choice Hypocrisy Map," Education Freedom Institute, February 5, 2020, https://www.efinstitute.org/maps/school-choice-hypocrisy-map/arizona/.

25 Loretta Hunnicutt, "Udall, John, Osborne Find New Way to Make School Choice Less Desirable for Many Families," *Arizona Daily Independent*, February 6, 2022, https://arizonadailyindependent.com/2022/02/06/udall-john-osborne-find-new-way-to-make-school-choice-less-desirable-for-many-families/.

26 Corey DeAngelis and Jason Bedrick, "School Choice Teaches Iowa Republicans a Big Lesson," Opinion, Fox News, June 16, 2022, https://www.foxnews.com/opinion/school-choice-teaches-iowa-republicans-lesson.

27 Ian Richardson, "Iowa Poll: Opposition Increases to Kim Reynolds' Proposal for Private School Scholarships," *Des Moines Register*, March 11, 2022, https://www.desmoinesregister.com/story/news/politics/iowa-poll/2022/03/11/iowa-poll-school-choice-taxpayer-private-scholarship-majority-iowans-oppose-bill-kim-reynolds/9431516002/; Corey DeAngelis and Jason Bedrick, "School Choice Teaches Iowa Republicans a Big Lesson," Opinion, Fox News, June 16, 2022, https://www.foxnews.com/opinion/school-choice-teaches-iowa-republicans-lesson.

28 "Reynolds Meets with Parents After School Board Passes Transgender Policy," KCCI Des Moines, Hearst Television, May 5, 2022, https://www.kcci.com/article/iowa-governor-kim-meets-with-marion-parents-after-school-board-passes-transgender-policy/39910146.

29 Jason Bedrick, "The Big School Choice Turnaround in Iowa That More States Should Follow," Opinion, Fox News, February 15, 2023, https://www.foxnews.com/opinion/big-school-choice-turnaround-iowa-more-states-should-follow.

30 Ibid.

31 "2022 Iowa State House—District 88 Republican Primary Results," *Des Moines Register*, June 7, 2022, https://www.desmoinesregister.com/elections/results/race/2022-06-07-state_house-R-IA-16647/.

32 Elijah Helton, "GOP Primary Hopefuls Debate in Gaza," *N'West Iowa Review*, May 8, 2022, https://www.nwestiowa.com/news/gop-primary-hopefuls-debate-in-gaza/article_6f84d25c-ceac-11ec-802e-17a6ce349faf.html.

33 "2022 Iowa State House—District 5 Republican Primary Results," *Des Moines Register*, June 7, 2022, https://www.desmoinesregister.com/elections/results/race/2022-06-07-state_house-R-IA-16496/.

34 Benjamin Toma, "Arizona School Choice Law Sets New Standard for Nation," Opinion, Fox News, July 6, 2022, https://www.foxnews.com/opinion/arizona-school-choice-law-standard-nation.

35 Yana Kunichoff, "Ducey Signs Universal School Vouchers into Law; Public Education Advocates Launch Referendum," *Arizona Republic*, July 7, 2022, https://www.azcentral.com/story/news/politics/arizona-education/2022/07/07/ariz-governor-signs-universal-school-voucher-law-advocates-vow-fight/7827019001/.

36 Jason Bedrick, "Arizona Parents Show How to Beat the Teachers' Unions," Heritage Foundation, October 7, 2022, https://www.heritage.org/education/commentary/arizona-parents-show-how-beat-the-teachers-unions.

37 Jason Bedrick, "School Choice Opponents Concede Defeat Just Days After Declaring Victory," *Daily Signal*, September 28, 2022, https://www.dailysignal

.com/2022/09/28/school-choice-opponents-concede-defeat-just-days-after-declaring-victory/.

38 Ibid.

39 Kathryn Joyce, "Arizona's School Privatization Battle Heats Up: Will the Voters Get to Decide?," Salon, September 20, 2022, https://www.salon.com/2022/09/20/arizonas-school-privatization-battle-heats-up-will-the-get-to-decide/.

40 Jason Bedrick, "Apparent Victory Rings Hollow for Group Opposing School Choice," *Daily Signal*, September 23, 2022, https://www.dailysignal.com/2022/09/23/apparent-victory-rings-hollow-for-group-opposing-school-choice/.

41 "Vouchers Hurt," Save Our Schools Arizona, https://sosarizona.org/vouchers-hurt/; "2023 Legislative Policy Priorities," Save Our Schools Arizona, May 2023, https://sosarizona.org/wp-content/uploads/2023/05/2023-Legislative-Policy-Priorities.pdf.

42 "Vouchers Hurt," Save Our Schools Arizona, Wayback Machine archived webpage from 2018, https://web.archive.org/web/20180309155730/https://sosarizona.org/vouchers-hurt/.

43 Save Our Schools AZ (@arizona_sos), "SOSAZ has always supported ESA vouchers for students with special needs, . . . " X (formerly known as Twitter), February 28, 2023, 7:12 p.m., https://x.com/arizona_sos/status/1630722584764461057.

44 Caitlin Sievers, Arizona Mirror September 24, and 2022, "Universal School Voucher Foes Turn in Signatures to Force a Public Vote in 2024," Arizona Mirror, September 24, 2022, https://www.azmirror.com/2022/09/24/universal-school-voucher-foes-turn-in-signatures-to-force-a-public-vote-in-2024/.

45 Corey DeAngelis, "Arizona School-Choice Opponents Admit Defeat," Opinion, *Wall Street Journal*, September 28, 2022, https://www.wsj.com/articles/school-choice-opponents-admit-defeat-in-arizona-katie-hobbs-signatures-vote-referendum-ducey-ballot-11664373189.

46 Jeremy Duda, "Parents Quick to Seek Universal ESAs, but They May Need a Backup Plan," *Axios Phoenix*, August 31, 2022, https://www.axios.com/local/phoenix/2022/08/31/parents-seek-universal-esa-potential-backup-plan.

47 John Brown, "Arizona Families Flocked to 'Universal' Voucher Program," *Tucson Sentinel*, December 6, 2022, https://www.tucsonsentinel.com/local/report/120622_voucher_rush/arizona-families-flocked-universal-voucher-program/.

48 Elenee Dao, "As ESA Expands, More Private Schools Pop Up Across Arizona," ABC15 Arizona (KNXV), August 1, 2023, https://www.abc15.com/news/local-news/as-esa-expands-more-private-schools-pop-up-across-arizona.

49 Raina Raskin, "GOP Voters in Arizona Punish Candidates Who Fell Out of Line on School Choice," *New York Sun*, August 3, 2022, https://www.nysun.com/article/gop-voters-in-arizona-punish-candidates-who-fell-out-of-line-on-school-choice.

50 "Joel John," Ballotpedia, 2022 data, https://ballotpedia.org/Joel_John; "Joanna Osborne," Ballotpedia, 2022 data, https://ballotpedia.org/Joanne_Osborne; "Michelle Udall," Ballotpedia, 2022 data, https://ballotpedia.org/Michelle_Udall.

51 "Texas Election Night Results," Texas Secretary of State, 2019, https://results.texas-election.com/races.

52 Pat McFerron, "Support for School Choice Continues to Increase | Cole Hargrave Snodgrass & Associates," *Sooner Survey* 34, no. 1 (March 1, 2022), https://chs-inc.com/sooner-survey-support-for-school-choice/.

53 "2022 Texas State House—District 85 Republican Primary Results," *Indy Star*, May 25, 2022, https://www.indystar.com/elections/results/race/2022-05-24-state_house-R-TX-49933/; "First Round of Endorsements for March 2022 Primaries," Texas American Federation of Teachers, January 13, 2022, Wayback Machine archived webpage, https://web.archive.org/web/20220419123600/https://www.texasaft.org/uncategorized/first-round-of-endorsements-for-march-2022-primaries/; "Texas House of Representatives District 85: 2022 Election Season," Republican Party Primary Runoff Election data, Transparency USA, Wayback Machine archived webpage, https://web.archive.org/web/20220603125611/https://www.transparencyusa.org/tx/race/texas-house-of-representatives-district-85.

54 Corey DeAngelis and Jason Bedrick, "Parents Wanted School Choice—and They Voted," *National Review*, June 2, 2022, https://www.nationalreview.com/2022/06/parents-wanted-school-choice-and-they-voted/.

55 "School Choice Supporters Advance in Texas Races," American Federation for Children, May 25, 2022, https://www.federationforchildren.org/school-choice-supporters-advance-in-texas-races/.

56 Patrick Svitek, "Republican Texas House Races Become High-Dollar Affairs as Tuesday's Primary Runoff Nears," *Texas Tribune*, May 19, 2022, https://www.texastribune.org/2022/05/19/texas-house-republican-runoffs/.

57 Niki Griswold, "Abbott, Cruz Split Endorsements in 3 Central Texas House Districts' GOP Runoff Races," *Austin American-Statesman*, May 16, 2022, https://www.statesman.com/story/news/2022/05/16/three-central-texas-house-districts-split-endorsements-gop-runoffs-abbott-cruz-republican-gop/9560421002/.

58 Corey A. DeAngelis (@DeAngelisCorey), "this fake Republican deleted his tweet saying he's a 'hard pass' on school choice and then blocked me.," X (formerly known as Twitter), February 4, 2022, 9:09 p.m., https://twitter.com/DeAngelisCorey/status/1489783227497816073.

59 Corey A. DeAngelis (@DeAngelisCorey), "Oklahoma Senator Jake Merrick (R) signed a pledge to support funding students instead of systems. He just voted against a school choice bill last week.," X (formerly known as Twitter), March 28, 2022, 10:32 a.m., https://twitter.com/DeAngelisCorey/status/1508452053961617410.

60 Corey A. DeAngelis (@DeAngelisCorey), "Oklahoma State Superintendent Republican Primary Election Results:," X (formerly known as Twitter), August 23, 2022, 10:36 p.m., https://twitter.com/DeAngelisCorey/status/1562267514897371136.

61 "Steve Rawlings—10 Report(s) Filed for the Position of State Representative 66th District," Kentucky Registry of Election Finance, https://secure.kentucky.gov/kref/publicsearch/CandidateSearch/CandidateReports/143618; "2022 Kentucky State House—District 66 Republican Primary Results," *Milwaukee Journal Sentinel*, May 18, 2022, https://www.jsonline.com/elections/results/race/2022-05-17-state_house-R-KY-18228/.

62 "School Choice Supporters Advance in Arkansas Primary," American Federation for Children, May 25, 2022, https://www.federationforchildren.org/school-choice-supporters-advance-in-arkansas-primary/; "School Choice Supporters Advance in Georgia Primaries," American Federation for Children, May 25, 2022, https://www.federationforchildren.org/school-choice-supporters-advance-in-georgia-primaries/; "School Choice Supporters Advance in Idaho Races," American Federation for Children, May 18, 2022, https://www.federationforchildren.org/school-choice-supporters-advance-in-idaho-races/; "School Choice Supporters Advance in Nebraska Legislative Races," American Federation for Children, May 11, 2022, https://www.federationforchildren.org/school-choice-supporters-advance-in-nebraska-legislative-races/; "School Choice Supporters Advance in Texas Races," American Federation for Children, May 25, 2022, https://www.federationforchildren.org/school-choice-supporters-advance-in-texas-races/.

63 Hart Research Associates, "AFT Education Survey," May 2022, https://s3.documentcloud.org/documents/22086577/education-poll.pdf.

64 Corey DeAngelis, "Ill Democratic Omens in Education Polls," Opinion, *Wall Street Journal*, July 22, 2022, https://www.wsj.com/articles/ill-democratic-omens-in-education-polls-teachers-union-randi-weingarten-gop-trust-parents-schools-aft-11658521717.

65 "House Battleground Poll," Democrats for Education Reform, July 2022, http://dfer.org/wp-content/uploads/2022/07/Baseline-Nationwide-BG-Education-Summer-2022-.pdf.

66 "New Polling: Reclaiming Education as Democratic Stronghold," memo, Education Reform Now Advocacy, Democrats for Education Reform, July 13, 2022, http://dfer.org/wp-content/uploads/2022/07/Polling-Memo-FINAL.pdf.

67 RJ Reinhart, "Americans Say Both Parties Have Core Issue Strengths," Gallup, June 26, 2017, https://news.gallup.com/poll/212795/americans-say-parties-core-issue-strengths.aspx.

68 "The 2022 Midterms & Biden's Job Performance, April 2022," Marist Poll, Marist Institute for Public Opinion, April 29, 2022, https://maristpoll.marist.edu/polls/npr-pbs-newshour-marist-national-poll-the-2022-midterm-elections-bidens-job-performance-april-2022/.

69 Kiera Butler, "The Most Powerful Moms in America Are the New Face of the Republican Party," *Mother Jones*, August 22, 2022, https://www.motherjones.com/politics/2022/08/the-most-powerful-moms-in-america-are-the-new-face-of-the-republican-party/.

70 Ibid.

71 Jessica Winter, "How 'Education Freedom' Played in the Midterms," *New Yorker*, November 9, 2022, https://www.newyorker.com/news/daily-comment/how-education-freedom-played-in-the-midterms.

72 Corey DeAngelis, "The School-Choice Election Wave," Opinion, *Wall Street Journal*, November 10, 2022, https://www.wsj.com/articles/the-school-choice-wave-midterm-2022-florida-desantis-education-freedom-parents-teachers-unions-illinois-pennsylvania-11668090033.

73 Ali Swenson, "Moms for Liberty's Focus on School Races Nationwide Sets Up Political Clash with Teachers Unions," Associated Press, July 2, 2023, https://apnews.com/article/moms-for-liberty-school-board-races-2024-5311cc11cd657a04e233216ac783d8f3.

74 "West Virginia State Senate Elections," Ballotpedia, 2022 data, https://ballotpedia.org/West_Virginia_State_Senate_elections; "West Virginia House of Delegates Elections, 2022," Ballotpedia, https://ballotpedia.org/West_Virginia_House_of_Delegates_elections,_2022.

75 "Iowa State Senate Elections, 2022," Ballotpedia, https://ballotpedia.org/Iowa_State_Senate_elections,_2022; "Iowa House of Representatives Elections, 2022," Ballotpedia, https://ballotpedia.org/Iowa_House_of_Representatives_elections,_2022.

76 "Florida State Senate Elections, 2022," Ballotpedia, https://ballotpedia.org/Florida_State_Senate_elections,_2022; "Florida House of Representatives Elections, 2022," Ballotpedia, https://ballotpedia.org/Florida_House_of_Representatives_elections,_2022.

77 Ben Felder, "Defeat of School Voucher Bill Sets Up Campaign Debates in Governor, Superintendent Races," *Oklahoman*, April 4, 2022, https://www.oklahoman.com/story/news/2022/04/04/private-school-vouchers-bill-key-issue-race-between-stitt-hofmeister-governor-superintendent-debate/7197022001/.

78 Andrea Eger, "Hofmeister Already on the Job," *Tulsa World*, November 10, 2014, https://tulsaworld.com/hofmeister-already-on-the-job/article_f1f28560-9655-522f-b796-cd6ad9d7871e.html; Corey A. DeAngelis (@DeAngelisCorey), "BREAKING: Oklahoma Democratic gubernatorial candidate Joy Hoffmeister opposes private school choice. She went to a private school," X (formerly known as Twitter), October 26, 2022, 10:54 p.m., https://twitter.com/DeAngelisCorey/status/1585464908224860162.

79 Ryan Walters (@ryanmwalters), "We are going to do more than any other state in the country to empower parents," X (formerly known as Twitter), November 11, 2022, 12:54 p.m., https://twitter.com/ryanmwalters/status/1591127197909413888.

CHAPTER 8: THE SCHOOL-CHOICE TIDAL WAVE

1 Andrew Prokop, "The Conservative Push for 'School Choice' Has Had Its Most Successful Year Ever," Vox, August 7, 2023, https://www.vox.com/politics/23689496/school-choice-education-savings-accounts-american-federation-children.

2 Max Eden, "The Red-State Education Revolution," Restoring America, *Washington Examiner*, March 7, 2023, https://www.washingtonexaminer.com/restoring-america/community-family/the-red-state-education-revolution.

3 State Sen. Adiran [*sic*] Dickey, "Debunking 'Lies' About School Choice Bill," *Southeast Iowa Union*, February 1, 2023, https://www.southeastiowaunion.com/guest-columnists/debunking-lies-about-school-choice-bill/.

4 Team Starting Line, "Republicans Said the Quiet Parts Out Loud During Voucher Debate," *Iowa Starting Line*, January 24, 2023, https://iowastartingline.com/2023/01/24/republicans-said-the-quiet-parts-out-loud-during-voucher-debate/.

5 Ibid.

6 Ibid.

7 Ibid.

8 Ibid.

9 Stephen Gruber-Miller and Katie Akin, "Jubilant Kim Reynolds Signs Iowa's Seismic 'School Choice' Bill into Law. What It Means:," *Des Moines Register*, January 25, 2023, https://www.desmoinesregister.com/story/news/politics/2023/01/24/iowa-governor-kim-reynolds-signs-school-choice-scholarships-education-bill-into-law/69833074007/.

10 Ibid.

11 Claire Celsi (@SenClaireCelsi), "I did go to a private school. That was my parents' choice. But they didn't ask taxpayers to pay for it," X (formerly known as Twitter), February 2, 2022, 12:17 p.m., https://twitter.com/SenClaireCelsi/status/1489028486312468480.

12 Claire Celsi (@SenClaireCelsi), "I had a word with Governor Reynolds this morning at her signing ceremony in the rotunda," X (formerly known as Twitter), January 24, 2023, 12:17 p.m., https://twitter.com/SenClaireCelsi/status/1617934579075284992.

13 Corey A. DeAngelis (@DeAngelisCorey), "Thank you for the shoutout @KimReynoldsIA—and for being an unapologetic education freedom fighter. Iowa is now a national leader on school choice," X (formerly known as Twitter), February 3, 2023, 1:48 p.m., https://twitter.com/DeAngelisCorey/status/1621581441954971651.

14 Jason Bedrick, "The Big School Choice Turnaround in Iowa That More States Should Follow," Opinion, Fox News, February 15, 2023, https://www.foxnews.com/opinion/big-school-choice-turnaround-iowa-more-states-should-follow.

15 Ibid.

16 Ibid.

17 Francesca Block, "Gov. Kim Reynolds Pushed 'Parental Rights' to Moms for Liberty Crowd. Protesters Pushed Back," The Des Moines Register, February 3, 2023, https://www.desmoinesregister.com/story/news/politics/2023/02/03/republican-lawmakers-join-moms-for-liberty-to-advocate-parental-choice-lgbtq-crt-school-choice/69860561007/.

18 Gov. Kim Reynolds (@IAGovernor), "Today marks an important milestone for Iowa's education system as universal school choice becomes a reality for Iowa Families!," X (formerly known as Twitter), May 31, 2023, 9:33 a.m., https://twitter.com/IAGovernor/status/1663901522072092673.

19 Adam Carros, "Iowa School Voucher Applications Surpass Expectations, Cost Likely to Follow," Ottumwa-Kirksville KYOU, MSN, June 9, 2023, https://www.msn.com/en-us/money/careersandeducation/iowa-school-voucher-applications-surpass-expectations-cost-likely-to-follow/ar-AA1clMFH.

20 The Editorial Board, "The Rising Demand for School Choice," Opinion, *Wall Street Journal*, July 30, 2023, https://www.wsj.com/articles/the-rising-demand-for-school-choice-arizona-florida-implementation-esa-1c47ce5f.

21 Associated Press, "It's Not Just Utah, Other Conservative States Are Seeing a School Choice Policy Push," KUER 90.1, January 27, 2023, https://www.kuer.org/politics-government/2023-01-27/its-not-just-utah-other-conservative-states-are-seeing-a-school-choice-policy-push.

22 Ibid.

23 Marjorie Cortez, "2 Bills Intended to Give Parents More Say in School Curriculum Expose Rift Between Educators, Parents Rights Organization," *Deseret News*, January 27, 2022, https://www.deseret.com/utah/2022/1/27/22904667/teachers-parents-rights-group-disagree-bills-teachers-required-to-post-curriculum-utah-legislature.

24 Ibid.

25 Ibid.

26 Ibid.

27 Lydia Saad, "Historically Low Faith in U.S. Institutions Continues," Gallup, July 6, 2023, https://news.gallup.com/poll/508169/historically-low-faith-institutions-continues.aspx.

28 Hannah Poling, "Utah School Administrators Admit to Deceiving Parents by Using 'Loopholes' to Teach Critical Race Theory in Classrooms," *Tennessee Star*, January 29, 2023, https://tennesseestar.com/news/utah-school-administrators-admit-to-deceiving-parents-by-using-loopholes-to-teach-critical-race-theory-in-classrooms/hpoling/2023/01/29/.

29 Heather Hunter, "Utah School Officials Caught in Video Pushing Woke Curriculum," *Washington Examiner*, January 29, 2023, https://www.washingtonexaminer.com/utah-school-officials-in-video-woke-curriculum; Brian Kilmeade (@kilmeade), "BUSTED: Utah administrators and union officials smugly brag about sneaking CRT into curriculum," X (formerly known as Twitter), January 27, 2023, 7:08 p.m., https://twitter.com/kilmeade/status/1619125136199909378.

30 Rep. Chris Stewart (@RepChrisStewart), "This is why so many people don't trust public education: arrogant teachers who think they know better than parents," X (formerly known as Twitter), January 30, 2023, 1:12 p.m., https://twitter.com/RepChrisStewart/status/1620122763750170624.

31 Courtney Tanner, "Utah House Pushes Through Controversial Voucher Bill After Suspending Rules," *Salt Lake Tribune*, January 20, 2020, https://www.sltrib.com/news/education/2023/01/20/utah-house-pushes-through/.

32 Ashley Fredde, "Gov. Cox Signs High-Profile Bills on Transgender Surgeries, School Choice Vouchers," *Deseret News*, January 28, 2023, https://www.deseret.com/utah/2023/1/28/23575685/gov-cox-signs-high-profile-transgender-surgeries-school-choice-voucher-bills.

33 Jason Bedrick, "State Legislative Push for School Choice Gains Momentum Nationwide," *Daily Signal*, February 16, 2023, https://www.dailysignal.com/2023/02/16/state-legislative-push-for-school-choice-gains-momentum-nationwide/.

34 Ibid.

35 "What You Need to Know about the Arkansas LEARNS Act," *Arkansas Democrat-Gazette*, March 10, 2023, https://www.arkansasonline.com/news/2023/mar/10/what-you-need-to-know-about-arkansas-learns/.

36 Jason Bedrick, "State Legislative Push for School Choice Gains Momentum Nationwide," *Daily Signal*, February 16, 2023, https://www.dailysignal.com/2023/02/16/state-legislative-push-for-school-choice-gains-momentum-nationwide/.

37 Rep. Ryan Rose (@ThePastorRyan), "LEARNS is law. As a candidate, I campaigned on increasing teacher pay & funding our public schools, focusing on improving reading skills..." X, August 4, 2023, 5:22 p.m., https://twitter.com/ThePastorRyan/status/1687574738565029888.

38 Corey A. DeAngelis (@DeAngelisCorey), "the chair of the Arkansas Democratic Party went to private school.," X (formerly known as Twitter), February 9, 2023, 12:30 a.m., https://twitter.com/DeAngelisCorey/status/1623554939434983426.

39 Ibid.

40 Austin Bailey, "Charter School Students Cheer as Governor Sanders and Voucher Evangelist Corey DeAngelis Sell 'School Choice,'" *Arkansas Times*, January 23, 2023, https://arktimes.com/arkansas-blog/2023/01/23/charter-school-students-cheer-as-governor-sanders-and-voucher-evangelist-corey-deangelis-sell-school-choice.

41 Sarah Huckabee Sanders (@SarahHuckabee), "It is now the law of the land in my state to educate, not indoctrinate, empower parents, not government, and prepare students for a high paying job, not a lifetime in poverty," X (formerly known as Twitter), March 9, 2023, 8:06 a.m., https://twitter.com/SarahHuckabee/status/1633816624892465159.

42 Kim Jarrett, "More than 5,400 Arkansas Students Applied for Education Freedom Accounts," Center Square, July 31, 2023, https://www.thecentersquare.com/arkansas/article_38e0b50e-2fea-11ee-911f-ebdf253e9260.html.

43 Corey A. DeAngelis (@DeAngelisCorey), "Letter calling to expand school choice to all Florida families:," X (formerly known as Twitter), January 23, 2023, 1:35 p.m., https://twitter.com/DeAngelisCorey/status/1617591769247670272/photo/2.

44 "This Week's Biggest Winners & Losers," City & State Florida, January 27, 2023, https://www.cityandstatefl.com/personality/2023/01/weeks-biggest-winners-losers/382262/.

45 Alexandra Tilsley, "America's Gradebook: How Does Your State Stack Up?," Urban Institute, March 2, 2020, https://apps.urban.org/features/naep/.

46 Paul Renner (@Paul_Renner), "@GovRonDeSantis signs HB 1, unlocking school choice for every FL student! Our model factors in the unique learning needs of every child and empowers parents and students," X (formerly known as Twitter), March 27, 2023, 4:10 p.m., https://twitter.com/Paul_Renner/status/1640446206617722911.

47 Never Back Down (@NvrBackDown24), "'As the father of a six, five, and a three-year-old, I don't care how big of a corporation you are, I don't care how powerful you are in this state. I am standing for our kids and I will not back down

from that.' —@RonDeSantis," X, September 6, 2023, 8:55 a.m., https://twitter.com/NvrBackDown24/status/1699405929874375054.

48 Kirby Wilson, "10 Times Ron DeSantis Changed Florida Education," *Tampa Bay Times*, February 8, 2023, https://www.tampabay.com/news/florida-politics/2023/02/08/desantis-education-covid-trump-common-core-woke-transgender/; William Mattox, "DeSantis Defends Values While Expanding Choice to De-escalate the Stakes," *Education Next* 23 no. 3, Summer 2023, https://www.educationnext.org/desantis-defends-values-while-expanding-choice-to-de-escalate-stakes-mattox-forum-desantis-education-record/.

49 "Education Freedom Report Card," Heritage Foundation, September 9, 2022, https://www.heritage.org/educationreportcard/.

50 The Editorial Board, "The Rising Demand for School Choice," Opinion, *Wall Street Journal*, July 30, 2023, https://www.wsj.com/articles/the-rising-demand-for-school-choice-arizona-florida-implementation-esa-1c47ce5f.

CHAPTER 9: THE GOVERNMENT SCHOOL EMPIRE STRIKES BACK

1 Timothy Nerozzi, "Randi Weingarten Says Parental Rights Bills Are 'the Way in Which Wars Start,'" Fox News, April 22, 2022, https://www.foxnews.com/us/randi-weingarten-parental-rights-bills-the-way-in-which-wars-start.

2 Corey DeAngelis, "These Parents Might Miss School Choice Revolution Because of One Politician," Opinion, Fox News, March 1, 2023, https://www.foxnews.com/opinion/these-parents-might-miss-school-choice-revolution-because-one-politician.

3 Ibid.

4 Kaitlyn Shepherd, "Senate Bill 1038—Freedom in Education Savings Accounts," Idaho Freedom Foundation, February 8, 2023, https://idahofreedom.org/senate-bill-1038-freedom-in-education-savings-accounts/.

5 Jason Bedrick, "State Legislative Push for School Choice Gains Momentum Nationwide," *Daily Signal*, February 16, 2023, https://www.dailysignal.com/2023/02/16/state-legislative-push-for-school-choice-gains-momentum-nationwide/.

6 Sadie Dittenber, "After Longwinded Debate, Idaho Senate Kills Controversial Education Savings Account Bill," *Idaho Capital Sun*, February 27, 2023, https://idahocapitalsun.com/2023/02/27/after-longwinded-debate-idaho-senate-kills-controversial-education-savings-account-bill/.

7 Rep. Heather Scott and Sen. Tammy Nichols, "Education Union Bosses Need to Get Out of the Way of Universal School Choice," Idaho Education News, February 9, 2023, https://www.idahoednews.org/voices/education-union-bosses-need-to-get-out-of-the-way-of-universal-school-choice/.

8 Corey DeAngelis, "Gov. Pritzker Flips on School Choice," Opinion, *Wall Street Journal*, October 19, 2022, https://www.wsj.com/articles/school-choice-jd-pritzker-gubernatorial-governor-race-election-illinois-charter-public-funding-teachers-unions-11666185999.

9 "Educational Freedom Institute Executive Director: Illinois Politicians Who Shut Down School Choice Funding Are 'a Bunch of Hypocrites,'" Prairie State Wire, May 31, 2023, https://prairiestatewire.com/stories/643263450-educational-freedom-institute-executive-director-illinois-politicians-who-shut-down-school-choice-funding-are-a-bunch-of-hypocrites.

10 Corey DeAngelis, "Gov. Pritzker Flips on School Choice," Opinion, *Wall Street Journal*, October 19, 2022, https://www.wsj.com/articles/school-choice-jd-pritzker-gubernatorial-governor-race-election-illinois-charter-public-funding-teachers-unions-11666185999.

11 The Editorial Board, "The Illinois Scholarship Scandal," Opinion, *Wall Street Journal*, May 26, 2023, https://www.wsj.com/articles/illinois-democrats-invest-in-kids-scholarship-program-school-choice-emanuel-chris-welch-don-harmon-teachers-unions-9b5b3933.

12 Ted Dabrowski, "Why Can Only 6 of Every 100 Chicago Black Students Do Math at Grade Level? Chicago Mayoral Candidate Brandon Johnson Offers Some Clues," Wirepoints, March 21, 2023, https://wirepoints.org/why-can-only-6-of-every-100-chicago-black-students-do-math-at-grade-level-chicago-mayoral-candidate-brandon-johnson-offers-some-clues-wirepoints/.

13 Tony Kinnett, "Analysis: As Schools Approach $30,000 per Student in Spending, Performance Plunges," Center Square, September 29, 2022, https://www.thecentersquare.com/national/article_1774b89a-4015-11ed-ad1d-a37426722af4.html.

14 Corey DeAngelis, "Democrat Josh Shapiro Defects on School Choice," Opinion, *Wall Street Journal*, September 19, 2022, https://www.wsj.com/articles/a-democrat-defects-on-school-choice-josh-shapiro-pennsylvania-lifeline-scholarship-education-savings-account-teachers-union-election-11663615562.

15 Ibid.

16 Jason Bedrick, "Pennsylvania Governor's Reversal on School Choice Betrays Voters, Children," Commentary, *Daily Signal*, July 6, 2023, https://www.dailysignal.com/2023/07/06/pennsylvania-governors-reversal-on-school-choice-betrays-voters-children/.

17 Corey A. DeAngelis (@DeAngelisCorey), "one of the plaintiffs in the case was president of the West Virginia teachers union's Raleigh County chapter," X (formerly known as Twitter), July 8, 2022, 10:29 p.m., https://twitter.com/DeAngelisCorey/status/1545595911241248768; Corey A. DeAngelis

(@DeAngelisCorey), "Education Law Center filed the lawsuit against the West Virginia school choice program," X (formerly known as Twitter), July 9, 2022, 3:43 p.m., https://twitter.com/DeAngelisCorey/status/1545856157394145280.

18 Corey A. DeAngelis (@DeAngelisCorey), "the judge who blocked the West Virginia school choice program also received funding from the teachers unions," X (formerly known as Twitter), July 8, 2022, 8:42 p.m., https://twitter.com/DeAngelisCorey/status/1545568956978642944.

19 Amanda Kieffer, "West Virginia Leading the States on School Choice," Real-Clear-Policy, October 21, 2022, https://www.realclearpolicy.com/articles/2022/10/21/west_virginia_leading_the_states_on_school_choice_860350.html.

20 *Commonwealth of Kentucky v. Holly M. Johnson*, Supreme Court of Kentucky, December 15, 2015, https://ij.org/wp-content/uploads/2021/06/KY-School-Choice-Supreme-Court-Decision.pdf.

21 *Arizona Christian School Tuition Organization v. Winn, Cornell Law School*, § 562 F. 3d 1002, reversed, U.S. Supreme Court, 2011.

22 Jason Bedrick, "State Legislative Push for School Choice Gains Momentum Nationwide," Heritage Foundation, February 21, 2023, https://www.heritage.org/education/commentary/state-legislative-push-school-choice-gains-momentum-nationwide.

23 EdChoiceKY (@EdChoiceKY), "'This House Majority will fund students... not systems.' @reposborne at the KY Chamber Day Dinner," X (formerly known as Twitter), February 12, 2023, 9:32 a.m., https://twitter.com/edchoiceky/status/1624778394800996352.

24 Steve Brawner, "CAPES Group Short of Signatures to Repeal LEARNS Act; New Initiative Planned," KUAR, NPR, August 1, 2023, https://www.ualrpublicradio.org/local-regional-news/2023-08-01/capes-group-short-of-signatures-to-repeal-learns-act-new-initiative-planned.

25 Caroline Downey, "Nebraska Teachers' Union Launches Misinformation Campaign to Shut Down School Choice," Independent Women's Forum, July 31, 2023, https://www.iwf.org/2023/07/31/nebraska-teachers-union-launches-misinformation-campaign-to-shut-down-school-choice/.

26 Jeremiah Poff, "School Choice Foes Turn to Ballot Referendums as States Expand Voucher Programs," *Washington Examiner*, September 4, 2023, https://www.washingtonexaminer.com/policy/education/school-choice-foes-ballot-referendums-states-voucher-programs.

27 Corey DeAngelis, "Teachers' Unions Show Desperation in Nebraska," *National Review*, July 27, 2023, https://www.nationalreview.com/2023/07/teachers-unions-shows-desperation-in-nebraska/.

28 Ibid.

29 Clarice Jackson (@voiceadvocacy), "To LIE to registered voters at a predominantly minority establishment and say the bill you are asking me to repeal doesn't give opportunity...," X (formerly known as Twitter), July 22, 2023, 5:46 p.m., https://twitter.com/voiceadvocacy/status/1682869751612055552.

30 Corey DeAngelis, "Teachers' Unions Show Desperation in Nebraska," *National Review*, July 27, 2023, https://www.nationalreview.com/2023/07/teachers-unions-shows-desperation-in-nebraska/.

31 Susan Corke, "Introduction: 2022 the Year in Hate and Extremism Comes to Main Street," Southern Poverty Law Center, June 6, 2023, https://www.splcenter.org/year-hate-extremism-2022/introduction#hateextremism.

32 Tyler O'Neil, "Target on Their Backs: Moms for Liberty Invests in Extra Security Ahead of Summit After Receiving Threats," *Daily Signal*, June 27, 2023, https://www.dailysignal.com/2023/06/27/target-backs-moms-liberty-invests-extra-security-summit-receiving-threats/.

33 Tyler O'Neil, "'I Will...Eradicate You': Moms for Liberty Threatened, Treated as 'Subhuman,' After SPLC Attack," *Daily Signal*, July 10, 2023, https://www.dailysignal.com/2023/07/10/exclusive-moms-for-liberty-undaunted-by-death-threats-being-treated-as-subhuman-after-splc-attack/.

34 Ibid.

35 U.S. Department of Homeland Security, "Secretary Mayorkas Appoints New Members to Academic Council to Advise DHS," press release, June 21, 2023, https://www.dhs.gov/news/2023/06/21/secretary-mayorkas-appoints-new-members-academic-council-advise-dhs.

36 Corey A. DeAngelis (@DeAngelisCorey), "Randi Weingarten was just appointed to a council to advise the Department of Homeland Security.," X (formerly known as Twitter), June 21, 2023, 10:52 p.m., https://twitter.com/DeAngelisCorey/status/1671712788903755776.

37 Breccan F. Thies, "Teachers Union Boss Randi Weingarten to Advise DHS on School Safety," *Washington Examiner*, June 22, 2023, https://www.washingtonexaminer.com/policy/education/teachers-union-boss-randi-weingarten-advise-dhs-school-safety.

38 Victor Nava, "Teachers Union Honcho Randi Weingarten Likens Parental Rights, School Choice Supporters to Segregationists," *New York Post*, September 14, 2023, https://nypost.com/2023/09/13/randi-weingarten-likens-parental-rights-and-school-choice-supporters-to-segregationists/.

39 Jason Bedrick, "The Real Roots of School Choice Lie in Inclusion and Integration," Engage by EdChoice, February 14, 2020, https://www.edchoice.org/engage/the-real-roots-of-school-choice-lie-in-inclusion-and-integration/.

40 Phillip W. Magness, "School Choice's Antiracist History," Opinion, *Wall Street Journal*, October 18, 2021, https://www.wsj.com/articles/school-choice-antiracist-history-integration-funding-segregation-11634568700.

41 Phillip W. Magness, "Freedom of Choice in Education: The Origins of a Slogan," American Institute for Economic Research, September 16, 2023, https://www.aier.org/article/freedom-of-choice-in-education-the-origins-of-a-slogan/.

42 Tyler O'Neil, "'Ministry of Truth': Conservatives Warn About Washington State's 'Domestic Terrorism' Effort," *Daily Signal*, September 17, 2023, https://www.dailysignal.com/2023/09/17/building-blocks-police-state-conservatives-raise-alarm-washington-states-domestic-terrorism-effort/.

43 Ibid.

44 Corey DeAngelis (@DeAngelisCorey), "CNN's Michael Smerconish:," Thread Reader, December 10, 2023, https://threadreaderapp.com/thread/1469162754552520707.html.

45 D'Angelo Gore, "Warren Misleads on Her Kids' Schooling," Factcheck.org, November 27, 2019, https://www.factcheck.org/2019/11/warren-misleads-on-her-kids-schooling/.

46 Corey A. DeAngelis (@DeAngelisCorey), "You went to Cranbrook, that's a private school.," X (formerly known as Twitter), August 5, 2021, 5:23 p.m., https://twitter.com/deangeliscorey/status/1423394317603856388.

47 Cranbrook Schools, "Bill Prady: Class of 1977," https://schools.cranbrook.edu/list-detail?pk=128370.

48 Dominic-Madori Davis, "Meet the Bidens: America's New First Family," Business Insider, November 12, 2020, https://www.businessinsider.com/meet-the-bidens-first-family-joe-jill-beau-hunter-ashley-2020-5/.

49 Jessica Chasmar, "Biden, Pelosi, Other Top Dems Sent Kids to Private School but Oppose School Choice," Fox News, June 16, 2022, https://www.foxnews.com/politics/biden-pelosi-top-dems-sent-kids-private-school-oppose-choice.

50 Ibid.

51 Robert Reich (@RBReich), "'School choice' sounds great, but it's a euphemism for defunding public schools and funneling the money to private, for-profit schools," X, September 27, 2023, 10:04 p.m., https://x.com/rbreich/status/1707214556681076882.

52 Corey A. DeAngelis (@DeAngelisCorey), images, X, September 28, 2023, 10:43 a.m., https://x.com/deangeliscorey/status/1707405612861026802.

53 Corey A. DeAngelis (@DeAngelisCorey), "NEW: The government relations director for the Illinois Education Association, the state's largest union, sends his kids to a private school," X, September 14, 2023, 11:15 a.m., https://twitter.com/DeAngelisCorey/status/1702340253481046364.

54 Corey DeAngelis, "Chicago Teachers Union Boss Picks Better School for Her Son, but Not Yours," Opinion, Fox News, September 13, 2023, https://www.foxnews.com/opinion/chicago-teachers-union-boss-picks-better-school-her-son-not-yours.

55 Anita Goswami, "Stacy Davis Gates: Chicago Teachers Union Chief Slammed for Sending Son to Private School After Calling It 'Fascist,'" MSN, September 9, 2023, https://www.msn.com/en-us/news/us/stacy-davis-gates-chicago-teachers-union-chief-slammed-for-sending-son-to-private-school-after-calling-it-fascist/ar-AA1gtn3Q.

56 Paul E. Peterson and Samuel Barrows, "Teachers More Likely to Use Private Schools for Their Own Kids," *Education Next*, January 11, 2016, https://www.educationnext.org/teachers-more-likely-to-use-private-schools-for-their-own-kids/.

57 Ibid.

58 Richard Innes, "Where Would Public School Teachers Like to Send Their Own Children to School?," *Bluegrass Institute* (blog), November 11, 2019, https://bipps.org/blog/where-would-public-school-teachers-like-to-send-their-own-children-to-school.

CHAPTER 10: RETURN OF THE PARENTS' PARTY

1 Matthew Ladner, "A 'Tiffany' with 1,000 Faces," reimaginED, October 9, 2019, https://www.reimaginedonline.org/2019/10/a-tiffany-with-1000-faces/.

2 Tyler Kingkade, "A Betsy DeVos–Backed Group Helps Fuel a Rapid Expansion of Public Money for Private Schools," NBC News, March 30, 2023, https://www.nbcnews.com/politics/politics-news/betsy-devos-american-federation-children-private-school-rcna76307.

3 Ibid.

4 Jonathan Mahler, "'The Most Dangerous Person in the World Is Randi Weingarten,'" *New York Times Magazine*, April 28, 2023, https://www.nytimes.com/2023/04/28/magazine/randi-weingarten-teachers-unions.html.

5 Tyler Kingkade, "A Betsy DeVos–Backed Group Helps Fuel a Rapid Expansion of Public Money for Private Schools," NBC News, March 30, 2023, https://www.nbcnews.com/politics/politics-news/betsy-devos-american-federation-children-private-school-rcna76307.

6 State of Oklahoma, "Governor Stitt Delivers 2023 State of the State Address," Office of Governor J. Kevin Stitt, transcript, February 6, 2023, https://oklahoma.gov/governor/newsroom/newsroom/2023/february2023/governor-stitt-delivers-2023-state-of-the-state-address.html; Corey A. DeAngelis (@DeAngelisCorey), "Oklahoma Gov. Kevin Stitt: 'Every child deserves a quality education that fits their unique needs, regardless of economic status, or background,'" X (formerly known

as Twitter), February 6, 2023, 2:00 p.m., https://twitter.com/DeAngelisCorey/status/1622671469753901076.

7 Ben Felder, "Governor Signs Private- and Home-School Tax Credit Bill, One of His Top Priorities.," *Oklahoman*, May 25, 2023, https://www.oklahoman.com/story/news/politics/government/2023/05/25/oklahoma-private-school-tax-credits-governor-kevin-stitt-signs-bill/70257151007/.

8 Madeline Leesman, "Undercover Video Shows Ohio Schools Teaching CRT and 'Tricking' Parents," Townhall, January 23, 2023, https://townhall.com/tipsheet/madelineleesman/2023/01/23/accuracy-in-media-undercover-crt-videos-n2618492.

9 Ken Blackwell, "Opinion: School Choice Is the Only Solution to What's Wrong with Public Schools," *Enquirer*, February 4, 2023, https://www.cincinnati.com/story/opinion/contributors/2023/02/05/opinion-school-choice-is-the-only-solution-to-whats-wrong-with-public-schools/69861665007/.

10 Accuracy in Media Staff, "Triumph in Ohio: AIM Investigation Leads to Universal School Choice in Buckeye State," Accuracy In Media, August 10, 2023, https://aim.org/2023/08/10/triumph-in-ohio-aim-investigation-leads-to-universal-school-choice-in-buckeye-state/.

11 Mark Powell, "South Carolina Senate Gets Serious about School Choice," *FITSNews*, February 7, 2023, https://www.fitsnews.com/2023/02/07/south-carolina-senate-gets-serious-about-school-choice/.

12 Corey DeAngelis, "2023 Is Already a Record Year for School Choice," Opinion, *Wall Street Journal*, March 10, 2023, https://www.wsj.com/articles/2023-is-already-a-record-year-for-school-choice-parent-student-nebraska-arkansas-dc10dc5a.

13 Jonathan Butcher and Jason Bedrick, "2023: The Year of Education Freedom," Heritage Foundation, September 11, 2023, https://www.heritage.org/education/report/2023-the-year-education-freedom.

14 Jason Bedrick, "Ohioans Declare Independence from the District School Monopoly," *Daily Signal*, July 5, 2023, https://www.dailysignal.com/2023/07/05/ohioans-declare-independence-district-school-monopoly/.

15 "A State of Emergency for Public Education: In Special Address, Governor Cooper Issues Call to Action to Protect Public Schools amid Spate of Extreme Legislation," NC Governor Roy Cooper (official website), press release, May 22, 2023, https://governor.nc.gov/news/press-releases/2023/05/22/state-emergency-public-education-special-address-governor-cooper-issues-call-action-protect-public.

16 T. Keung Hui, "NC Students Drop to Historic Lows on National Tests. Two Decades of Gains Were Lost.," *News & Observer*, October 24, 2022, https://www.newsobserver.com/news/politics-government/article267593777.html.

17 David N. Bass, "Crime and Violence Spike 24% in NC Public High Schools," *Carolina Journal*, March 3, 2023, https://www.carolinajournal.com/crime-and-violence-spike-24-in-nc-public-high-schools/.

18 Kristina Watrobski, "'This Is Immoral': Pastor Slams NC School Board over 'Pornographic' Library Book," WTVC, May 17, 2023, https://newschannel9.com/news/local/this-is-immoral-pastor-slams-nc-school-board-over-pornographic-library-book-john-amanchukwu-north-caolina-asheville-city-perfectly-normal; Kristina Watrobski, "Mom Confronts North Carolina School Board over 'Vulgar' Library Books," WCTI, June 19, 2023, https://wcti12.com/news/nation-world/mom-confronts-north-carolina-school-board-over-vulgar-library-books-wake-county-public-system-asheville-city-schools-what-girls-are-made-of-elana-arnold-john-amanchukwu-pastor.

19 Kyle Morris, "NC Gov Roy Cooper Faces Scrutiny for Sending Daughter to Private School amid Opposition to School Choice Bill," Fox News, May 24, 2023, https://www.foxnews.com/politics/nc-gov-roy-cooper-faces-scrutiny-sending-daughter-private-school-amid-opposition-school-choice-bill.

20 Corey DeAngelis, "Education Freedom in North Carolina," Opinion, *Wall Street Journal*, April 9, 2023, https://www.wsj.com/articles/education-freedom-in-north-carolina-public-schools-democratic-party-switch-cotham-choice-universal-7b9a3a8.

21 "Durham Public Schools Will Provide 'Learning Centers' for K–5 Students Who Need Supervision in Remote Learning," WRAL News, August 14, 2020, https://www.wral.com/durham-public-schools-will-provide-learning-centers-for-k-5-students-who-need-supervision-in-remote-learning/19235986/.

22 John Fund, "Decisive Party Switch Gives North Carolina School Choice a Big Boost," *National Review*, April 5, 2023, https://www.nationalreview.com/corner/decisive-party-switch-gives-north-carolina-school-choice-a-big-boost/.

23 T. Keung Hui, "Wake Democrats Delete Tweet That Accused School Board Critics of Spreading Conspiracies," *News & Observer*, January 20, 2022, https://www.newsobserver.com/news/politics-government/article257483359.html.

24 John Fund, "Decisive Party Switch Gives North Carolina School Choice a Big Boost," *National Review*, April 5, 2023, https://www.nationalreview.com/corner/decisive-party-switch-gives-north-carolina-school-choice-a-big-boost/.

25 Corey A. DeAngelis (@DeAngelisCorey), "it's time for North Carolina to fund students, not systems.," X (formerly known as Twitter), May 3, 2023, 8:03 p.m., https://twitter.com/DeAngelisCorey/status/1653913296032997376.

26 Dawn Baumgartner Vaughan, "NC State Budget Passes GOP-Controlled Legislature, Cooper Will Let It Become Law. Here's Why.," *News & Observer*, September 22, 2023, https://www.newsobserver.com/news/politics-government/article279635739.html; Jazper Lu et al., "NC Republicans Override Cooper to Pass

6 New Laws After Debate over LGBTQ+ Youth," *News & Observer*, August 16, 2023, https://www.newsobserver.com/news/politics-government/article277096128.html.

27 Corey A. DeAngelis (@DeAngelisCorey), "Governor Abbott calls for UNIVERSAL SCHOOL CHOICE as an EMERGENCY ITEM:," X (formerly known as Twitter), February 16, 2023, 8:22 p.m., https://twitter.com/DeAngelisCorey/status/1626391713588584448.

28 James Wesolek, "Legislative Priorities for 2023–2024," Republican Party of Texas, press release, June 22, 2022, https://texasgop.org/legislativepriorities88/.

29 Corey A. DeAngelis (@DeAngelisCorey), "BREAKING: Charlie Johnson: 'My phone was lighting up from rural House members... "take a breath, just got off the phone with [Governor Abbott], he ain't gonna push a voucher bill.,"'" X (formerly known as Twitter), April 19, 2022, 8:49 p.m., https://twitter.com/DeAngelisCorey/status/1516579701271285766.

30 Greg Abbott (@GregAbbott_TX), "1. I don't know who this person is. 2. I've never talked to this person. 3. He and I did not speak as he claims.," X (formerly known as Twitter), April 20, 2022, 1:40 a.m., https://twitter.com/GregAbbott_TX/status/1516653036784996352.

31 Brandon Waltens, "Abbott Says He Supports School Choice and 'Fully Funding' Public Schools," *Texas Scorecard*, May 10, 2022, https://texasscorecard.com/state/abbott-says-he-supports-school-choice-and-fully-funding-public-schools/.

32 Corey A. DeAngelis (@DeAngelisCorey), "BREAKING: Texas Governor Greg Abbott: 'Empowering parents means giving them the choice to send their children to any public school, charter school, or private school with state funding following the student.,'" X (formerly known as Twitter), May 9, 2022, 8:02 p.m., https://twitter.com/DeAngelisCorey/status/1523815669841674241.

33 Jay P. Greene and Jason Bedrick, "What's Behind the Recent Surge in School-Choice Victories," *National Review*, February 4, 2023, https://www.nationalreview.com/2023/02/whats-behind-the-recent-surge-in-school-choice-victories/.

34 Erin Anderson, "State Investigating School District's Shenanigans to Boost Billion-Dollar Bond," *Texas Scorecard*, May 11, 2022, https://texasscorecard.com/local/state-investigating-school-districts-shenanigans-to-boost-billion-dollar-bond/.

35 Ibid.

36 Corey A. DeAngelis (@DeAngelisCorey), "it's time for Texas to fund students, not systems.," X (formerly known as Twitter), July 26, 2022, 2:41 p.m., https://twitter.com/DeAngelisCorey/status/1552001238836936704.

37 Jeannie Kever, "Hobby School Survey Gauges Public Support for School

Vouchers," University of Houston, January 30, 2023, https://uh.edu/news-events/stories/2023/january-2023/01302023-school-vouchers.php.

38 Matthew Ladner and Jason Bedrick, "Texas Families Deserve School Choice," Heritage Foundation, August 25, 2023, https://www.heritage.org/education/report/texas-families-deserve-school-choice; Corey A. DeAngelis (@DeAngelisCorey), "Texas Republican primary voter school choice support in the 10 most rural counties:," X (formerly known as Twitter), March 2, 2022, 5:48 p.m., https://twitter.com/DeAngelisCorey/status/1499154728189628417.

39 Brian Lopez, "At Parental Rights Event, Gov. Greg Abbott Sheds Light on How He'd Implement 'School Choice' Policy," *Texas Tribune*, January 31, 2023, https://www.texastribune.org/2023/01/31/greg-abbott-school-choice-public-education/.

40 "Governor Abbott Delivers 2023 State of the State Address," Office of the Texas Governor, press release, February 16, 2023, https://gov.texas.gov/news/post/governor-abbott-delivers-2023-state-of-the-state-address.

41 Texas House Democrats (@TexasHDC), "'Vouchers drain money from Texas' already underfunded schools,' @GinaForAustin said.," X (formerly known as Twitter), February 19, 2023, 3:40 p.m., https://twitter.com/TexasHDC/status/1627407802636414985.

42 Corey A. DeAngelis (@DeAngelisCorey), "the money doesn't belong to the government schools.," X (formerly known as Twitter), February 19, 2023, 8:23 p.m., https://twitter.com/DeAngelisCorey/status/1627478932810235905.

43 Gina Hinojosa (@GinaForAustin), "I know you don't live in Texas @DeAngelisCorey but what you disparagingly call "government schools" are Texas public schools enshrined in our Texas constitution," X (formerly known as Twitter), February 19, 2023, 11:20 p.m., https://twitter.com/GinaForAustin/status/1627523529611612160.

44 Corey A. DeAngelis (@DeAngelisCorey), "Texas Senate Education Committee considering UNIVERSAL SCHOOL CHOICE: 'The money doesn't belong to the institutions. Education funding is meant for educating children, not for protecting a particular institution. We should fund students, not systems.," X (formerly known as Twitter), March 22, 2022, 11:32 p.m., https://twitter.com/DeAngelisCorey/status/1638745606813536257.

45 Corey A. DeAngelis (@DeAngelisCorey), "you went to private school.," X (formerly known as Twitter), March 23, 2023, 11:10 a.m., https://twitter.com/DeAngelisCorey/status/1638921101232291840.

46 Jay Leeson (@jayleeson), "School Choice in Texas: @DeAngelisCorey, a shameless and known #BetsyDeVos, Wall Street, and K Street puppet looking to upheave what Texas Revolutionary heroes fought for," X (formerly

known as Twitter), April 16, 2023, 2:39 p.m., https://twitter.com/jayleeson/status/1647670944406597634.

47 Corey A. DeAngelis (@DeAngelisCorey), "Texas House Democrats Chair Trey Martinez Fischer: 'if defunding education with vouchers is his dream, we're his nightmare.,'" X (formerly known as Twitter), February 18, 2023, 12:06 a.m., https://twitter.com/DeAngelisCorey/status/1626810460837117952; Corey A. DeAngelis (@DeAngelisCorey), images, X (formerly known as Twitter), February 18, 2023, 12:07 a.m., https://twitter.com/DeAngelisCorey/status/1626810631516028928.

48 Ibid.

49 Doug P., "Corey DeAngelis Has a Reminder About Texas Dem State Rep Opposing School Vouchers," twitchy, February 15, 2023, https://twitchy.com/dougp-3137/2023/02/15/corey-deangelis-has-a-reminder-about-texas-dem-state-rep-opposing-school-vouchers/.

50 Ibid.

51 Beto O'Rourke (@BetoORourke), "'School choice' isn't really about choice—it's a ploy to funnel funds reserved for public education into private schools.," X (formerly known as Twitter), April 9, 2018, 7:09 p.m., https://twitter.com/BetoORourke/status/983481977541017600.

52 "School Choice Bibliography," EdChoice, last modified June 7, 2023, http://www.edchoice.org/school-choice-bibliography.

53 Corey A. DeAngelis (@DeAngelisCorey), "Texas Representative Travis Clardy ('R') is a school choice hypocrite.," X, September 24, 2023, 2:40 p.m., https://twitter.com/DeAngelisCorey/status/1706015812891369776; Corey A. DeAngelis (@DeAngelisCorey), "BREAKING: Texas Representative Travis Clardy ('R'), a school choice opponent, sent his kids to a private school.," X, September 15, 2023, 11:17 a.m., https://twitter.com/DeAngelisCorey/status/1702703095455588647.

54 Libs of TikTok, "REVEALED: TX Rep Travis Clardy (R) Voted Against School Choice, Is Funded by Teacher's Unions, Sends His Kids to Private School," Libs of Tiktok, September 24, 2023, https://www.libsoftiktok.com/p/-tc.

55 "Joanne Shofner: The True Texas Conservative Woman: 'It Is an Honor to Meet You!,'" Joanne Shofner for Texans, https://joannefortexans.com/.

56 Corey A. DeAngelis (@DeAngelisCorey), "The Texas Senate has 12 Democrats," X, October 13, 2023, 9:58 p.m., https://twitter.com/DeAngelisCorey/status/1713011435884699892.

57 Corey DeAngelis, "School Choice in Texas: The Easy or Hard Way," Opinion, *Wall Street Journal*, September 24, 2023, https://www.wsj.com/articles/school-choice-the-easy-way-education-elections-gop-9faedaad.

58 Jayme Lozano Carver, "Ted Cruz Urges Passage of a School Choice Measure in Texas," *Texas Tribune*, September 23, 2023, https://www.texastribune.org/2023/09/23/ted-cruz-texas-tribune-festival/.

59 Patrick Svitek, "Senate Fast-Tracks Passage of Vouchers and Border Security Legislation," Texas Tribune, November 9, 2023, https://www.texastribune.org/2023/11/09/texas-senate-vouchers-border-security/.

60 Patrick Svitek, "Texas House Committee Advances School Voucher Bill, Overcoming Key Hurdle," Texas Tribune, November 10, 2023, https://www.texastribune.org/2023/11/10/texas-house-vote-committee-school-vouchers/.

61 Zach Despart and Brian Lopez, "Texas House Votes to Remove School Vouchers from Massive Education Bill," Texas Tribune, November 16, 2023, https://www.texastribune.org/2023/11/16/texas-house-school-vouchers/#:~:text=The%20House%20voted%2084%2D63,to%20private%20and%20religious%20schools.

62 Corey A. DeAngelis (@DeAngelisCorey), "BREAKING: 18 of the 21 Texas House 'Republicans' who voted against school choice were endorsed by the teachers union.," X, November 18, 2023, 10:13 p.m., https://twitter.com/DeAngelisCorey/status/1726076207991574806.

63 Brandon Waltens, "Every School Choice Opponent in Texas House Earns a Primary Challenger," *Texas Scorecard*, December 12, 2023, https://texasscorecard.com/state/every-school-choice-opponent-in-texas-house-earns-a-primary-challenger/.

64 The Editorial Board, "Texas and the Politics of School Choice," Opinion, *Wall Street Journal*, December 7, 2023, https://www.wsj.com/articles/texas-school-choice-greg-abbott-primary-endorsements-house-republicans-049d97cb.

65 Ibid.

66 Corey DeAngelis, "Another Democrat Leaves Her Party to Stand Up for Parents," Opinion, Fox News, July 14, 2023, https://www.foxnews.com/opinion/democrat-leaves-party-stand-parents.

67 "New Poll: School Choice Support Soars from 2020," American Federation for Children, press release, July 11, 2023, https://www.federationforchildren.org/new-poll-school-choice-support-soars-from-2020/.

68 Rich Calder, "Pols Seek to Study Subsidizing Private School Tuition—to Keep Families from Fleeing NYC," *New York Post*, September 9, 2023, https://nypost.com/2023/09/09/new-bill-could-pave-way-to-nyc-paying-private-school-tuitions/.

69 Deirdre Bardolf and Susan Edelman, "Kindergarten Enrollment Rates Among Highest Declines as Families Flee NYC DOE," *New York Post*, August 5, 2023, https://nypost.com/2023/08/05/families-fleeing-public-schools-starting-with-kindergarten/.

70 Rich Calder, "Pols Seek to Study Subsidizing Private School Tuition—to Keep Families from Fleeing NYC," *New York Post*, September 9, 2023, https://nypost.com/2023/09/09/new-bill-could-pave-way-to-nyc-paying-private-school-tuitions/.

71 Juan Perez Jr., "'We've Lost Our Advantage on Education': Democrats Grasp for Wins on Public Schools," *Politico*, September 17, 2023, https://www.politico.com/news/2023/09/17/education-democrats-school-choice-cardona-biden-00116385.

72 Ibid.

73 Andrew Prokop, "The Conservative Push for 'School Choice' Has Had Its Most Successful Year Ever," Vox, August 7, 2023, https://www.vox.com/politics/23689496/school-choice-education-savings-accounts-american-federation-children.

74 Corey A. DeAngelis (@DeAngelisCorey), "BREAKING: Randi Weingarten: 'So if you listen to one thing that I say today, remember this name: Christopher Rufo. Rufo and DeAngelis. By the way, Corey DeAngelis tweets or posts at me. Like last year I think was, what was it, Asher, 5,000 times last year?,'" X, December 16, 2023, 2:36 p.m., https://twitter.com/DeAngelisCorey/status/1736107950303793504.

75 "Asher Huey, Digital Director," Union Employee Details, Center for Union Facts, https://www.unionfacts.com/employee/American_Federation_of_Teachers/ASHER/HUEY.

CONCLUSION: *THE PARENT REVOLUTION* CONTINUES

1 Max Eden, "Move School Board Elections On-Cycle to Restore Local Control," American Enterprise Institute, October 18, 2021, https://www.aei.org/research-products/report/move-school-board-elections-on-cycle-to-restore-local-control/.

2 Elizabeth Held, "School Reopening Debate Shows Power of Local School Boards," Opinion, *USA Today*, August 7, 2020, https://www.usatoday.com/story/opinion/2020/08/07/schools-reopening-importance-local-school-board-column/5531093002/.

3 Max Eden, "Move School Board Elections On-Cycle to Restore Local Control," American Enterprise Institute, October 18, 2021, https://www.aei.org/research-products/report/move-school-board-elections-on-cycle-to-restore-local-control/.

4 Mike Desmond, "Pressure Increases to Move Buffalo School Board Election," WBFO, February 5, 2019, https://www.wbfo.org/education/2019-02-05/pressure-increases-to-move-buffalo-school-board-election.

5 "Model School Board Policy on Parental Rights in Education and Safety, Privacy, and Respect for All Students in the District," Heritage Foundation, https://www.heritage.org/model-school-board-policy-parental-rights-education-and-safety-privacy-and-respect.

6 Ibid.

7 "Academic Transparency," Goldwater Institute, https://www.goldwaterinstitute.org/issues/academic-transparency/academictransparency/.

8 William A. Jacobson, "Nicole Solas Anti-SLAPP Hearing Against Teachers Union—Judge Doubts NEA-RI Ever Had Claim to Prevent Records Release but Reserves Decision," Legal Insurrection, December 1, 2021, https://legalinsurrection.com/2021/12/nicole-solas-anti-slapp-hearing-against-teachers-union-judge-doubts-nea-ri-ever-had-claim-to-prevent-records-release-but-reserves-decision/.

9 Chrissy Clark, "Minnesota Public School District Tried to Charge Concerned Parents More than $900,000 for Records," *Daily Caller*, November 28, 2021, https://dailycaller.com/2021/11/28/minnesota-public-school-concerned-parents-900000-records-crt/.

10 "Academic Transparency Act," Goldwater Institute, June 8, 2022, https://www.goldwaterinstitute.org/wp-content/uploads/2022/07/Academic-Transparency-Act-2022-Model-Legislation-6-22.pdf.

11 Erika Sanzi, "Make Intrusive School Surveys 'Opt-In' Rather Than 'Opt-Out,'" American Enterprise Institute, March 9, 2022, https://www.aei.org/research-products/report/make-intrusive-school-surveys-opt-in-rather-than-opt-out/.

12 Ibid.

13 "Independent Women's Voice and WoLF Introduce the Women's Bill of Rights," Women's Liberation Front, March 31, 2022, https://womensliberationfront.org/news/iwv-wolf-womens-bill-of-rights.

14 Mary Margaret Olohan, "Vermont High School Under Fire as Girls, Parents Push Back Against Biologically Male Trans Student Using Female Locker Room," *Daily Signal*, October 2, 2022, https://www.dailysignal.com/2022/10/02/vermont-high-school-under-fire-as-girls-parents-push-back-against-biologically-male-trans-student-using-female-locker-room/; "Silenced for Their Discomfort: New *Daily Signal* Video Tells Story of Vermont High School Girls Attacked for Protesting the Male in Their Locker Room," Heritage Foundation, October 13, 2022, https://www.heritage.org/press/silenced-their-discomfort-new-daily-signal-video-tells-story-vermont-high-school-girls; Dana Kennedy, "Vermont HS Volleyball Team Banned from Own Locker Room over Transgender Dispute: Reports," *New York Post*, October 1, 2022, https://nypost.com/2022/10/01/vermont-hs-volleyball-team-banned-from-locker-room-over-transgender-dispute/.

15 "The Given Name Act," Heritage Foundation, https://www.heritage.org/the-given-name-act; Jason Bedrick and Jonathan Butcher, "Protecting Parents' Rights with the Given Name Act," Heritage Foundation, February 14, 2023, https://www.heritage.org/education/report/protecting-parents-rights-the-given-name-act.

16 "List of School District Transgender—Gender Nonconforming Student Policies," Parents Defending Education, March 7, 2023, https://defendinged.org/investigations/list-of-school-district-transgender-gender-nonconforming-student-policies/.

17 Jason Bedrick and Jonathan Butcher, "Protecting Parents' Rights with the Given Name Act," Heritage Foundation, February 14, 2023, https://www.heritage.org/education/report/protecting-parents-rights-the-given-name-act.

18 "Protecting K–12 Students from Discrimination," Heritage Foundation, https://www.heritage.org/protecting-k-12-students-discrimination.

19 "Education Licensure Certificate Act," National Association of Scholars, https://www.nas.org/policy/model-education-licensure-code/education-licensure-certificate-act.

20 Robert Gordon, Thomas J. Kane, and Douglas O. Staiger, "Identifying Effective Teachers Using Performance on the Job," The Brookings Institution: The Hamilton Project, Discussion Paper 2006-01, April 2006, https://www.brookings.edu/wp-content/uploads/2016/06/200604hamilton_1.pdf.

21 "Education Licensure Certificate Act," National Association of Scholars, https://www.nas.org/policy/model-education-licensure-code/education-licensure-certificate-act.

22 Lindsey M. Burke, PhD, "Why Do We Send Teachers for Re-Education?," Heritage Foundation, September 23, 2022, https://www.heritage.org/education/commentary/why-do-we-send-teachers-re-education.

23 Frederick M. Hess, "Defund the Teacher-Trainers," *National Review*, August 11, 2022, https://www.nationalreview.com/magazine/2022/08/29/defund-the-teacher-trainers/.

24 Ibid.

25 Max Eden, "My Gender Is 'Rock,'" *City Journal*, September 19, 2023, https://www.city-journal.org/article/gender-ideology-in-k-12-schools.

26 Asaf Orr, Joel Baum, et al., *Schools in Transition: A Guide for Supporting Transgender Students in K–12 Schools*, ed. Beth Sherouse (ACLU, Gender Spectrum, Human Rights Campaign Foundation, National Center for Lesbian Rights, National Education Association, n.d.), p. 14, https://hrc-prod-requests.s3-us-west-2.amazonaws.com/files/assets/resources/Schools-In-Transition.pdf.

27 Ibid., p. 32.

28 Adam Andrzejewski, "Substack: Invent Your Own Gender. Governor Gavin Newsom Encourages Youth with Millions in Taxpayer Support," Open The Books, September 15, 2023, https://www.openthebooks.com/substack-invent-your-own-gender-governor-gavin-newsom-encourages-youth-with-millions-in-taxpayer-support.

29 Franklin Delano Roosevelt, "Text of FDR Letter Opposing Public Employee (Government) Unions," National Center for Public Policy Research, February 19, 2011, https://nationalcenter.org/ncppr/2011/02/19/blog-text-of-fdr-letter-opposing-public-employee-government-unions/.

30 Daniel DiSalvo, "The Trouble with Public Sector Unions," *National Affairs*, Fall 2010, https://www.nationalaffairs.com/publications/detail/the-trouble-with-public-sector-unions.

31 Terry M. Moe, "Collective Bargaining and the Performance of the Public Schools," *American Journal of Political Science* 53, no. 1 (January 2009), Stanford University, Wayback Machine archived webpage, https://web.archive.org/web/20160611071647/https:/files-politicalscience-stanford-edu.s3.amazonaws.com/s3fs-public/collectivebargainingpublishedversion.pdf.

32 Michael F. Lovenheim and Alexander Willén, "The Long-Run Effects of Teacher Collective Bargaining," American Economic Association, October 2017, https://www.aeaweb.org/conference/2018/preliminary/paper/ShD4d8GY.

33 Larry Sand, "It's Time to Abolish the Teachers Unions," Opinion, Heartland Institute, January 4, 2022, https://heartland.org/opinion/its-time-to-abolish-the-teachers-unions/; See also: Andrew J. Coulson, "The Effects of Teachers Unions on American Education," *Cato Journal* 30, no. 1 (Winter 2010), http://www.ctenhome.org/wp-content/uploads/2018/12/CoulsonCato-Journal.pdf.

34 "Collective Bargaining Laws," National Council on Teacher Quality, January 2019, https://www.nctq.org/contract-database/collectiveBargaining.

ABOUT THE AUTHOR

Corey A. DeAngelis is a senior fellow at the American Federation for Children and a visiting fellow at Stanford University's Hoover Institution. He has been labeled the "school choice evangelist" and called "the most effective school choice advocate since Milton Friedman." He is a regular on Fox News and frequently appears in the *Wall Street Journal*. DeAngelis is also the executive director at Educational Freedom Institute, a senior fellow at Reason Foundation, an adjunct scholar at Cato Institute, and a board member at Liberty Justice Center. He holds a PhD in education policy from the University of Arkansas.